THE COHERENCE OF THE BOOK OF MICAH
A Literary Analysis

SOCIETY
OF BIBLICAL
LITERATURE

DISSERTATION SERIES
J. J. M. Roberts, Old Testament Editor
Charles Talbert, New Testament Editor

Number 89

THE COHERENCE OF THE BOOK OF MICAH

by
David Gerald Hagstrom

David Gerald Hagstrom

THE COHERENCE OF
THE BOOK OF MICAH
A Literary Analysis

Scholars Press
Atlanta, Georgia

THE COHERENCE OF THE BOOK OF MICAH
A Literary Analysis

David Gerald Hagstrom

Ph.D., 1982
Union Theological Seminary in Virginia

Advisor:
James L. Mays

© 1988
Society of Biblical Literature

Library of Congress Cataloging-in-Publication Data

Hagstrom, David, 1954–
  The coherence of the book of Micah.

  (Dissertation series ; no. 89)
  Bibliography: p.
  1. Bible. O.T. Micah—Criticism, interpretation,
etc. I. Title. II. Series: Dissertation series (Society
of Biblical Literature) ; no. 89.
  BS1615.2.H34 1988   224'.93066   86-26107
  ISBN 0-89130-972-1 (alk. paper)
  ISBN 0-89130-973-X (pbk. : alk. paper)

Printed in the United States of America

Contents

List of Tables

Acknowledgments

Many people have provided guidance, encouragement, and support in the course of work on this dissertation. To the following few I wish to acknowledge my special debt of gratitude:

Dr. James L. Mays, my supervisor, a wise counselor whose searching questions so often opened up new vistas and led the way from obscurity to clarity and whose deep and evident caring has made working with him an experience of great joy.

Drs. Patrick D. Miller and W. Sibley Towner, my readers, who provided valuable criticism and helpful suggestions at various stages in this project.

My fellow graduate students and faculty members in the Biblical Department at Union Theological Seminary who provided a nurturing community of support during these past four years and in dialogue with whom many parts of this dissertation were refined and clarified.

The administration and staff of the Library of Union Theological Seminary and especially Mrs. Martha B. Aycock who gave freely of her time and energy both in the research and manuscript preparation phases of this project.

Both Union Theological Seminary and The American Lutheran Church for fellowships and other forms of financial assistance which aided greatly in making this project feasible.

Gerald and Arlene Hagstrom, my parents and faithful supporters, whose love, encouragement, and constant support in prayer have helped to sustain me throughout my years of schooling and to whom I owe more than I can possibly express.

Jane Louise, my wife and best friend, who joined me amid this project, expressed encouragement, love, and patience during the time of its research and writing, and who has to these years brought new and unexpected joy.

List of Abbreviations

BDB	F. Brown, S. R. Driver, and C. A. Briggs, *A Hebrew and English Lexicon of the Old Testament*
BHS	*Biblia Hebraica Stuttgartensia*
Ges.	*Gesenius' Hebrew and Chaldee Lexicon to the Old Testament Scriptures,* trans. with additions by S. P. Tregelles, 1952
JBL	*Journal of Biblical Literature*
JPS	Jewish Publication Society of America, *A New Translation of the Holy Scriptures according to the Traditional Hebrew Text,* 2d section: *The Prophets: Nebi'im*
JSOT	*Journal for the Study of the Old Testament*
JSOTSup	Journal for the Study of the Old Testament Supplement Series
KB	L. Koehler and W. Baumgartner, eds., *Lexicon in Veteris Testamenti Libros* with *Supplementum,* 2d ed., 1958
LXX	Septuagint
MT	Masoretic Text
NEB	*New English Bible*
OT	Old Testament
OTL	Old Testament Library
OTWSA	Die Ou-Testamentiese Werkgemeenskap in Suid-Afrika, *Old Testament Studies: Papers Read at Eleventh Meeting Held at the University of Pretoria, January 1968*
RSV	Revised Standard Version
Syr	Syriac Peshitta
Vg	Latin Vulgate version
VT	*Vetus Testamentum*
VTSup	Supplements to Vetus Testamentum
ZAW	*Zeitschrift für die alttestamentliche Wissenschaft*
ZDMG	*Zeitschrift der Deutsche Morgenländischen Gesellschaft*

All biblical translations are those of the author except where otherwise specified.

1
Introduction

The custom in the field of biblical studies has been to deal with the book of Micah in terms of its variety and parts rather than its coherence; it has more often been viewed as a collection of pericopes than as a unified book. Contrary to this tendency, I shall seek by means of a literary analysis to establish the following thesis: The book of Micah in its final form is so shaped as to render the book a unified, coherent whole; that is, the individual units of Micah are so shaped, structured, and linked together as to make it possible to read the book as a unit.

I. TRENDS WITHIN THE FIELD

As stated, the primary focus of this study will be a literary analysis of the book of Micah. Before proceeding, however, with a description of the problem along with a statement of the procedure to be employed in this analysis, I should like briefly to locate my research within the field of biblical studies. In particular, this study reflects and addresses at least two major currents or issues of present concern within the field.

First, I shall seek to deal with the *whole book* of Micah as a unit for interpretation. Of late, since the publication of his *Introduction to the Old Testament as Scripture,* this current is perhaps most closely identified with Brevard Childs[1] There have, however, been quite a number of studies which have reflected a more synthetic trend, that is, away from the more common focus on isolated form-critical units reflecting oral Gattungen, seeking instead to deal with larger—and often, admittedly composite—wholes. For example, "kerygmatic exegesis," associated with von Rad, Wolff, and Brueggemann, among others, dealt largely with whole tradition strands.[2] More prominent of late have been those studies identified by the labels literary or rhetorical criticism—such as those by Ackerman on the birth narratives of Moses, Gunn on the stories of King

---

[1] Brevard S. Childs, *Introduction to the Old Testament as Scripture* (Philadelphia: Fortress Press, 1979).

[2] See, for example, Walter Brueggemann and Hans Walter Wolff, *The Vitality of the Old Testament Traditions* (Atlanta: John Knox Press, 1975).

David and King Saul, or Holladay on Jeremiah 1-20.[3] On the level of whole books, one thinks of the work of Good on Hosea, Trible on the Song of Songs and Ruth, and Wharton on Job.[4]

Secondly, I shall be dealing solely with the *final form* of the book. Of course, literary critics in general share this concern for the final form of the book. Moreover, though he distinguishes his approach from those of literary critics in other ways, Childs also displays this same concern "to do justice to the integrity of the text itself."[5] In addition, some redactional studies would also claim to

---

[3] James S. Ackerman, "The Literary Context of the Moses Birth Story," in *Literary Interpretations of Biblical Narratives,* ed. Kenneth R. R. Gros Louis, James S. Ackerman, and Thayer S. Warshaw, The Bible in Literature Courses (Nashville: Abingdon Press, 1974) 74-119; David M. Gunn, *The Story of King David: Genre and Interpretation,* JSOTSup, no. 6 (Sheffield: JSOT Press, 1978); idem, *The Fate of King Saul. An Interpretation of a Biblical Story,* JSOTSup, no. 14 (Sheffield: JSOT Press, 1980); William L. Holladay, *The Architecture of Jeremiah 1-20* (Lewisburg: Bucknell University Press, 1976). See also Phyllis Trible, "A Love Story Gone Awry" [Gen 2-3], in *God and the Rhetoric of Sexuality,* Overtures to Biblical Theology (Philadelphia: Fortress Press, 1978) 72-143; Brevard S. Childs, "On Reading the Elijah Narratives," *Interpretation* 34 (1980) 128-37, James L. Crenshaw, *Samson: A Secret Betrayed, a Vow Ignored* (Atlanta: John Knox Press, 1978); Richard G. Bowman, "The Crises of King David: Narrative Structure, Compositional Technique, and the Interpretation of II Samuel 8:15-20:26." (Th.D. dissertation, Union Theological Seminary, Richmond, Virginia, 1981); Jan P. Fokkelman, *Narrative Art and Poetry in the Books of Samuel: A Full Interpretation Based on Stylistic and Structural Analyses,* vol. 1: *King David (II Sam. 9-20 & 1 Kings 1-2)* (Assen: Van Gorcum, 1981); idem, *Narrative Art in Genesis: Specimens of Stylistic and Structural Analysis* (Assen: Van Gorcum, 1975).

[4] Edwin M. Good, "The Composition of Hosea," *Svensk Exegetisk Årsbok* 31 (1966) 21-63; Trible, "Love's Lyrics Redeemed" [Song of Songs] and "A Human Comedy" [Ruth], in *God and the Rhetoric of Sexuality,* idem, pp. 144-65 & 166-99; James A. Wharton, "The Unanswerable Answer: An Interpretation of Job," in *Texts and Testaments: Essays on the Bible and Early Church Fathers,* ed. W. Eugene March (San Antonio, TX: Trinity University Press, 1981) 37-70. Note also Norman R. Petersen, *Literary Criticism for New Testament Critics,* Guides to Biblical Scholarship (Philadelphia: Fortress Press, 1978) 49-80; idem, "When Is the End Not the End?," *Interpretation* 34 (1980) 151-66; Francis I. Anderson and David N. Freedman, *Hosea,* Anchor Bible, vol. 24 (Garden City, NY: Doubleday, 1980).

[5] Childs, *Introduction,* p. 74. Indeed, one important factor which contributed to my initial interest in investigating the thesis stated above was an attraction to the approach to interpretation being developed by Childs. A preliminary evaluation tended to confirm the importance and value of this approach. This led in turn to an attempt to catalog and classify the various elements discussed by Childs in his *Introduction* under the rubric of "canonical shape" in order to provide a taxonomy of its constituents which might be of help in developing criteria for use in an analysis of the book of Micah. In the process of this investigation, I concluded that Childs's approach is fundamentally literary-critical in character. (Childs's article "On Reading the Elijah Narratives" also displays a strong kinship to literary criticism.) The dominant role of literary concerns in Childs's analysis

emphasize the final form of the book by focusing on the level of the latest redaction and treating the book as a product of its compositional history. At this point, however, a careful distinction must be made; for it should not be assumed that the final form of the book will reflect at every point the intention of the final redactor. As Wharton notes with respect to the book of Job: "no single tradition or individual . . . has succeeded in bending the entire work to its purpose. The final book has achieved a baroque unity which no individual seems to have intended."[6] One could reasonably expect this to be the case for other composite texts as well.

II. THE PROBLEM

It will be helpful first to define, at least in broad terms, what is meant by unity or coherence. One may say that a literary work displays coherence or unity when it is capable of being construed as a unit. A piece of literary discourse is capable of being construed as a unit when there are features within the text that hold it together, that make it cohere, that provide keys as to how it might be construed. Such keys function in several ways. They may be keys of consonance — features in different parts of the text that are like each other, or refer to each other. There are those of dissonance, as two parts the proximity of which underscores an adversative relation between them. Again, there may be features which serve to link one part to another sequentially — for example, as in logical sequence. In the course of this study I shall specify such features as they occur within the book of Micah with much greater precision.

---

led me to inquire further with regard to the rather new trend toward literary investigation of biblical literature.

In fairness to Childs, however, it should be noted that his is not a "strictly" literary-critical approach. As he notes, "the canonical approach differs from a strictly literary approach by interpreting the biblical text in relation to a community of faith and practice for whom it served a particular theological role as possessing divine authority" (*Introduction,* p. 74). Childs's approach may be clearly located within the historical-critical tradition by virtue of this concern to locate a particular level of the text which may in turn be related to a particular community who read the text on this level and preserved the tradition with the *intention* that it be so interpreted. In addition, he is careul to note where and to what extent the final text retains the historical particularity of earlier levels thus perhaps providing warrant itself for interpreting the text at more than one level. However, he deems historical-critical results most helpful when and to the extent that they shed light on the final, resultant text.

⁶ Wharton, "Unanswerable Answer," p. 38. To this contrast the approach of Willis who focuses on the intent of the final redactor and regards as secondary an element of the final form of the text which does not correspond to the emphasis intended by this redactor (John T. Willis, "The Structure, Setting, and Interrelationships of the Pericopes in the Book of Micah" [Ph.D. dissertation, Vanderbilt University, 1966] 232–33 n. 2. Hereafter cited as Willis, Dissertation.).

Of course, one may also distinguish different types of coherence. For example, one might say that the book of Proverbs and the book of Psalms display coherence in that they are made up of the same kinds of material (i.e., psalms and proverbs). Yet it is not self-evident in what way one might interpret the parts in relation to each other or to the whole as a literary unit in either case. They appear more as collections of similar units. (Of course, this is not to deny that some closer relation might be discovered.) While such similarity might be considered a certain type of coherence, such "coherence" would be trivial from the standpoint of the present study. Thus, properly speaking, my question is not simply "Is the book of Micah coherent?," but rather "What kind of coherence does the book of Micah display?" and, in particular, "Does the book of Micah display a certain significant type of coherence which renders it capable of meaningful construal as a unit?"

Literary critics generally begin with the assumption that the text to be interpreted is a coherent unit.[7] However, in light of the historical-critical tradition, it is far from self-evident that this assumption is valid with regard to biblical books. Certainly I have no intention of defending this assumption with regard to biblical books in general. Rather I shall seek to determine whether the book of Micah displays such coherence. One reason, however, for choosing the book of Micah is that its relatively long period of development provides a challenge to the thesis that the book in its present form and taken as a whole can be shown to communicate a coherent message. Should the book of Micah be found to display such coherence one could reasonably expect to find such coherence displayed elsewhere within the canon as well (though not of necessity and certainly not in every case).

I readily admit that the book of Micah is a composite text with an extended compositional history. It is also clear that such a composite nature may give rise to certain difficulties in interpreting the text. For example, as Alter acknowledges in his discssion of composite narrative texts:

> There are passages of biblical narrative that seem to resist any harmonizing interpretation, leading one to conclude either that there were certain circumstances in the transmission and editing of ancient Hebrew texts which could on occasion lead to intrinsic incoherence, or that the biblical notion of what constituted a meaningful and unified narrative continuum might at times be unfathomable from the enormous distance of intellectual and historical evolution that stands between us and these creations of the early Iron age.

Indeed, one might find this to be the case for the book of Micah. Nevertheless, Alter's study of biblical narrative provides warrant for a more optimistic outlook; for, in his evaluation, "insoluble cruxes deriving from the composite

---

[7] Leland Ryken, "Literary Interpretation of the Bible: Some Fallacies," in *Literary Interpretations of Biblical Narratives,* ed. Kenneth R. R. Gros Louis, James S. Ackerman, and Thayer S. Warshaw, The Bible in Literature Courses (Nashville: Abingdon Press, 1971) 26–27, 33–35.

nature of the text are a good deal rarer than scholars tend to assume."[8] Moreover, with regard to the book of Micah in particular, further reason for optimism may be noted in that several modern scholars have suggested that its present form displays a certain type of coherence.[9] Mays, for example, contends that:

> When the book is studied carefully with an interest, not in what makes it come apart, but in what holds it together, then a variety of integrating features begin to appear. . . .
> Beyond these features there is an arrangement of the material which employs them in a movement of proclamation that flows through the entire book. The structure of this arrangement does not, of course, have the clarity and coherence of an original composition where the movement of thought creates the material. But there does seem to be a discernable pattern in the material which is the result of an accumulative and sustained intention to say something which incorporates all the smaller parts into a larger message.

Thus, in his comment on individual passages, Mays seeks to point "to the way the sayings are related to their literary context as part of the whole."[10]

In carrying out a thorough examination of this proposal regarding the coherence of the final form of the book of Micah, I am motivated by much the same concern as Wharton has expressed with regard to the book of Job; that is:

> . . . the present, tattered, cluttered book of Job as an entity . . . has a right to be respected and listened to for its own sake, just as it is . . . since the conclusion of its complex history of formation and transmission, Job has functioned in the life of the Jewish and Christian communities as a word of address, the word of God to his people. Even if one did not share that faith, one should recognize that the book as it is represents a unique and complete literary *datum*, a *de facto* entity that has a right to be heard and interpreted on its own terms![11]

Quite aware of the difficulties involved in interpreting a composite text, Wharton proposes

---

[8] Robert Alter, *The Art of Biblical Narrative* (New York: Basic Books, 1981) 133.

[9] Note, for example: Willis, Dissertation; idem, "The Structure of the Book of Micah," *Svensk Exegetisk Årsbok* 34 (1969) 5-42; Leslie C. Allen, *The Books of Joel, Obadiah, Jonah and Micah,* New International Commentary on the Old Testament (Grand Rapids, MI: William B. Eerdmans Publishing Co., 1976); James L. Mays, *Micah: A Commentary,* OTL (Philadelphia: Westminster Press, 1976).

[10] Mays, *Micah,* pp. 2-3.

[11] Wharton, "Unanswerable Answer," p. 37. Childs's concern also is not with any particular editorial layer of the text, but with the final resultant product. Moreover, Childs (*Introduction,* pp. 75-77) suggests several additional reasons as to why this final shape is of special significance; in particular: 1) it alone displays the full history of revelation witnessed to by Scripture; 2) in it the community has exercised its critical judgment on the received traditions and modified them accordingly; and 3) by showing how the text was actualized by generations removed from the original event and composition of the writings the canonical shape may provide a hermeneutical key as to how we may actualize the text in our day.

... to explore again the possibility that the sequence from prologue to the voice from the whirlwind to the epilogue is capable of a relatively coherent reading, one that embraces a number of apparent contradictions even if it does nor resolve or eliminate them![2]

Of course, the fact that such a coherent reading is possible does not guarantee that this reading was intended by any given writer or redactor. Indeed, Wharton admits that the unity he does find in the book of Job is such as "no individual seems to have intended."[13] Even so (and here I follow many literary critics and depart from Childs), I also am seeking to discern within the text guides to construability, not necessarily intentionality. I shall ask: What possibilities for construal are suggested by the language of the text itself? and What features of the text might serve as guidelines for the reader in preferring one possibility over another?[14]

III. PROCEDURE

As stated above, in this study I shall seek to investigate the literary coherence of the final form of the book of Micah and to show how that coherence is

---

[12] Wharton, "Unanswerable Answer" p. 42.

[13] Ibid., p. 38. Note also Gunn's discussion (*Fate of King Saul,* p. 15) of the relation between authorial intentionality and the results of literary analysis. As regards his own analysis, Gunn concludes: "When I find subtlety in this story it is not necessarily the deliberate contrivance of a master narrator that I am exposing, though that may also be the case, rather it may be a subtlety created unconsciously in the dialectical process by which the story is created, a subtlety which is the logical resolution of the variously nuanced contributions and not a property of the contributions themselves."

[14] Thus, the emphasis of this study will not be on the recovery of an intention operative behind the text (although such a recovery is, of course, the basis of the standard historical-critical paradigm for interpretation). Neither, however, shall I advance an epistemological argument for the semantic autonomy of the text (i.e., that the text has meaning of itself apart from the intention of an author) such as do some contemporary literary critics. I have no intention of entering into the epistemological debate as to which of these interpretive paradigms is correct or even preferable (i.e., the historical-critical or the purely literary-critical).

To address the question of construability is a simpler and less conjectural business than seeking to determine intentionality. For this study I have chosen to adopt literary methods and to seek only to determine keys to construal which inhere within the text itself. As mentioned above, it is possible that the final form of the book may be found to be coherent but in such a way as not intended by any particular author or editor. Of course this would present no barrier to interpretation for one who holds for the semantic autonomy of the text. On the other hand, after determining the unique shape of the text and noting the keys which it provides as to its construal, the possibility also remains open of looking back in the other direction and re-examining the question of intentionality from a new perspective.

Another issue in general hermeneutics, the possibility of multiple meanings in a text, is also related to this study though outside of its proper scope.

expressed in terms of concrete literary features. To this end, I shall proceed inductively. That is, I shall seek by means of an analysis of the language of the book of Micah itself to compile features constitutive of coherence and thus to provide a description in terms drawn from the book itself.[15]

To begin, however, I seek to arrive at a working hypothesis regarding the overall structure of the book of Micah. The resulting structural hypothesis will then function as a framework for the continuing investigation of the coherence of the book. In the process of this investigation, the hypothesis itself will also be assessed and confirmed or modified.

Next, because chapter three of Micah has been noted by several scholars as that portion of the book which displays the most visible signs of unity or coherence,[16] the detailed analysis begins with Micah 3. That is, because this chapter clearly does exhibit coherence, it serves as a helpful starting place to begin marking features which contribute to coherence (as opposed to beginning with one of the problem spots in the book). Moreover, to begin with a passage generally acknowledged as being coherent helps guard against circular argumentation. Thus, the purpose of chapter 3 is twofold. First, I shall seek to demonstrate the coherence of Micah 3. To this end, I shall begin on the "lower" levels of the text analyzing what makes a sentence cohere, then move "upward" by stages investigating the coherence of smaller and then larger literary units. Secondly, and equally important in the scope of this study, I shall seek to identify and catalog those features of the text which contribute to this coherence and to analyze this data in such a way as to be of service in the investigation of the book as a whole.

The bulk of the analysis is presented in the following three chapters. Chapters 4 and 5 deal with the coherence of Micah 1-5 and 6-7 respectively. Then, in chapter 6, I seek to display the relations between these major sections which serve to bind them together into a coherent whole.

Finally, in chapter 7, I gather together and evaluate the significance of results reached in the preceding analysis. In particular, it is expected that this study might contribute to the field in several areas, including: 1) establishing the literary coherence of the book of Micah in its final form and suggesting some of the implications of this for the interpretation of the book; 2) providing a more precise understanding of the literary features which contribute to the unity of biblical books in general and of Micah in particular; 3) sorting out and evaluating the various scholarly proposals regarding the organization of the book of Micah, and 4) drawing implications regarding the helpfulness and

---

[15] While this study will proceed inductively, I shall nevertheless make free use of both methodological and exegetical studies which either point out specific features in the book of Micah relevant to my analysis or suggest features present in other biblical literature which might also play a significant role in the book of Micah.

[16] See Claus Westermann, *Basic Forms of Prophetic Speech*, trans. Hugh C. White (Philadelphia: Westminster Press, 1967) 174-75; Willis, "Structure," pp. 14, 38.

adequacy of interpretive approaches currently being developed which would deal with biblical books as coherent wholes. For example, after determining the shape of the text itself in its final form, it may be instructive to re-examine Childs's program asking "Do Childs's notion of a canonical intentionality and the ways in which he has discerned intentionality with respect to particular books indeed square with the possibilities for construal which are determined by a more purely literary study of the text itself, i.e., which are signalled by literary features of the text?"

IV. EXCURSUS: THIS PROJECT IN COMPARISON WITH WILLIS'S DISSERTATION

The present study bears some similarity to Willis's dissertation, "The Structure, Setting, and Interrelationships of the Pericopes in the Book of Micah." Both studies deal with the final or present form of the book and seek to investigate, indeed to demonstrate, its coherence. From this point, however, the studies diverge.

Willis's dissertation centers around a two-part thesis. He contends, first, that "the book of Micah in its present form exhibits a type of coherence." In particular, the book is arranged symmetrically according to an ABA pattern. Secondly, Willis argues that this coherence is the result of a literary process — primarily the result of the final redaction. The ABA pattern stems from a particular sixth century redactor who gave the book its present arrangement in order to speak to a specific community in a particular historical setting. This *Sitz-im-Leben*, i.e., the community and historical situation which pertain to the decisive, "final" redactor provides the proper context for interpreting the final form of the book. After understanding the final form of the book in relation to the community of the final redactor, one may then work back to earlier forms of the book.[17]

My purpose in seeking to analyze the coherence of the book of Micah differs markedly. Although Willis may well be correct that the distinctive shape of the book may be traced to a particular sixth century redactor, that is not of present concern. In fact, all such genetic arguments which understand the text as the product of what it came from run askew of my purpose in this study.[18] My concern is rather to discern the possibilities for construal presented by the language of the text itself. Although I do not seek an "original" literary unity,[19]

---

[17] Willis, Dissertation, pp. 103–6, 190, 248, 314.

[18] Cf. James L. Mays, "What is Written: A Response to Brevard Childs' *Introduction to the Old Testament as Scripture*," *Horizons in Biblical Theology* 2 (1980) 156–57.

[19] On my part, I readily grant that the book of Micah stems from a number of hands operating over a period of several centuries. A basic core of material stemming from Micah of Moresheth is agreed upon in principle if not always with respect to its precise scope. So too, the presence of exilic material has been argued quite convincingly. Thus, the

the coherence I seek is literary in nature in the sense that it is expressed in literature and by literary means, i.e., in the form of written language and by means of stylistic and rhetorical devices. As described above, I shall proceed inductively by examining the language of the final form of the book of Micah in order to isolate specific literary features which contribute to its coherence and seeking to determine whether such features so pervade the text as to make it possible to construe the book as a unit.

While much of his analysis is correct and helpful, Willis tends to overdraw the parallels between sections of the book. In attempting to prove coherence, he emphasizes their "affinities," i.e., the typical elements these sections hold in common. By overdrawing parallels, Willis tends to lose the distinctiveness of the sections—thus obscuring their true relation. In order to understand the nature of the book's coherence and its inner dynamics, it is necessary also to explicate what is unique and distinctive in the text in its various parts. The present study will seek to provide a more precise description of the literary features which contribute to the coherence of the book of Micah.[20] Such increased precision will help clarify the inner relations within the book.

This study also seeks to be of service in evaluating the helpfulness for biblical interpretation of recent approaches which would deal with biblical books as coherent wholes. That is, if the book of Micah in its final form does 1) display a type of coherence and 2) provide keys as to how it might best be construed, then an approach such as Childs's would seem more plausible. Whereas Willis would seek to read the final form of the book in relation to the community of the final redactor and then work back to earlier forms, Childs would seek to read the book as a totality which expresses via its language the fullness of the community's life over a period of time and which contains within itself the keys for its construal. According to this model, the final redaction may be decisive or it may be relatively unimportant; the resultant shape of the whole is given priority. Now, I shall not attempt to show that the latter is the correct way to read a text; however, such an approach might seem more worthy of credence if it could be demonstrated that the text displays such coherence as to render it construable as a unit.

coherence I seek is not that displayed in discourse written by a single author to a particular situation.

Moreover, as Childs (*Introduction*, p. 74) has observed: "the biblical texts were often shaped in such a way that the original poetic forms were lost, or a unified narrative badly shattered.

[20] For example, Willis tends to analyze "concepts" or "ideology," and in the course of his discussion brings up particular themes and motifs (without labelling them as such). Such concepts, as analyzed by Willis, tend to be general; themes and motifs are more particular. Moreover, concepts relate to intentionality and thus betray Willis's predisposition toward analyzing the purpose of a particular redactor. In order to avoid this loss of particularity and to deal with the resultant text, rather than a particular redactional layer, I intend to deal with explicit themes and motifs. Cf. Willis, "Structure," p. 40.

2
The Summons "Hear" and the Structure of the Book of Micah

The purpose of this chapter is to arrive at a working hypothesis concerning the overall structure of the book of Micah in its present form. This structural hypothesis will then function as a framework for my continuing investigation of the coherence of the book. In the process of this investigation, the hypothesis itself will also be assessed and confirmed or modified. To begin, I shall summarize the various scholarly positions held with regard to the structure of the book of Micah.

I. SCHOLARLY APPRAISALS OF THE STRUCTURE OF THE BOOK OF MICAH

The Structure of the Book of Micah as a Function of its Formation

Nearly all scholarly appraisals of the book of Micah consider its present structure primarily as a product of its compositional history. Moreover, the theory proposed with regard to the formation of the book often has a direct bearing on a scholar's evaluation of the coherence and significance of the resultant structure. For this reason, despite the independence of the present study from such genetic concerns, it will be helpful briefly to characterize the various theories proposed with regard to the formation of the book of Micah.

Willis summarized such theories in terms of five basic models. Of these, two explicitly deny the coherence of the book in its final form. First, some scholars posit an original, coherent book of Micah the order of which has somehow been confused in the course of its transmission rendering the received form of the book essentially incoherent. Advocates of this approach seek by rearrangement to recover the original order of the material and thus to restore the book's lost coherence. A second model, that most commonly subscribed to according to Willis, holds that the book of Micah is essentially "a collection of pericopes from different eras and circumstances, which came together in piecemeal fashion without any purposeful objective or coherence."[1] J. M. P. Smith, for example,

---

[1] Willis, Dissertation, pp. 46-100 (p. 57 quoted). As advocates of rearrangement, Willis cites Haupt, Fichtner, Hanon, Elhorst, Skipwith, Halevy, Schmidt, and Wiener; for a

exemplifies this attitude with regard to the coherence of the book in its final form. Concerning Micah 4–5, he writes: "The chapters . . . seem to contain a miscellaneous collection of fragments gathered up from various sources, and having little in common other than a hopeful outlook for the future." Similarly, Micah 6–7 appears to Smith as "a collection of miscellaneous fragments, coming from widely scattered periods and at least four different authors." Moreover, "There is no logical unity within chs. 6 and 7; they resolve themselves into seven sections, no one of which connects closely with either its preceding or its following sections."[2]

Yet, despite the prevalence of this latter view, there are also scholars who view the final form of the book in a positive light. For example, some suggest that the book of Micah is structured chronologically. It is divided into several major sections, each of which contains oracles reflecting the same general historical period of Micah's ministry. Though "untenable" in his evaluation, Willis nevertheless maintains the significance of this model as evidence "that scholars have been able to find a type of coherence in the book."[3]

The final two categories do not of necessity either affirm or deny the coherence of the book. According to the "compilation theory," various oracles were gathered into two or more independent collections which, in turn, were eventually compiled to form the present book of Micah. The fifth model considers the book of Micah to have developed from an original core of authentic Micah material which has been expanded and revised by a series of redactors. As exponents of the latter view who also assert the coherence of the book, Willis cites George, Weiser, Ungern-Sternberg, and Schilling.[4] The commentary of J. L. Mays serves as an example of a more recent treatment which combines the last two models regarding the book's compositional history and also asserts the coherence of the whole.[5]

---

survey of their various hypotheses, see pp. 46–56 (also idem, "Structure," pp. 5–6). As subscribing to variations of the second model, which he terms the "disconnected pericope theory," Willis cites thirty-eight scholars; see pp. 56–65 (also idem, "Structure," pp. 6).

[2] John M. P. Smith, *A Critical and Exegetical Commentary on the Books of Micah, Zephaniah and Nahum,* International Critical Commentary (Edinburgh: T. & T. Clark, 1911) 12, 15, 16.

[3] Willis, Dissertation, p. 100. As proponents of this approach, Willis (pp. 83–92) lists G. A. Smith, van Hoonacker, and Clamer. (See also idem, "Structure," pp. 10–11.) More recently, Rudolph has advocated a position which mediates between the chronological order and disconnected pericope approaches, whereas van der Woude combines chronological order and compilation theories; see the summaries in Knud Jeppesen, "New Aspects of Micah Research," *JSOT* 8 (1978) 14–16, 20–23.

[4] Willis, Dissertation, pp. 108–10, 27–30. More generally, see pp. 65–75 (also idem, "Structure," p. 6) for a survey of compilation hypotheses and their proponents; similarly, with regard to the latter model, see pp. 75–83 (also idem, "Structure," pp. 7–10).

[5] Mays, *Micah,* pp. 2–12, 21–33. In particular, Mays (p. 3) notes "a discernable pattern in the material which is the result of an accumulative and sustained intention to say

The matter of the compositional history of the book of Micah will not be addressed in this study. Rather I shall focus on the literary coherence of the book. From the point of view of this study, the significance of the above mentioned studies has to do with their assessment of the coherence of the book of Micah and, in the present context, especially with regard to their proposals as to the structural outline of the book.

Proposals Regarding the Structure of the Book of Micah

Recognizing that there exist many variations and a few exceptions, it is nevertheless the case that nearly all scholarly proposals regarding the structure of the present form of the book of Micah belong to one of four basic types. I shall describe and briefly evaluate each of these, taking note of the rationale behind each as well as their relative strengths and weaknesses. In this way I shall seek either to arrive at a clear preference as to which proposed structural outline will be most suitable as a working hypothesis or to establish the need for a fresh alternative.

Dividing 1-3 / 4-5 / 6-7.

It is frequently suggested that the book be divided into three sections as follows: chaps. 1-3, 4-5, and 6-7.[6] In support of this partitioning, the factors most frequently cited are differences in content, historical provenance, and style; or, as George Adam Smith puts it, "by their subject matter, by their temper and standpoint, and to a less degree by their literary form."[7] Of these, differentiation on the basis of content is by far the most frequent. The following statement by J. M. P. Smith is quite typical: "Chaps. 1-3 contain almost exclusively denunciations of sin and threats of punishment; chaps. 4-5 are made up prevailingly of words of hope and encouragement; while chaps. 6-7 mingle threat and promise."[8]

Secondly, the significance of genetic reasons for this partitioning is very evident in Robinson according to whom these three sections were originally independent collections of material differing in historical provenance as well as in content.[9] The significance of historical reasons for J. M. P. Smith's division

something which incorporates all the smaller parts into a larger message."

[6] See Willis (Dissertation, pp. 120-21 n. 3) for a catalog of scholars who partition the book in this way. Or, see idem, "The Structure of Micah 3-5 and the Function of Micah 5:9-14 in the Book," *ZAW* 81 (1969) 195-96. To this list one may add Theodore H. Gaster, s.v. "Micah," *The Universal Jewish Encyclopedia*, 1942, 7:528-29.

[7] George A. Smith, *The Book of the Twelve Prophets*, vol. 1: *Amos, Hosea, and Micah*, rev. ed. (New York: Harper & Bros., 1928) 383.

[8] John M. P. Smith, *A Commentary on the Books of Amos, Hosea, and Micah*, The Bible for Home and School (New York: Macmillan Co., 1914) 158.

[9] Theodore H. Robinson und Friedrich Horst, *Die zwölf kleinen Propheten*, 3. Aufl., Handbuch zum alten Testament, 1. Reihe, Nr. 14 (Tübingen: Verlag von J. C. B. Mohr [Paul Siebeck], 1964) 127. (The commentary on Micah is by Robinson.)

of the book is well supported by his separate treatments of the history of critical study for each section![10] And, while G. A. Smith does derive nearly all of the book of Micah from differing periods in the ministry of Micah himself, he also takes into account the critical discussion observing that the authenticity of chaps. 1–3 [less 2:12–13] is unchallenged and, in discussing the history of critical study of chaps. 4–7, noting the different problems and critical evaluation of 4–5 and 6–7![11]

Finally, as regards stylistic differences, G. A. Smith observes that "a series of oracles" in chaps. 1–5 is succeeded in chaps. 6–7 by "a series of conferences or arguments, by several speakers."[12] On the other hand, J. M. P. Smith cites a marked difference in style between Micah 1–3 and 4–7. The style of chaps. 1–3 he describes as "straightforward and vigorous," as "discourse in the highest degree vivid, strong, and logically effective;" by contrast, chaps. 4–7 "proceed from a less vigorous mind," display less "vividness and passion," and lack the stylistic unity of 1–3![13]

Despite certain helpful comments with regard to the literary form of the text made by its advocates, this partitioning of the text is quite inadequate. Of late, Childs, Willis, and Smend have all objected to this critical partitioning of the book on two grounds: First, it is based primarily on a critical evaluation of its compositional history, rather than its present shape![14] Secondly, this proposal also involves the elimination (or relocation) of 2:12–13 as a misplaced later interpolation![15] Furthermore, it remains a mystery why one should divide the book between chaps. 3 and 4 on the basis of content (chaps. 1–3 being predominantly threat, 4–5 promise) yet maintain 6–7 as a single section of mixed threat and hope. To mark a division between chaps. 3 and 4 and not between 7:6 and 7:7 is simply inconsistent application of this content criterion. Moreover, as Willis notes, "an analysis of the book composed of a section of doom, then a section of hope, then a section of doom-hope is not really as symmetrical as a doom, hope, doom, hope or a doom-hope, doom-hope pattern."[16] This partitioning thus tends to obscure the logical literary arrangement of the book.

---

[10] J. M. P. Smith, *Micah, Zephaniah and Nahum*, pp. 9–16.

[11] G. A. Smith, *Amos, Hosea, and Micah*, pp. 384–86.

[12] Ibid., p. 395.

[13] J. M. P. Smith, *Amos, Hosea, and Micah*, p. 158. Cf. idem, *Micah, Zephaniah and Nahum*, pp. 6–8.

[14] Childs, *Introduction*, p. 431, Willis, Dissertation, p. 121; Rudolph Smend, *Die Entstehung des Alten Testaments*, Theologische Wissenschaft, Bd. 1 (Stuttgart: Verlag W. Kohlhammer, 1978) 179. As G. A. Smith (*Amos, Hosea, and Micah*, p. 383) acknowledges, "literary form" plays a lesser role in this partitioning.

[15] Childs, *Introduction*, p. 431; Smend, *Entstehung des Alten Testaments*, p. 179. Willis (Dissertation, pp. 118–20) raises this issue in conjunction with the partitioning 1–3/4–5/6:1–7:6/7:7–20, but also suggests the possibility that 2:12–13 may have been moved subsequent to the "final" redaction of the book.

[16] Willis, Dissertation, p. 122.

Finally, Willis also raises the issue of whether a division should be drawn between chaps. 3 and 4 at all:

... the contrasts between 3:9-12 and 4:1-5 are so striking that one is almost compelled to conclude that the final redactor intended for chaps. 3 and 4 to be taken together. By making a major division between these chapters, one destroys the full effectiveness of these contrasts.[17]

For all the above reasons, this first structural proposal is to be regarded as inadequate and rejected.

Dividing 1-3 / 4-5 / 6:1-7:6(7) / 7:7(8)-20 (and variants).

Numerous scholars have suggested that the book of Micah be divided 1-3, 4-5, 6:1-7:6(7), 7:7(8)-20.[18] Once again the chief rationale put forth in support of this outline has to do with content. Thus Weiser writes:

We can distinguish in the book of Micah four groups of oracles: (1) Chapters 1-3 denunciations and threats (with one exception in 2:12 f.); (2) chapters 4-5 promises with an eschatological tinge; (3) 6-7 [sic] denunciations and threats; (4) chapters 7:7-20 a promise.[19]

Again, this partitioning is also argued on the basis of the history of the formation of the book of Micah. For example, according to Fohrer, these sections represent three separate collections of oracles formed independently in different periods plus a prophetic liturgy. Eventually, these collections were put together: first, 4-5 was appended to the authentic Mican collection, 1-3; later, the latter two sections were added.[20] Finally, stylistic features are also —

---

[17] Ibid., pp. 121-22; note the specific contrasts Willis mentions in n. 1.

[18] As proponents of this partitioning, Willis (ibid., p. 116 n. 3) cites: Baudissin, Kent, Steurnagel, Sellin, Bentzen, Pfeiffer, Deden, Fichtner, George, Kuhl, Kapelrud, Hanon, Leslie, Schilling, Bright, Weiser, and Deissler. To this list I would add: W. Nowack, s.v. "Micah," *Dictionary of the Bible*, ed. James Hastings, 1906, 3:359-60; B. Renaud, *Structure et Attaches littéraires de Michée IV-V* (Paris: J. Gabalda et Cie., 1965) 100-3; Rolf F. von Ungern-Sternberg, *Der Rechtsstreit Gottes mit seiner Gemeinde: Der Prophet Micha,* Die Botschaft des Alten Testaments, Bd. 23/3 (Stuttgart: Calwer Verlag, 1958) 5-6. Eissfeldt, Meyer, Lippl, and Gehman follow a standard variation of this proposal (see n. 22 below). Also related are the proposals of Gailey (Balmer H. Kelly, ed., *The Layman's Bible Commentary,* 25 vols. [Richmond: John Knox Press, 1962] vol. 15: *Micah, Nahum, Habakkuk, Zephaniah, Haggai, Zechariah, Malachi,* by James H. Gailey, pp. 10, 12) and W. Robertson Smith (see Willis, Dissertation, p. 66).

[19] Artur Weiser, *Introduction to the Old Testament* [London: Darton, Longman & Todd, 1961] 253.

[20] Georg Fohrer, *Introduction to the Old Testament,* initiated by Ernst Sellin, completely revised and rewritten by Georg Fohrer, trans. David E. Green (Nashville: Abingdon, 1968) 444-47.

The genetic basis for this partitioning arises quite easily from the early period of Micah criticism: Georg H. A. von Ewald (*Commentary on the Prophets of the Old Testament,*

though less often — cited in support of this outline.[21]

This partitioning is certainly an improvement over the first proposal in that the criterion of content and tone is applied more uniformly (though 2:12-13 is still excluded). However, application of this criterion also gives rise to a major variant of this outline: Eissfeldt, along with several others, divides 1-3, 4:1-5:8, 5:9-7:6, 7:7-20;[22] i.e., these scholars take 5:9-14 as a threat rather than a promise. It will later be shown, after a close analysis of the present form of 5:9-14 and its function in context, that this oracle is better taken as essentially positive in tone.[23] The partitioning 1-3, 4-5, 6:1-7:6, 7:7-20 is thus to be preferred over its variant.

Further, that the prime concern of the present study is for the literary shape of the book does blunt the force of genetic arguments in favor of a structural proposal. Nevertheless, the fact that this partitioning is backed up by historical arguments does not in any way tend to invalidate it either.

However, there remain several problems with this proposal. Two of the arguments against the first proposal apply also with regard to this one. To draw a major division between chaps. 3 and 4 obscures the clear contrastive relationship between 3:9-12 and 4:1-5. Moreover, proponents of this partitioning also regard 2:12-13 as not in its proper context and thus to be either moved or

---

5 vols., trans. J. Frederick Smith [London: Williams & Norgate, 1876] 2:323-26) suggested the division between chaps. 1-5 and 6-7, assigning the latter to an anonymous prophet during the reign of Manasseh; Bernhard Stade ("Bemerkungen über das Buch Micha," *ZAW* 1 [1881] 161-76) argued that authentic Micah material is limited to chaps. 1-3, 4-5 stemming largely from the exilic period, and the break between 7:6 and 7:7 stems from Julius Wellhausen (ed., Friedrich Bleek's *Einleitung in das Alte Testament*, 4. Aufl., p. 426, as cited and translated by Samuel R. Driver, *An Introduction to the Literature of the Old Testament*, International Theological Library, 6th ed. [New York: Charles Scribner's Sons, 1897] 333) who, noting that the historical situation presumed in 7:7-20 is radically different from that represented in 7:1-6, concluded that "Between v. 6 and v. 7 there yawns a century."

[21] It should be noted, however, that the argument from compositional history derives in part from the pioneering work of Ewald (see n. 20 above and p. 17 below) whose argument for the break between chaps. 5 and 6 was largely stylistic in nature.

[22] Otto Eissfeldt, *The Old Testament: An Introduction*, trans. Peter R. Ackroyd (London: Harper & Row, 1965) 409; Joseph Lippl und Johannes Theis, *Die zwölf kleinen Propheten*, Die Heiligen Schrift des Alten Testamentes, 8. Bd., 3. Abt./1. Hälfte (Bonn: Peter Hanstein Verlagsbuchhandlung, 1937) 182 (the commentary on Micah is by Lippl); R. Meyer, s.v. "Michabuch," *Die Religion in Geschichte und Gegenwart*, 3. Aufl., 4:929-31; Henry S. Gehman, s.v. "Micah, The Book of," *The New Westminster Dictionary of the Bible*, (1970) 615-16 (Gehman also suggests partitioning 1-2/3-5/6-7).

[23] See pp. 67-68 below. See also Willis (Dissertation, pp. 111-16) who argues quite convincingly against a break between 5:8 and 5:9.

eliminated.[24] Finally, to divide in such a four-fold manner tends to obscure the parallel content of the first and third, and second and fourth, sections. Even advocates of this outline seem to realize this. For example, while advocating a four-part division, Fohrer also notes: "Structurally, the book follows the two-part eschatological schema, twice repeated."[25] Thus, while this proposal is a definite improvement over the first, it is still in need of modification. This leads to a third proposal regarding the structure of the book of Micah.

Dividing 1-5 / 6-7.

A number of scholars have divided the book of Micah into two maor sections: chaps. 1-5 and 6-7.[26] Of these, Ewald was the first. In summary form, his arument was: (1) Chapters 1-5 form a complete unit of themselves; (2) the two sections appear to arise out of different historical situations; (3) the style of the two sections is different; some literary features characteristic of chaps. 1-5 are lacking in 6-7; and (4) chaps. 6-7 are dramatic in form, 1-5 are not.[27]

S. R. Driver supports the same basic partitioning. However, he subdivides each of the two major sections so that his structural outline is similar to that described above, especially the repeated two-part eschatological schema referred to by Fohrer, Lippl, and Weiser. Though Driver displays an awareness of the critical discussion regarding the disparate historical provenance of various portions of the book, his arguments for this structural outline are strictly literary in character, drawing on the criteria of content, tone, point of view, and literary form.[28]

---

[24] For example, Artur Weiser (*Das Buch der zwölf kleinen Propheten*, Bd. 1, *Die Propheten Hosea, Joel, Amos, Obadja, Jona, Micha*, Das Alte Testament Deutsch, Tbd. 24 [Göttingen: Vandenhoeck & Ruprecht, 1949] 203) writes: "Mit Ausnahme von 2,12 f. enthalten Kapitel 1-3 Drohung;" and Lippl (*Zwölf kleinen Propheten*, 1:182) rearranges so that "1,1-3,12 stehen, abgesehen von 2,12 f., Drohungen; 4,1-5,8 + 2,12-13 Verheissungen." See also Willis, Dissertation, p. 119 n. 1.

[25] Fohrer, *Introduction*, p. 447. Lippl (*Zwölf kleinen Propheten*, 1:182) and Weiser (*Zwölf kleinen Propheten*, 1:202), among others, support the same viewpoint.

[26] Willis (Dissertation, p. 120) cites Nöldeke, Ewald, Kleinert, W. Robertson Smith, Driver, Findlay, Hölscher, Burkitt, Mowinckel, George, Orelli, and G. W. Anderson. To this list I would add: Mays, *Micah*, p. 3; A. S. van der Woude, "Deutero-Micha: ein Prophet aus Nord-Israel?" *Nederlands Theologisch Tijdsschrift* 25 (1971) 365-78 (see also the review of his work on Micah in Jeppesen, "New Aspects of Micah Research," pp. 20-23); Theodor Lescow, "Redaktionsgeschichtliche Analyse von Micha 1-5," *ZAW* 84:46-85, idem, "Redaktionsgeschichtliche Analyse von Micha 6-7," *ZAW* 84:182-212; William Wright, s.v. "Micah," *Cyclopedia of Biblical Literature*, ed. John Kitto, 10th ed., 2:334; John Jahn, *An Introduction to the Old Testament*, additional references and notes by Samuel Turner & William Whittingham (New York: G. & C. Carvill, 1827) 331-33.

[27] Ewald, *Prophets*, 2:324-26; J. M. P. Smith, *Micah, Zephaniah and Nahum*, p. 12.

[28] Driver, *Introduction*, pp. 326, 330-31.

More recently, James L. Mays has argued quite forcibly in support of this two-part partitioning of the book of Micah. His primary argument is also literary in character depending primarily on the arrangement of the material.

> The book is composed of two major parts, 1.2–5.15 and 6.1–7.20. Each part opens with an introductory summons to hear which identifies its audience (1.2 and 6.1a). Each is arranged so as to unfold a revelation of YHWH's way in the world. . . . Each section is rounded off by a passage which concludes its movement, the first with the threat of YHWH's vengeance on the disobedient nations (5.15) and the second with a hymn to the compassion of God. Within each section there is evidence in the arrangement and shaping of the material that a persistent intention has been at work to bring the individual units under the control of broader kerygmatic purposes.

In addition, Mays notes a basic stylistic difference between 1–5 and 6–7; the latter presents "an antiphonal alternation of voices." Further, within each of these major sections Mays notes a pivot, i.e., between 3:12 and 4:1 and again at 7:7. Yet, he cautions against drawing too sharp a division at these points. To divide 1–5 and 6–7 each into a simple alternation of judgment and salvation tends to obscure "the many inner relationships within the two blocks and the significance of the content of one for the other."[29]

While the above arguments are strictly literary in character, Mays is not unconcerned with genetic questions. As such matters relate to the structure of the book, Mays's crucial conclusion, following the redactional studies of Lescow, is that the two parts were formed separately prior to their being compiled into one book.[30] Thus, while Mays carefully separates his discussions of "the form of the book" and "the formation of the book," he also discovers that the two are clearly interrelated: some of the same features contribute to both analyses; moreover, with regard to the partitioning of the book, the latter does tend to confirm and support the former.

This option is clearly superior to either of the preceding two. In fact, of the objections raised in the preceding sections, there remains only that regarding how to construe 2:12–13. The three scholars I have used as examples in this section deal with this problem in three different ways. Ewald, following the lead of Ibn Ezra, considered these words as spoken by Micah's opponents, the false prophets, "as an example of their deceptive security."[31] Driver is unable to construe these verses in their present context and simply acknowledges the difficulty.[32] Finally, contrary to the consensus which perceives in 2:12–13 a hopeful tone, Mays reads this unit as an oracle of doom.[33]

---

[29] Mays, *Micah,* pp. 3, 9, 4.
[30] Ibid., pp. 22–23.
[31] Driver, *Introduction,* p. 328; Ewald, *Prophets,* 2:306–7, 309.
[32] Driver, *Introduction,* pp. 327–28.
[33] Mays, *Micah,* pp. 5, 73–76. See also the discussion on pp. 51–54 below.

Dividing 1-2 / 3-5/ 6-7.

Finally, it has also been suggested that the book be partitioned 1-2, 3-5, 6-7.[34] Divided in this manner, each major section opens with a summons beginning with the imperative שִׁמְעוּ and a specification of addressee. Moreover, each of these three sections displays the pattern "judgment + salvation." This partitioning is thus based on two factors: the content or tone of the oracles and the use of the summons "Hear."

In his 1966 Vanderbilt dissertation, Willis carried out a structural analysis of the final form of the book of Micah and further refined this partitioning emphasizing the role of symmetry in the arrangement of the book:

> The general arrangement of the book seems to conform to a [sic] A (1-2)-B (3-5)-A (6-7) pattern. In the first and third divisions, the doom sections are much longer than the hope sections, whereas in the central division, the hope section is much longer than the doom section. It is striking that the first and third sections are composed of four pericopes each: (a) a covenant lawsuit (1:2-7 in I and 6:1-8 in III), (b) a lament (1:8-16 in I and 7:1-6 in III); (c) an explanation (*Begründung*) for the impending catastrophe in the form of a reproach (2:1-11 in I and 6:9-16 in III), and (d) a hope oracle (2:12-13 in I and 7:7-20 in III). To include ch. 3 as part of the first section or portions of ch. 5 as part of the last would destroy this symmetry.[35]

Since the publication of Willis's article, "The Structure of the Book of Micah," this outline, favored also by Keil and many earlier interpreters, has enjoyed new popularity.[36]

---

[34] Willis (Dissertation, p. 123) cites Barnes, Farrar, Beck, Chambers, Rupprecht, Halevy, Eiselen, Zenon, Rösler, Farley, McFadyen, Zeller, Gehman, Ridderbos, Copass-Carlson, Young, Unger, and Ginn. To these I would add: V. Ermoni, s.v. "Michée (Le Livre de)," *Dictionnaire de la Bible* (1908) vol. 4, cols. 1064–67; William A. Wright, s.v. "Micah," *Smith's Dictionary of the Bible* (1888) 3:1914–17; G. Campbell Morgan, *Introduction: Job to Malachi*, The Analyzed Bible (New York: Fleming H. Revell Co., 1908) 218–19; George C. M. Douglas, *The Six Intermediate Minor Prophets: Obadiah-Zephaniah*, Handbooks for Bible Classes and Private Students (Edinburgh: T. & T. Clark, n.d.) 4; W. J. Deane and S. D. Hillman, *Micah*, pp. ii–iii, viii, *The Pulpit Commentary*, vol. 30 (New York: Anson D. F. Randolph & Co., [1881–90]) (exposition by Deane); Paul Fabianke, Hrsg., *Praktische Bibelerklärung* (Konstanz: Christlicher Buch u. Kunstverlag, n.d.), T. 2, Bd. 17b: *Die Propheten: Jonah, Micha, Nahum, Habakkuk, Zephaniah, Zechariah, Malachi*, von S. Zeissig, A. Hering P. Fabianke, B. Keller, u. W. Joft (Micha erklärt von A. Hering) 11; and Carl F. Keil, *The Twelve Minor Prophets*, vol. 1, Clark's Foreign Theological Library, 4th series vol. 17, trans. James Martin (Edinburgh: T. & T. Clark, 1885) 422. For recent proponents of this partitioning, see n. 36 below.

[35] Willis, "Micah 3-5," p. 197. See idem, Dissertation, chaps. II-IV.

[36] See Smend, *Entstehung des Alten Testaments*, p. 179; Allen, *Books of Joel . . .*, pp. 257–58; Wilhelm Rudolph, *Micha-Nahum-Habakkuk-Zehanja*, Kommentar zum alten Testament, Bd. 13/3 (Gütersloh: Gütersloher Verlagshaus Gerd Mohn, 1975) 24, 63–65; Childs, *Introduction*, p. 431. For earlier proponents of this partitioning, see n. 34 above.

In its favor, it may be noted that this analysis is based primarily on literary criteria, especially the use of the summons "Hear" and the alternation of sections of judgment and salvation. Conversely, it may legitimately claim independence of genetic arguments. In this regard it must be emphasized, however, that such independence does not of necessity imply special merit or guarantee better results even from a strictly literary standpoint.

Another apparent advantage of this partitioning is that it explains the significance of 2:12-13 in its present context. Following this analysis, these verses need be neither moved nor excised. So Rudolph observes:

> Der Aufbau des Michabuches ist wohlüberlegt. Seine Dreiteilung gilt schon seit lange als ausgemacht, aber in der Form: 1-3; 4/5; 6/7. Dabei ist aber die Funktion von 2,12f. übersehen, das nicht ein ungeschickter und störender Einschub ist, sondern im Gesamtaufbau seine bestimmte Funktion hat, nämlich auch den ersten Teil mit einer Heilsweissagung abzuschliessen (siehe bei 2,12f.). Damit bekommen wir die Einteilung 1/2; 3-5; 6/7, wobei jeder Teil nicht nur formal mit "Höret" anfängt, sondern auch nach dem Schema: Unheil-Heil angeordnet ist . . .[37]

Yet, its treatment of 2:12-13 might also be argued as a point against this proposal; it may place too much weight on these verses. According to Willis, Rudolph, and others who analyze the structure of Micah in this fashion, each of the three major sections of the book follows the pattern "judgment + salvation." Then 2:12-13 is viewed as the salvation portion of the first section, the corresponding salvation portions of sections two and three being 4:1-5:15 and 7:7-20. One is hard pressed, however, to see the two verses of 2:12-13 as constituting a subsection comparable to the latter two salvation subsections.

Finally, it should be noted that whereas critical scholars have uniformly held Micah 1-3 together as a unit which is entirely authentic Micah material, this partitioning splits this material. In this regard, Willis notes:

> . . . granting for argument's sake that the prophet Micah is responsible for materials in chaps. 1-3 alone, this would not preclude the possibility that a later redactor could have taken this material and for his own purposes divided it in his own arrangement of that larger corpus of prophetic oracles which forms the present composition of the book.[38]

Now, what Willis suggests is certainly possible. But is it the case? While the authenticity of the material is of no concern to the present analysis, I shall argue that chaps. 1-3 function as a coherent unit even in the final form of the book.[39]

---

[37] Rudolph, *Micha,* p. 24; note also pp. 63-65. Cf. Smend (*Entstehung des Alten Testaments,* p. 179) who exhibits the same concern, but appears to misrepresent Rudolph: "Es scheint, als liege hier dreimal, jeweils mit 'hört' eingeleitet, das Kompositionsschema Unheil/Heil vor (RUDOLPH; nach der herkömmlichen Auffassung, die 2:12f. vernachlässigt, zweimal)."

[38] Willis, Dissertation, p. 121.

[39] See pp. 45-59 below. Willis himself notes some reasons for maintaining Micah 1-3 as a unit; see his Dissertation, pp. 116-20; or "Micah 3-5," p. 197.

Reading 2:12-13 as an oracle of salvation and dividing between chaps. 2 and 3 creates an unnatural tension; 1:1-2:11 and 3:1-12 then seem to reach out for each other across the break. Moreover, this division also disregards the function of ויאמר in 3:1 which serves to link chaps. 1 and 2 to chap. 3.[40]

Summary

Of the four structural proposals treated above, the latter two are clearly the better options. However, despite the fact that I may have signalled my own preference, from the analysis above no compelling reason emerges to prefer one of these two options over the other. Both present certain advantages; both entail certain difficulties.

To divide 1-5/6-7 displays an even application of the content/tone criterion combined with an awareness of the symmetry expressed by the pattern "judgment + salvation" twice repeated. It recognizes the clear distinction between the judgment and salvation portions of each major section; yet, within each major section, it also takes into account the links between the two portions. Moreover, this proposal recognizes the parallel structures of the two major sections without obscuring their stylistic differences. Nevertheless, following this analysis, the problem of 2:12-13 looms large; to relocate or excise this unit is a major departure from the present form of the book. Yet, to follow Mays and construe 2:12-13 as an oracle of doom could alleviate this problem.

On the other hand, the partitioning 1-2/3-5/6-7 may lay claim to being based on an explicit stylistic marker (the summons to hear), displaying a symmetrical structure to the book, and presenting one way to resolve the problem of how to construe 2:12-13 in its present context. Yet, this construal of 2:12-13 appears to overload the text at this point. Furthermore, there are a number of constraints against drawing a major division between chapters two and three.

What is needed at this point is some way of breaking the deadlock between these two proposals. Several issues appear as crucial in this regard. How is 2:12-13 to be construed? Are chapters 1-3 a unit, or is there a break after chapter two? Does the summons "Hear" function in the book of Micah in the way Willis contends? Now, while it will be important eventually to explore each of these questions, it will suffice at present to focus on one. Thus, I propose that an

---

[40] In his article "A Note on ויאמר in Micah 3:1" (*ZAW* 80 [1968] 50-54), Willis rehearses the positions taken on the significance of ויאמר and, in the light of his theory regarding the structure of the book of Micah, dismisses them all in favor of his own suggestion that a redactor inserted ויאמר here in order to indicate a major break between sections, i.e., between chaps 2 and 3. He adduces Amos 1:2 as an analogous situation in which ויאמר is used to introduce a major section of a prophetic book.

In my opinion, however, ויאמר in Amos 1:2 serves as a transition; it opens the first major section of Amos, but at the same time links it to the introduction given in 1:1. To interpret ויאמר in Mic 3:1 as signalling a major break is to disregard the syntax of the waw consecutive which ordinarily serves the function of linking. ויאמר also serves here to identify the speaker of the following oracles; this is helpful given the interchange of voices in 2:6ff.

analysis of the function of the summons "Hear" be employed as a discriminant to tilt the balance between the structural options indicated above.

II. THE FUNCTION OF THE SUMMONS
"HEAR" IN THE BOOK OF MICAH

Each major section of the book of Micah begins with a summons of the form: "Hear" + addressee.[41] This is true whether one partitions the book 1-5/6-7 or 1-2/3-5/6-7. In fact, such a summons introduced by the imperative שמעו occurs five times within the book of Micah, in 1:2; 3:1, 9; 6:1-2, 9. The RSV reads:

1:2   Hear, you peoples, all of you;
      hearken O earth, and all that is in it;
    and let the LORD GOD be a witness against you,
      the Lord from his holy temple.
    For behold . . .

3:1   And I said:
    Hear you heads of Jacob
      and rulers of the house of Israel!
    Is it not . . .

3:9   Hear this, you heads of the house of Jacob
      and rulers of the house of Israel,
    who abhor . . .

6:1-2   Hear what the LORD says:
    Arise, plead your case before the mountains,
      and let the hills hear your voice.
    Hear, you mountains, the controversy of the LORD,
      and you enduring foundations of the earth;
    for the LORD has a controversy with his people,
      and he will contend with Israel.

6:9   The voice of the LORD cries to the city—
      and it is sound wisdom to fear thy name:
    "Hear, O tribe and assembly of the city!
      Can I forget . . .

---

[41] The occurrence of the summons שמע is frequent in the prophetic literature (qal imperative of שמע occurs ninety-three times in the prophets; see, e.g., Isa 1:2; Amos 3:1; Hos 4:1 Jer 2:4) and often functions structurally. For example, Samuel R. Driver (ed., *The Books of Joel and Amos*, 2d ed., Cambridge Bible for Schools and Churches [Cambridge: Cambridge University Press, 1915] 97, 159) notes that the book of Amos is composed of three parts; of these, the second (chaps 3-6) is composed of three discourses each introduced by the summons to hear (Amos 3:1; 4:1; 5:1).

The present task is to analyze these occurrences of the summons to see how they function within the book and whether they tend to support one structural proposal over the other.

To begin, it is immediately apparent that this summons occurs only within the judgment sections of the book. Thus, its role as a structural indicator is clearly limited; one dare not overlook the clear significance of the transitions from judgment to salvation as structural keys. The summons may be an important structural feature; it is not the only such feature.

Now, let us assume that Willis's analysis of the structure of the book of Micah is substantially correct; that is, Micah is divided into three major sections: 1-2; 3-5; and 6-7. The occurrences of the summons in 1:2; 3:1; and 6:1 are cited as one primary indicator of this structure. This leads immediately to the question: If the summons to hear is so important for the structure of Micah, then what about the occurrences of this summons in 3:9 and 6:9? Nowhere does Willis address this problem directly, though he comes close with respect to 3:9 (see below). However Leslie Allen—who also partitions the book 1-2/3-5/6-7— addresses this question briefly: "The imperative also occurs in 3:9; 6:9, where its appearance is of secondary structural importance, serving as an echo of the key word in 3:1; 6:1."[42] But is this in fact the case?

Consider first 3:9. Though Willis nowhere discusses directly the question of why 3:9 is not structurally significant like the three which open his major sections, he does hint at how he might deal with this question when he refers to 3:9-12 as a summary oracle.[43] Perhaps the repetition of the summons is a result of the oracle's summing up 3:1-4 and 3:5-8. Indeed, the additional summons in 3:9 is not a major problem for Willis's analysis; there are several indications that 3:9 is integrally connected with and resumes 3:1. Notice: 1) the addressee of 3:1 is repeated almost verbatim in 3:9; 2) chapter three exhibits—with respect to its addressees—a clear A B A' structure (vv 1-4/5-8/9-12) where the addressees of A' are the same as those in A, except that in v 11 this group (i.e., the addressees of A') is expanded to include also the prophets—the subjects of B; and 3) the beginning of the unit is actually not "Hear" in 3:1, but "And I said" which is not repeated in 3:9. With regard to 3:9, Allen may well be correct that it echoes 3:1 and is of lesser importance structurally.

It is not nearly so easy, however, to dismiss 6:9 as of secondary structural importance. Whereas the summons in 3:1 is repeated nearly verbatim in 3:9, 6:1 and 6:9 are quite different. To term 6:9 an "echo" of 6:1 is at best imprecise, and perhaps quite misleading. For now, it will suffice simply to note that this proposal does not supply an adequate explanation of the function of 6:9.

This is not, however, the only problem with Willis's proposal in relation to the summons. It should also be noted that 3:1 and 9 are not completely parallel to 1:2 and 6:1-2. In each case one observes the summons "Hear" + addressee.

---

[42] Allen, *Books of Joel . . .* , p. 258.
[43] Willis, Dissertation, pp. 274-75.

However, in 1:2 and 6:1-2 the addressees are summoned to function as witnesses (though the role of the witnesses is not identical in the two texts);[44] the summonses in chap. 3 are addressed to the accused, i.e., the defendants. Moreover, the legal terminology ("witness," "plead your case," "controversy") so prominent in 1:2 and 6:1-2 is not evident in 3:1, 9. Of course, Willis does outline the structure of Micah as ABA, section two being somewhat different than sections one or three. Nevertheless, these differences are significant enough to make it doubtful that the summons in 3:1 functions in the same way as those in 1:2 and 6:1-2.

Thus, there seems to be adequate reason to question whether the proposal of Willis and Allen is the best way to account for the several occurrences of the summons to hear. In order to facilitate further comparison of these five texts, I have listed in table 1 a number of features which accompany the summons. This should help clarify the similarities and differences involved in the several uses of this summons in the book of Micah.

---

[44] The role of the addressee in 1:2 is a question open to debate. The various positions taken on the issue are rehearsed by Willis in "Some Suggestions on the Interpretation of Micah 3:1," *VT* 18 (1968) 372-79. Willis concludes (p. 377) that in 1:2 the addressees "are the defendants or the accused in the lawsuit." They are not parallel to the mountains in 6:1-2 which function rather as "*legal* witnesses."

In my opinion, Willis's careful analysis of עד ... ב (pp. 375-78) is quite correct; the phrase must surely be translated "Let the Lord be a witness against you." Thus, the addressees cannot function in a manner strictly parallel to that of the mountains in 6:1-2, i.e. (p. 377; following Huffmon and others), as "*legal* witnesses who testify to the accuracy or truthfulness of the plaintiff's (Yahweh's) accusation against the defendant (Israel)."

Seeking to elaborate on the relation between YHWH and the addressees of 1:2, Willis writes (p. 378): "Such a summons to the nations is quite appropriate in an oracle which announces impending doom on Israel, because the prophets considered Yahweh's punishment of Israel a model or pattern for Yahweh's future punishment of the nations. The nations are to see Yahweh's *witness against* (accusation of) them (vv 2-4) in His punishment of His own people (vv 5-7). If Yahweh does not spare His own people, the nations need not expect that He will spare them." Again, I agree.

However, I disagree with Willis's conclusion regarding the role which the nations (Surely Willis is also correct that the nations are the referent of עמים and ארץ ומלאה) play in this text. Beginning with 1:5 and throughout chaps. 1-3 it is abundantly clear that Israel is the defendant; the trial is initiated because of "the transgression of Jacob" and "the sins of the house of Israel" (1:5). The nations function as learning witnesses who, by observing the accusation and judgment of Israel, see that they also stand under the accusation of YHWH. Israel is on trial; but her trial serves also as YHWH's witness against the nations.

TABLE 1
FEATURES ATTENDING THE VARIOUS OCCURRENCES OF
THE SUMMONS "HEAR" IN THE BOOK OF MICAH

1:2   a) lacking introduction
       b) addressees: three parallel expressions ("peoples," "earth," "all in it")
       c) language to evoke picture of courtroom setting[45]
       d) role of addressees: learning witnesses who are also accused[46]
       e) accusation: general
       f) description of theophany

3:1   a) introduced by ואמר
       b) addressees: two parallel expressions ("heads of Jacob," "rulers of the house of Israel"; more specific than 1:2
       c) lacking legal terminology
       d) role of addressees: defendants
       e) accusation: sins specified
       f) lacking description of theophany

3:9   a) lacking introduction
       b) addressees: two parallel expressions ("heads of the house of Jacob," "rulers of the house of Israel")
       c) lacking legal terminology
       d) role of addressees: defendants
       e) accusation: sins specified
       f) lacking description of theophany

6:1-2 a) lacking introduction
       b) addressees: three separate addressees (of which only the "mountains"/"foundations" are explicitly identified)[47]

[45] Cf. Mays, *Micah,* pp. 40, 129.
[46] See n. 44 above.
[47] The three part summons in 6:1-2 is quite complex and presents several difficulties for the interpreter. Here is just a brief sampling of opinions regarding the identity of the speaker(s) and addressees involved:

		Speaker	Addressees
Renaud	1a	prophet	
	1b	God	prophet (to relay to the people)
	2	prophet	mountains and hills
Mays	1a		general audience
	1b	YHWH	people of YHWH
	2	YHWH	mountains and hills
Watson	1a		audience
	1b	*	plaintiff and defendant
	2	*	mountains and hills

(* the prophet or a court official)

          c) court setting described

          d) role of addressees: mountains are legal witnesses[48]

          e) accusation by way of testifying to own covenant faithfulness

          f) lacking description of theophany

6:9   a) extended introduction

          b) addressees: two parallel expressions ("tribe," "assembly of the city")[49]

          c) lacking legal terminology

          d) role of addressees: accused, i.e., defendants; specific groups (versus 1:2 and 6:1-2 which are general)

          e) accusation: sins specified

          f) lacking description of theophany

The extremely close relation between 3:1 and 3:9 has been discussed above. In anticipation of chaps. 3 and 4, I would note further that within the context of chap. 3, 3:9 functions to resume 3:1 and also as a focus marker which signals the climactic oracle of the unit. Moreover, within the larger unit of chaps. 1-3, 3:9 is the third member of a triad,[50] again functioning as a focus marker signalling the climax of this larger unit also. Thus, it does function structurally, but in a manner somewhat different than the other four.

Between any pair of the four remaining summonses both similarities and differences may be noted. However, two general observations may also be made: 1) 1:2; 3:1; and 6:1-2 do not all function on one level distinguishable from that of 6:9; 2) rather, one may observe parallels between 1:2 and 6:1-2 and between 3:1 and 6:9. The latter pair is distinguished from the former by a) an introduction, b) a more narrowly circumscribed group of addressees, c) the lack of legal language evoking a courtroom setting, d) more specific accusations, and e) addressees clearly having the role of defendants on trial.

(B. Renaud, *La Formation du Livre de Michée: Tradition et Actualisation,* Etudes Bibliques [Paris: J. Gabalda et Cie., 1977] 301-2; Mays, *Micah,* p. 128; Paul Watson, "Form Criticism and an Exegesis of Micah 6:1-8," *Restoration Quarterly* 7 [1963] 64.)

My own tendency is to consider the speaker as constant throughout, most likely the prophet functioning as an official of the court. As for the addressees, I would suggest that v 1a is addressed to the defendant (Israel), v 1b to the plaintiff (YHWH), and v 2 to the legal witnesses (the mountains and hills; see n. 44 above). For further discussion, see pp. 89-91 below.

[48] See n. 44 above. Cf. Watson, "Form Criticism."

[49] "Assembly of the city:" Reading ומועד העיר instead of MT's ומי יעדה עוד with partial support of LXX (cf. *BHS*). The MT appears confused; however, it is possible to see how it might have resulted from the restored text via a series of errors of transmission. The emended reading not only makes sense, but also restores parallelism.

[50] Regarding the significance of such triads, see p. 40 n. 32 below.

The above analysis has uncovered a number of problems with partitioning the book of Micah 1-2/3-5/6-7. Conversely, this analysis is fully consistent with that proposal which divides the book 1-5/6-7. The summons "Hear" is indeed a key element in the structure of the book of Micah; however, it functions somewhat differently than Willis, et al., would lead one to believe. First, 1:2 and 6:1-2 function to introduce new major sections; they set the scene by means of language which evokes an image of the courtroom setting. Thus, the book of Micah falls into two major sections: chaps. 1-5 and 6-7. Each of these begins with a summons and is composed of a section of judgment followed by promises of salvation. I would add, however, that each of the judgment sections is subdivided by a second summons. 3:1 and 6:9 each function as continuations of the legal disputes introduced in 1:2 and 6:1-2. They also function as transitions: a more narrowly defined group is singled out for further accusation (i.e., the leaders, those who bear greater responsibility) and their sins are more clearly specified. Thus, one might sketch an outline of the book of Micah as in table 2.

TABLE 2
A STRUCTURAL OUTLINE OF THE BOOK OF MICAH

I. Chaps. 1-5 The First Dispute
  A. Chaps. 1-3 Judgment
    1. Chaps. 1-2
    2. Chap. 3
  B. Chaps. 4-5 Salvation
II. Chaps. 6-7 The Second Dispute
  A. 6:1-7:6 Judgment
    1. 6:1-8
    2. 6:9-7:6
  B. 7:7-20 Salvation

In conclusion, while the summons to hear does play a role as a structural indicator in the book of Micah, my analysis has shown that its significance in this respect must be carefully qualified. First, it is important to note that the summons is variously employed in its several occurrences. Not all occurrences of the summons are to be taken as functioning on the same level. Its significance varies. Secondly, the summons "Hear" simply will not bear the weight of the structure of the book of Micah when considered alone. In the discussion above I have noted a number of features which contribute to the structure of the book of Micah. More such features will be adduced in succeeding chapters. Their significance ought not be minimized. Finally, in light of the above, I have demonstrated that the two-part partitioning of the book of Micah, 1-5/6-7, is to be preferred over the three-part partitioning, 1-2/3-5/6-7. This two-part partitioning will thus serve as a working hypothesis in the chapters which follow.

3
The Coherence of Micah 3

As stated above, the purpose of this chapter is twofold: to demonstrate the coherence of Micah 3 and to identify those features of the language of the text which contribute to this coherence. To this end, I shall first investigate the coherence of each of its component units. An examination of the relations which obtain between these units will follow.

To begin, Micah 3 may be divided into three units consisting of vv 1-4, 5-8, and 9-12. The limits of these units are clear and the partitioning is generally agreed upon. Briefly, each unit exhibits a clear introduction: vv 1-4 and 9-12 begin with the summons שמעו נא ; 5-8 with the formula כה אמר יהוה. Basically parallel in structure, the units continue with a specification of addressees (in vv 5-8 a specification of those under indictment), a list of charges against said persons, and an announcement of YHWH's judgment. To this basic structure, vv 5-8 add Micah's self-recommendation in which he contrasts his own prophetic authority and vocation with those of the prophets under indictment;[1] this is linked to the preceding verses of the unit by the conjunction ו functioning adversatively together with the pronoun אנכי which emphasizes the contrast.

I. UNIT ANALYSIS

Verses 1-4

My thesis, that the book of Micah in its final form is construable as one coherent unit, does indicate a predisposition in favor of the received text (as opposed to a reconstructed earlier level).[2] Nevertheless, there is no merit in the preservation of textual confusion. Where textual problems seem to reflect scribal errors I shall not hesitate to emend the text.[3] In general, any necessary

[1] See Hans W. Wolff "Wie Verstand Micha von Moreschet sein prophetisches Amt?," in *Congress Volume: Göttingen 1977* of the International Organization for the Study of the Old Testament, VTSup, vol. 29 (Leiden: E. J. Brill, 1978) 414-15.

[2] For example, I am fairly confident that the phrase רוח יהוה in 3:8 is an editorial addition and not part of the "original" oracle. Yet it is part of the book in its final form. Thus, given my purpose to demonstrate the coherence of the book as a whole in its final form, I shall not excise this phrase.

[3] A distinction is thus being drawn between editorial activity which is inherent to the final form of the text and errors of transmission which are not. Errors of transmission may

clarifications, textual problems, and emendations will be explicated in notes. However, the presence in this unit of a significant textual problem necessitates a more extended discussion.

The Arrangement of vv 2-3

The MT of vv 2-3 is possible, though quite difficult, to construe. The major problem is the lack of an antecedent for the third masculine plural suffixes in v 2bc. The intended referent appears to be "my people" as iterated in v 3.[4] The antecedent thus follows rather than precedes the suffix. The syntax of the text is also somewhat difficult to follow. Verse 2bc appears to function as an extension of the vocative in v 2a. The sequence is then further extended by the relative in v 3 —whether through 3e or only 3c is unclear.

Several ways of dealing with this problem have been suggested. Renaud prefers to retain the MT. In support of the MT he argues that it is possible to make sense of the flow of the text without emendation if one recognizes that the oracle was spoken before it was written and is thus subject to the conventions of oral —rather than literary—discourse. Thus, in response to the problem of the lack of antecedents in v 2bc, Renaud suggests that since the oracle was originally spoken (perhaps on the occasion of 2:6-11), the antecedents are to be located within this original Sitz-im-Leben.[5] Granted, it is possible that antecedents clearly within some oral setting of the oracle are obscured by its literary form. Yet, from a literary standpoint, this argument is quite unsatisfying. The question of the literary antecedents for v 2bc remains unresolved.[6]

A second option is to excise v 2bc.[7] Thus Wellhausen eliminates v 2bc as a

---

distort the continuity of the text and/or result in a loss of coherence. (A loss of coherence may even function as one criterion for distinguishing between the "final form" of the text and subsequent errors of textual transmission.) In such cases emendation may serve as a vehicle to recovering a proper understanding of the final form of the text. Such emendation is to be distinguished from that which would shorten the text by removing redactional additions; the latter process leads one to construe a different text—rather than the final form.

[4] Keil (*Twelve Minor Prophets,* 1:450) suggests as referent בית ישראל in v 1.

[5] Renaud, *Formation,* p. 127. Even if one grants this argument of Renaud, another problem remains: What is the referent of אז (v 4)? In response, Renaud suggests that אז is here employed as a logical, rather than temporal, articulation. In support of this interpretation of אז, he argues (pp. 127-28) that this usage parallels some instances of אתה (*sic;* ועתה). I find this argument unconvincing also.

[6] The lack of literary antecedents for v 2bc might be taken as one argument against the literary coherence of the book of Micah. In response, one might argue that in this case the antecedent is in the following verse or, following Keil (see n. 4 above), that the antecedent is to be found in v 1.

[7] See Renaud's discussion (*Formation,* p. 125). As Renaud notes, Lescow makes a similar suggestion, i.e., to eliminate v 3b as a doublet which repeats much from v 2b. (See Lescow, "Micha 1-5," pp. 17-48.)

gloss.[8] Nowack, Marti, Guthe, and J. M. P. Smith all follow suit.[9] Willi-Plein suggests that v 2bc is an interpretive gloss intended to replace v 3de; however, v 3de was retained and v 2bc moved.[10] While it is certainly possible that v 2bc may be an editorial addition, to excise it for this reason runs counter to my intention to deal with the final form of the text.

Thirdly, one may opt to rearrange the text.[11] Thus Weiser transposes v 2bc to a position after v 3 and suggests reading the perfect form of the verb ("*gasēlû*") in v 2b.[12] Mays suggests the same transposition; however, he would alter the verb form in v 2b to "*yigzēlû*" and translate it as having an indefinite subject, thus "The skin will be torn off them . . ."[13] The latter is basically the same emendation as that suggested by Elliger in *BHS*.[14] Emending the text following Elliger's notes 2a3a does yield a much clearer text. If v 2bc is taken after v 3, the antecedent problem is resolved. Moreover, v 2bc can then be understood to provide the circumstance which evokes the cry of distress in v 4a. The resulting switch from direct address to third person address in v 3a creates no real problem; it is then analogous to the clear structure of the text in 3:11. Furthermore, while one might invoke the principle of *lectio difficilior* to oppose the emendation, the principle's force is muted in this case by circumstances which render a scribal error easily understandable. The multiple incidence of verbal repetition between v 2bc and v 3abc could easily confuse a copyist resulting in the transposition. After that, the insertion of ואשר in v 3a probably followed as an attempt to bind the parallel lines 2bc and 3abc into a common structure and to avoid the switch to third person address.[15] Renaud does raise several objections to this option.[16] As I see it, however, the clarity gained by the

[8] Julius Wellhausen, *Skizzen und Vorarbeiten*, 5. Heft: *Die kleinen Propheten übersetzt, mit Noten*, 2. Aufl. (Berlin: Georg Reimer, 1893) 23, 137.

[9] See J. M. P. Smith, *Micah, Zephaniah and Nahum*, p. 71 (wherein he also cites the others mentioned).

[10] Ina Willi-Plein, *Vorformen der Schriftexegese innerhalb des Alten Testaments*, Beiheft zur Zeitschrit für die alttestamentliche Wissenschaft, no. 123 (Berlin: Walter de Gruyter, 1971) 80–81. See also the summary and critique in Renaud, *Formation*, p. 125.

[11] Renaud (*Formation*, p. 126) suggests that this is the option followed by most scholars who seek to conserve the whole text in a more logical and coherent form; in particular, he cites Lindblom, Weiser, Vuilleumier, and Jeremias. Note also Willis, Dissertation, pp. 146–47.

[12] Weiser, *Zwölf kleinen Propheten*, 1:225.

[13] Mays, *Micah*, pp. 76, 79–80.

[14] Mays differs from Elliger with respect to ואשר in v 3a; he would prefer to retain it on two grounds: a) meter; and b) the construction parallels v 5b.

[15] Another possibility is to retain ואשר and construe it as introducing a causal clause; but cf. n. 16 below.

[16] In particular, Renaud (*Formation*, p. 126) objects that while such a transpositon would supply the necessary antecedents for v 2bc, it would also engender a number of other problems 1) In spite of the fact that the active participle גזלי fits following שׁואי, the transposition hypothesis requires that it be changed to יגזלו; 2) the transposition also

transposition more than offsets its concommitant problems. The following discussion will thus reflect the emended text.

Partitioning the Unit.

Referring to vv 1-4 as a unit implies of necessity that any divisions discernible within vv 1-4 will be of lesser weight relatively speaking than those which identify the unit itself vis-à-vis its context. Nevertheless, a unit on the level of vv 1-4 is still susceptible of further division into units on at least three lower levels: 1) those units which, for convenience sake, will here be termed "subunits"; 2) individual sentences; 3) clauses; and, beyond that, into phrases and words.

Verses 1-4 may be partitioned into the following subunits: 1a-2a, 3a-2c, and 4a-4d.[17] The first division, between 2a and 3a, is signalled by the shift from direct address in 1a-2a to third person (or indirect) address in 3a-4d. Now, it would be tempting to make the second division after 3e since it terminates the invective and the sentence begins in 2b. Moreover, 2bc is linked to 4a by the adverbial אז (in 4a referring back to 2bc). Nevertheless, two factors indicate the above partitioning. First, the imagery of cannibalism is continuous within 3a-2c. And secondly, while the adverbial אז does serve to link 4a-d to 2bc, on this level adverbials also indicate transition points.

Prior to analyzing the individual subunits, I should note that on the subunit level perhaps the primary indicators of coherence are grammatical and syntactical features, especially those rhetorical devices, or "tropes," which are

---

requires that one translate יגזלו as impersonal so that the natural subjects (i.e., the persecutors in v 3ab) now become the persecuted, similarly the referent of the verbal suffixes is altered also; and 3) one looks in vain for a term in v 2b signalling a shift from accusation to sentence.

To Renaud's third objection one might respond by retaining ואשר in v 3a and arguing that it introduces a causal clause. Then the shift to the imperfect in v 2b would signal the independent clause, the result of v 3.

However, ואשר should probably not be interpreted in this fashion. First, causal clauses usually begin with כי, יען, combinations of the above with אשר, or with באשר. They do sometimes begin with אשר alone (Note the examples in Ronald J. Williams, *Hebrew Syntax: An Outline*, 2d ed. [Toronto: University of Toronto Press, 197b] 89 [§533]; and William Gesenius, *Hebrew Grammar,* ed. and enlarged by E. Kautzsch, trans. and rev. in accordance with the 28th German ed. by A. E. Cowley [Oxford: Clarendon Press, 1910] 492 [§158b]); but I know of no such case in which אשר is preceded by the conjunction ו. Secondly, the Masoretes have noted that ואשר occurs twelve times in the prophets beginning a clause (יב ר״ם). In each of the other eleven cases it functions as a relative. This would seem to suggest that it most likely functions as a relative here also — as it indeed does function if v 2bc is left in place.

[17] Throughout this discussion, verse subdivisions refer to individual cola. For ease of reference a translation of Micah 3 with verse subdivisions labelled is provided in the appendix.

structural elements of Hebrew poetry![18] Such tropes also facilitate the partitioning of units into subunits. That is, by tying certain lines together, they indicate
clearly many places where subunit divisions ought not be drawn. Nevertheless,
because these devices play their role in establishing coherence primarily on the
lower levels and are thus of lesser significance with regard to the aim of this
study, they will be excluded from the following discussion.

Vv 1a-2a.

In addition to the above mentioned features, this subunit is unified by means
of its structure and flow of thought. In particular, it is composed of a quotation
marker, וָאֹמַר; an imperative plus vocatives, serving as a summons addressed to
the leaders of Jacob/Israel; and a question directed to the above addressees
inquiring as to the nature of their responsibility coupled with vocatives which,
in effect, accuse these leaders of violating their responsibility![19]

Vv 3a-e, 2bc

The image of cannibalism is the most prominent unifying characteristic of
this subunit. Two other notable features serve to enhance this unity: first, repetition of vocabulary: שיר in 3a, 3d, 2c; עורם in 3b, 2b; עצמות in 3c, 2c; and
מעליהם in 3b, 2b; and secondly, the repeated third masculine plural suffixes and
third common plural subjects of verbs.

Moreover, given the rearranged text,[20] yet another feature comes to the fore,
the correspondence of crime and punishment. Note that the four verbs in 3a-e
are all third common plural perfect. But, according to the emended text, this
sequence is broken in 2b by a shift to the imperfect aspect (without ו conjunction). This shift has been adduced to justify translating יגזלו as having an
indefinite subject — the effect being that the leaders who are the subjects of the
verbs (i.e., the persecutors) in v 3 now become the persecuted. That is, the
prophetic invective in 3a-e leads to an appropriate sentence, according to the
principle of *jus talionis,* in 2bc.

V 4a-d

The coherence of this subunit is expressed most prominently in terms of
syntactic dependency and semantic parallelism. One may note also an internal
referent; the phrase בעת ההיא refers back to אז, thus tying 4c back to 4a.

---

[18] See Michael P. O'Connor, *Hebrew Verse Structure* [Ph.D. dissertation, University of
Michigan, 1978] (Winona Lake, IN: Eisenbrauns, 1980).

[19] I interpret the preposition ל as expressing obligation; see Williams, *Hebrew Syntax,*
p. 51 (§284).

[20] See the appendix for a translation of the text which follows this rearrangement.

Internal Relations

Following the movement of thought through the unit reveals several features which contribute to its overall coherence. First, continuity of theme plays a major role: vv 1a–2a set forth the major theme, the responsibility of the leaders with respect to justice and their violation of this responsibility; then, via the imagery of cannibalism, their perversion of justice is elaborated; and finally, YHWH's response is motivated precisely by their evil deeds, i.e., the violation of their responsibility with respect to justice.

Secondly, consider the role of the chiefs/rulers. In vv 1a–2a they are summoned and addressed directly. But in v 3a–e there is a shift from direct address to indirect address; the prophet now couches his accusation of the leaders in the form of a speech to the whole assembly *about* those summoned. And in v 4a–d, the "You" addressed (vv 1a–2a) who are the "they" accused (v 3a–e) become the "they" sentenced.

Thirdly, the principle of *jus talionis* is at work on two levels. Within vv 3a–2c, the cannibals of v 3a–e become the cannibalized of v 2bc. Again, because the leaders turn away from YHWH by forsaking their God-given responsibility for justice, YHWH also turns away from them: both by the shift from direct to indirect address and by his refusal to respond in their time of need.[21]

Finally, there are a number of internal references within the unit. אז, in v 4a, refers back to the leaders' time of trouble described in v 2bc. Verse 4d, the causal clause, refers back to the evil deeds depicted in v 3a–e. Moreover, the third common plural subjects of the verbs and third masculine plural suffixes (which have been sorted out above as to when they refer to the leaders and when to עמי) should also be noted.

Verses 5–8

This unit is clearly divisible into three subunits: vv 5a–f, 6a–7d, and 8a–d. Each subunit has a different function: 5a–f is an accusation; 6a–7d functions as a sentence; 8a–d constitutes a boast. And each is set off by an opening adverbial; respectively, כה, לכן, and ואולם. (At first glance there also appears to be a shift in discourse style; but there is not—which will be discussed later.)

V 5a–f

The initial clause of this subunit employs a speech-act verb which appears to function as a quotation marker; after 5a one expects a quote. But the quotation is deferred while the prophet describes, and thus also accuses, the prophets. First Micah makes a general accusation: the prophets lead "my people" astray. He then specifies: in particular, the prophets misuse their sacred office for their

---

[21] See Renaud, *Formation*, p. 127.

own material gain (cf. v 11). With respect to theme and function, the subunit is thus unified as a description/accusation of the prophets.

Vv 6a–7d

While the imagery of v 6 differs from that of v 7, the two are held together by a common theme, judgment. Verse 6 makes use of the image of night to describe YHWH's judgment upon the prophets. On the semantic level, 6a and 6b are parallel: it will be night/darkness. Likewise 6c and 6d: the sun goes down/it becomes dark. As night signifies privation with respect to light, so the judgment upon the prophets will be privation with respect to divine communication. (Note the use of privative מ.) Verse 7 describes the perplexity and shame of the prophets which results from the judgment. On the semantic level 7a–c are all parallel expressions of shame.[22]

Two other features also contribute to the coherence of this subunit. First, 7d is a causal clause which refers back to v 6 cementing the two verses together by a logical tie. And vocabulary provides another link: החזים in 7a points back to מחזון in 6a, הקסמים in 7b to מקסם in 6b.

In sum, in addition to features of poetic structure (reflected by parallelism on the semantic level), the coherence of this subunit is expressed by: continuity of theme; a sustained use of imagery; an internal reference which provides a logical tieback; and repeated vocabulary.

V 8a–d

These four lines are linked by syntactic dependency. Moreover, this subunit is also held together by unity of theme: i.e., the gifts and purpose which Micah (in contrast to the prophets of vv 5–7) brings to the prophetic office.

Internal Relations

These three subunits are in turn bound together by continuity of discourse style, linking adverbials, a clear flow of thought, and thematic continuity.

Line 5a appears to introduce a quotation. However, the anticipated divine speech is deferred by Micah's description of the prophets in v 5b–f. Neither does the quote begin in v 6a. Or, at least, there is no direct marker indicating so, such as the addition of לאמר at the end of v 5f would provide. Moreover, v 7 refers to God in the third person. Finally, v 8 is clearly the words of the prophet; yet there is no introductory ויאמר Thus, there is no quotation. Verses 5–8 present neither an interchange of voices nor a discourse within which a quotation is employed, but rather a sustained discourse spoken by a single voice. The tension created by the lack of the anticipated divine speech may be resolved by

---

[22] One might distinguish, of course, between the statements of shame in v 7ab and the prophets' expression of shame in v 7c.

understanding v 5a as the prophet's appeal to YHWH as the source of the message of judgment proclaimed in vv 5-7.

Again, the adverbials לכן and אולם provide clear links between the subunits. The articulation לכן establishes the relation between v 5 and vv 6-7 as cause and effect. And ואולם sets forth a clear contrastive relation between vv 5-7 and v 8.

These linkages, then, help make explicit the flow of thought within the unit as a whole which moves from accusation (in the form of a description of the prophets' misuse of their office) to judgment and finally to Micah's boast or self-recommendation.[23]

Finally, the theme of prophecy is continuous throughout the unit. Lines 5a-f establish that the oracle is concerned with those prophets who misuse the prophetic office. Lines 6a-7d describe the resulting judgment: their prophetic gift ceases; God refuses to answer. To all the above, lines 8a-d offer as a contrast the gifts which empower Micah for the prophetic office and his consistent message regarding the sins of Jacob/Israel (versus the message in v 5c-f: peace or war according to whether or not you pay).

Verses 9-12

This unit also is composed of three subunits: vv 9-10, 11, and 12. Shifts in poetic structure, i.e., from bi-cola to tri-cola, and in form of address, i.e., from direct address in vv 9-10 to third person address in v 11, mark the first division. The second partition is indicated by the articulation לכן בגללכם and a shift back to direct address at the beginning of v 12.

The Problem of בנה in v 10

Before discussing the coherence of the individual subunits of this unit, it will be helpful to clear up one textual difficulty. In the midst of a plural context v 10 begins with a singular participle. Partly for this reason, most commentators follow the versions and emend the text to בני, the construct form of the plural participle.[24] At least two apparent gains result from this emendation. The text then reads smoothly as another relative clause continuing the description begun in v 9a. Moreover, this change alters the metric value of the bi-cola (based on stress count analysis to 2+2 yielding a more even rhythmic flow in vv 9-10.

[23] See Wolff, "Wie Verstand Micah von Moreschet sein prophetisches Amt?," pp. 414-15.

[24] For example, J. M. P. Smith (*Micah, Zephaniah and Nahum*, p. 79) adopts this emendation and, in its support, cites also Wellahusen, Graetz, Oort, Nowack, Marti, Halevy, Sievers, Duhm, Löhr, van Hoonacker, and Guthe. To these one may add: Robinson, *Zwölf kleinen Propheten*, p. 138; Lippl, *Zwölf kleinen Propheten*, 1:198; R. F. Horton, *The Minor Prophets: Hosea, Joel, Amos, Obadiah, Jonah, and Micah*, Century Bible (Edinburgh: T. C. & E. C. Jack, [1904]) 242; Ernst Sellin, *Das Zwölfprophetenbuch*, 1. Hälfte: *Hosea-Micha*, 2d & 3d Aufl., Kommentar zum alten Testament, Bd. 12 (Leipzig: A. Deichertsche Verlagsbuchhandlung D. Werner Scholl, 199) 326.

However, there is no support for this reading among the Hebrew manuscript evidence. Moreover, it is difficult to see why an original בני would have been altered to the more problematic בנה. And finally, as shall be seen, the reading בנה is capable of meaningful construal. Under these conditions, to emend the text violates the text critical principle of *lectio difficilior,* i.e., that one tends to prefer the more difficult reading.

If then one opts to keep בנה, how is the text to be construed? Mays, for one, does retain the reading בנה. He then construes this clause as in apposition to the previous clause. In support of retaining בנה he also cites the parallel text Hab 2:12 (which does, however, use the singular consistently throughout). This construal does seem quite plausible.[25]

Yet, without altering the radicals of the MT [i.e., בנה), another construal is possible based on the syntactic function of the clause. The parallel clauses in v 10 seem to function as further specification of the actions described in v 9b. Now, neither the traditional grammars nor Meek's articles on coordinate adverbial clauses allow the use of a participle in such a clause; rather, one expects either an infinitive absolute or a finite verbal form.[26] Since it does not require a change in the consonantal text, I suggest that בֹנֶה simply be repointed as an infinitive absolute, i.e. בָּנֹה. The clause then makes perfect sense as an adverbial clause of manner which further specifies the action described in v 9a.[27]

Vv 9a–10b

In vv 9–10, a summons and its addressees (9a) are continued by four coordinate clauses which together function subordinately to provide a vivid description of the sins of the addressees. These four clauses may be divided into two pairs each of which displays synonymous parallelism. Moreover, the latter pair functions adverbially in relation to the former. In sum, the subunit is one coherent sentence unified with respect to theme and function as a description/accusation of the leaders of Jacob/Israel.

V 11a–f

This subunit consists of two groups of three lines. The first three lines are parallel with respect to both grammatical construction and thought: each group

---

[25] Mays, *Micah,* p. 86.

[26] Theophile J. Meek, "The Co-ordinate Adverbial Clause in Hebrew," *Journal of the American Oriental Society* 49 (1929) 156–59; idem, "The Co-ordinate Adverbial Clause in Hebrew," *American Journal of Semitic Languages* 47 (1930/31) 51–52. See also Gesenius, *Hebrew Grammar,* pp. 41, 350–51, 386–87; and Paul Joüon, *Grammaire de L'Hébreu Biblique,* deuxième édition anastatique corrigée (Rome: Institut Biblique Pontifical, 1947) 353–54 (§123r; cf. §121).

[27] See the translation in the appendix. Rudolph (*Micha-Nahum-Habakuk-Zephanja,* p. 68) also points this as an infinitive absolute (following Kleinert and Ehrlich).

of leaders accepts money to carry out their function—i.e., to give a ruling, teach, or prophesy—to the advantage of those who pay.

The next group of three lines build on each other in order to express the attitude and theology of the groups addressed. The first line begins with the conjunction ו attached to a non-verbal element of the clause which, in this case, signals a disjunctive sequence used here to express an adversative relation to what precedes; that is: "Nevertheless (in spite of the blatant impropriety just described), they lean upon YHWH." The line then ends with לאמר introducing the rationale of the groups under accusation given in the form of direct speech in the succeeding two lines. The speech begins with a rhetorical question expecting the very definite positive answer: "YHWH is indeed in our midst."[28] And the final line completes the speech by expressing the expected consequence of the previous line in accordance with their theology; i.e., YHWH's presence ensures safety.

In summary, the unity of this subunit is expressed by means of: the clear synonymous parallelism of the first group of three lines; a coherent development of thought within the second; thematic continuity within each group; and a clear antithetical relation between the two groups showing the ironic relation between the actions and theology of the leaders. In addition, one may note an internal referent which links the two groups: the third masculine plural subject of the verb in v 11d refers back to the chiefs, priests, and prophets of v 11a-c.

V 12a-d

This subunit is unified with respect to theme and function. It functions as a sentence or verdict. After the introductory articulation (v 12a), the following three lines are parallel expressions of the same theme—the destruction of Jerusalem.

Relations between Subunits

A number of features work to bind these subunits together and thus to create a coherent unit. To begin, the adverbial לכן serves to link and, in so doing, to clarify the relationship between v 12 and vv 9-11; i.e., the description in vv 9-11 is to be understood as the basis for the judgment announced in v 12.

Coherence is also expressed by means of terms which are repeated within the unit or which refer to terms used earlier within the unit. The terms "Zion" and "Jerusalem" are employed in vv 10 and 12; moreover, they are implicitly present in the first three lines of v 11, being the referent of the third person feminine singular suffixes. Again, the term ראש is introduced in v 9 and repeated in v 11. Finally, the third person plural suffix of בגללכם refers the reader back to the leaders addressed in the preceding verses.

---

[28] Gesenius, *Hebrew Grammar,* p. 474 (§150e).

Finally, the unit displays a clear overall structure and a logical progression of thought. The basic structural outline of the unit follows the progression "indictment + לכן + specification of punishment." In particular, the unit begins with a summons and direct address followed by a description/indictment of those addressed. There is then a shift to the third person form of address (perhaps the prophet is now speaking to the court assembly) and the indictment is expanded by listing charges against specific groups of leaders and by an exposé of the ironic relation between their actions and their theology. Finally, returning to direct address, the prophet (acting as messenger of YHWH, the divine judge) specifies the coming judgment.

II. RELATIONS BETWEEN THE UNITS

Having examined the internal coherence of each of the three units of Micah 3, I shall in this section describe the features which serve to bind these units into one larger, coherent unit.

Common Topic[29]

In all three units the basic topic of discourse is wicked leaders. Verses 1-4 deal with chiefs and rulers, 5-8 with prophets; and 9-12 mention all of the above (and add priests).

Parallel Structure

In each of the three units a clear introduction is followed by a specification of addressees (in vv 5-8 a specification of those under indictment), a list of charges against them, and an announcement of YHWH's judgment. To this basic structure, vv 5-8 add Micah's boast or self-recommendation.

Continuity of Theme

The speaker's concern for justice is a major theme in all three units. In lines 1c and 9c the speaker makes it explicit both that justice is the proper concern of the leaders and that it is expressly their violation of this responsibility that is the basis of the coming judgment. And contrasting himself to the prophets, the speaker identifies himself as being "filled with justice" — thus establishing his authority vis-à-vis both the prophets (cf. vv 5-7, 11) and the other leaders (cf. vv 1-4, 9-11). The theme is thus prominent in all three units.

---

[29] In this section I employ three different words — topic, theme and motif — to refer to the subject of discourse in the text. Of these, topic is the broadest (or least definite) of the three. Theme will refer to a subject, idea, or proposition developed and of primary concern within the text. Motif denotes a recurring idea, phrase, or subject of discourse. See *Webster's New Dictionary of Synonyms* (1978) s.v. "subject," pp. 790-91.

Common Motifs[30]

1) In vv 1–3 the chiefs and rulers are indicted for perverse use of their office, i.e., for violation of their God-given responsibility. The same accusation is leveled against the prophets in v 5. 2) Verse 4bc pronounces the word of judgment that YHWH will not answer the leaders' cry; rather he will "hide his face." Similarly, the judgment announced in v 6 is the absence of divine communication and in v 7 "no answer from God." These two motifs serve to bind together vv 1–4 and 5–8; another binds 5–8 and 9–12. 3) In v 5 the speaker accuses the prophets of having a favorable word for whoever will feed them. Verse 11 states the same: they prophesy for pay. (The illegitimacy of their activity is emphasized by use of the verb קסם.[31])

Repeated Vocabulary

(A) With respect to vv 1–4 and 5–8, note especially: עמי in vv 3, 5; and ענה in vv 4, 7. (B) With respect to vv 5–8 and 9–12, note: נביא in vv 5, 6, and 11; and קסם in vv 7, 11. (C) With respect to vv 1–4 and 9–12, note: ראש in vv 1, 9, 11; קצין in vv 1, 9; and שמע in vv 1, 9. (D) Finally, occurring in all three units are: משפט in vv 1c, 8b, and 9c; יעקב and ישראל in vv 1ab, 8cd, and 9ab; and יהוה in vv 4, 5, 8, and twice in v 11.

Rhetorical Form

Various features of Micah 3 also contribute to an overall mode of discourse or rhetorical form. Note, for example, the repeated two line summons beginning with שמעו נא which opens the first and third units, enclosing vv 5–8 in a ring pattern. Again, the first two units accuse and announce judgment upon two particular and different groups of leaders; vv 9–12 encompasses all the leaders. Moreover, the chapter is composed of three units of parallel structure dealing with the same topic; such triadic form is a common device to underscore the third element of the series as its culmination.[32] The chapter thus moves toward

---

[30] I have offered a brief definition of motif in n. 29 above. To confirm that this is indeed the way in which the term is used by literary critics, I cite the following. Karl L. Beckson and Arthur Ganz (*Literary Terms: A Dictionary* [New York: Farrar, Straus, & Giroux, 1975] 152) define motif as "A theme, character, or verbal pattern which recurs in literature or folklore." Similarly, according to C. Hugh Holman (*Handbook to Literature*, 3d ed. [Indianapolis: Odyssey Press, 1972] 329), "In literature, recurrent images, words, objects, phrases, or actions that tend to unify the work are called *motives*."

[31] J. M. P. Smith (*Micah, Zephaniah and Nahum*, p. 75) notes in connection with vv 6–7 that קסם is "never used of legitimate prophetic activity."

[32] In his analysis of the rhetorical style of II Isa, James Muilenburg ("Isaiah 40–66: Introduction," in *The Interpreter's Bible*, 5:390, ed. George A. Buttrick [New York: Abindon Press, 1956]) notes a "copius use of words, phrases, sentences, and larger units in triadic form." He adds: "The purpose of this device is to bring the thought to a climax or to give special emphasis to the culminating member."

a climax; the severe, but penultimate, judgments in vv 2bc, 4, and 6–7 lead to the ultimate judgment, the destruction of Jerusalem, in v 12. The opening ויאמר, to be discussed later,[33] also contributes to the rhetorical form of the chapter.

All these features contribute to an overarching unity which characterizes chapter three of the book of Micah. Together they establish the thesis that Micah 3 may be read as a connected, coherent whole.

III. CONCLUSIONS REGARDING
THE PHENOMENON OF COHERENCE

In the previous two sections I have demonstrated the coherence of Micah 3 and, in so doing, identified specific features of the language of the text which contribute to this coherence. The present task is to analyze the above data in such a way as to be of service in the continuing investigation of the coherence of the book as a whole.

TABLE 3
LITERARY FEATURES CONTRIBUTING TO
THE COHERENCE OF MICAH 3

	Level		*Features*
Subunit	*Unit*	*Chapter*	
*			grammatical/syntactical conventions
*			troping
*			semantic parallelism
*			syntax of sentences
*	*		flow of thought
*	*	*	structure
*	*		grammatical antecedents
*	*	*	repeated vocabulary
*			sustained use of imagery
*	*		principle of *jus talionis*
*			syntax of relating sentences
*	*		internal referent (non-grammatical)
*	*	*	continuity of theme
*			unity of function
	*		linking adverbials
	*		continuity of speaker (i.e., of discourse style)
*			use of irony
		*	recurrence of motif
		*	continuity of topic
		*	rhetorical form

---

[33] See pp. 57–58 below.

To begin, those features observed as contributing to the coherence of Micah 3 are so listed in table 3 as to display on which of three levels they operate: 1) the subunit level—features which contribute to the relation of words, clauses, and sentences within a subunit; 2) the unit level—features which contribute to the relation of subunits within a unit;[34] and 3) the chapter level—features which contribute to the relation of units within Micah 3 as a whole (the larger unit).

One clear result of this analysis is the fairly obvious, but nonetheless important, observation that coherence functions on a variety of levels and encompasses a plethora of different phenomena. Moreover, the means of expressing coherence varies from level to level. Coherence on the level of the sentence and coherence on the level of extended discourse do show a family resemblance, but they are certainly not identical twins. Some of their similarities and differences are apparent from table 3. Some features appear to be restricted to a given level; others contribute to the coherence of the text on several levels. For example the poetic feature of semantic parallelism operates over a range of two or three lines and thus is noted only on the subunit level. On the other hand, thematic continuity may be observed on all three levels. Of course, to extend the above analysis over a greater range of text would probably alter the above profile somewhat; nevertheless, it provides a helpful starting point.

Secondly, one may observe that a number of the features listed above are related. For example, "continuity of theme," "continuity of topic," and "recurrence of motif" all have to do with a commonality of subject matter or content. Hence, I offer the following tentative categorization:

Poetic Devices
　　E.g., semantic parallelism

Syntax of Sentences
　　I.e., basic grammatical and syntactical conventions

Syntax of Relating Sentences
　　E.g., linking adverbials,
　　grammatical antecedents between sentences

Stylistic Devices
　　E.g., continuity of discourse style,
　　internal referents (non-grammatical),
　　repeated vocabulary,
　　use of irony

---

[34] While here used particularly in reference to the component units of Micah 3, the term "unit" is employed generally throughout this study as a level-neutral term to refer to a coherent piece of literary discourse. Eventually, I shall demonstrate that it may be applied in this manner to the book of Micah as a whole.

Rhetorical Form
    E.g., structure,
    flow of thought,
    unity of function,
    movement to a climax

Commonality of Subject Matter
    E.g., thematic continuity,
    recurrence of motif,
    continuity of topic,
    (repeated vocabulary)
    (recurrence of principle of *jus talionis*)

This list may serve as a starting point — suggesting some features for which to be alert in investigating the coherence of the rest of the book of Micah. However, since the analysis which follows will focus on the "higher" levels of the text, features which are operative primarily on the "lower" levels will largely be left out of consideration. Moreover, features other than those observed so far may come into play.

4
The Coherence of Micah 1-5

The purpose of this chapter is to establish the coherence of the first major section of the book of Micah, i e., chaps. 1-5. Following the structural outline proposed in table 2 (p. 27), I shall examine first the coherence of Micah 1-3 and then that of Micah 4-5. Finally, I shall seek to display those relations between them which serve to bind these sections into an integrated whole.

I. THE COHERENCE OF MICAH 1-3

The pattern of this section will mirror that of the chapter—albeit on a smaller scale. That is, I shall first focus on Micah 1-2, then review my results concerning Micah 3, and finally examine those relations which, by operating over their combined domain, effectively link Micah 1-2 and Micah 3 into one larger coherent unit.

The Coherence of Micah 1-2

Linear Analysis of Micah 1-2

One final procedural note will be of help. Recall that chapter 3 described in detail the coherence of Micah 3 by first breaking the text down into clauses and then gradually building it back up taking note of those features which bind clauses into sentences, sentences into small units, and small units into increasingly larger units. Among the most important features noted were continuity of topic, flow of thought, and syntactical relations—including, but not restricted to, the use of connectives. Now, rather than breaking Micah 1-2 down into its component sections, subsections, etc., I propose to make use of those features noted above and simply follow the linear continuity of the text, just as the reader encounters it. I shall take special note of transitions which signal the flow of thought by establishing logical relations. At various points this linear continuity will become less clear or even be lost entirely. At such points I shall mark the break and continue reading. Later, I shall look back for features which might serve to relate the sections thus divided in another manner and thus establish an overarching coherence.

1:1/1:2. No connective joins these in such a way as to identify them as successive components of a logical argument or flow of events. Rather, Micah

1:1 stands apart as a superscription.[1] The body of the book begins in 1:2.

1:2/1:3–4. The connective כי הנה here indicates a causal relation. In particular, the theophany in vv 3–4 provides reason or motivation for the audience to respond to the summons in v 2.

1:3–4/1:5. כל זאת in v 5 refers back to the events reported in vv 3–4. The theophany is occasioned by the "transgression of Jacob" and the "sins of the house of Israel." Note also the verbal correspondence between במותי ארץ in v 3 and במות יהודה in v 5 which serves as a further link between the theophany and the situation which prompts it.[2]

1:5/1:6–7. While no logical connective is employed at this juncture, the conjunction ו clearly carries the force of לכן, "therefore." The sin mentioned in v 5 calls forth the judgment described in vv 6–7. The verbal repetition of נגד (1:4, 6) and אש (1:4, 7) bear witness to a certain continuity of imagery between the theophany and the judgment of Samaria.

1:6–7/1:8–16. At this point the picture becomes less clear. Some, who divide the chap. 2–9/10–16,[3] consider כל זאת in v 8 as a reference back to the destruction of Samaria as the cause for the prophet's lamentation. This partitioning, however, has the result of separating the lament (vv 10ff.) from its announcement in v 8. Others would prefer to divide the chapter 2–7/8–16.[4] The demonstrative זאת is then read as referring forward to the content of the lament stated *in nuce* in v 9.[5] In this manner, the lament is connected closely to its announcement, but the connective על זאת is construed in an unnatural way.[6] A third option is to divide the chapter 2–7/8–9/10–16, taking vv 8–9 as a transition related to both

---

[1] The significance of this superscription is considered on pp. 122–24 below.

[2] Cf. Mays, *Micah*, p. 45.

[3] For example, Fohrer (*Introduction*, pp. 444–45), Allen (*Books of Joel . . .* , p. 261), J. M. P. Smith (*Micah, Zephaniah and Nahum*, pp. 32, 41) divide Micah 1 in this manner. Roland E. Wolfe ("The Book of Micah: Introduction and Exegesis," in *The Interpreter's Bible*, ed. George A. Buttrick [New York. Ab:ngdon Press, 1956] 6:900) divides vv 5–9/10–16.

[4] Eissfeldt (*Introduction*, p. 407), Lippl (*Zwölf kleinen Propheten*, 1:183, 185, 187), Weiser (*Zwölf kleinen Propheten*, 1:211–12), and Bernhard Duhm (*Israels Propheten*, 2. Aufl. [Tübingen: J. C. B. Mohr (Paul Siebeck), 1922] 120) divide Micah 1 in this manner. Mays (*Micah*, p. 50) also divides between vv 7 and 8.

[5] Mays, *Micah*, pp. 50–51.

[6] Cf. Renaud, *Formation*, pp. 38–41. Following an exhaustive study of the OT occurrences of על זאת, Renaud concludes (p. 40): "l'expression résume toujours ce qui précède et tire les conséquences d'une situation ou d'un événement précis. Et ceci sans aucune exception." Moreover, although על זאת often occurs at the beginning of a verse or phrase, it is never found at the beginning of an argument; rather, its proper place is within a logical development where it functions to introduce a new step in the progression.

vv 2–7 and 10–16, but not a part of either.[7] Among these options, none emerges as a clear best choice; the third merely holds in tension the problems of the first two.

Renaud, however, offers another option. The dilemma results from a misconstrual of both the structure of the lament and the relation between vv 8 and 9. He observes a close correspondence between vv 8 and 16 which function as an inclusio, framing the lament:

> On notera aussitôt l'inclusion des versets 8 et 16: chacun d'eux comporte l'évocation de gestes de deuil: "déchaussé et nu" en 8, tonsure et rasure en 16. Dans les deux cas, la comparaison est tirée du monde animal: chacal, autruches en 8, vautour en 16.[8]

Again, he suggests that v 9 is part of the lament proper which corresponds to and functions in the same manner as v 12b.[9] In particular, he observes:

> . . . tous les deux commencent par *ky*, évoquent l'intervention divine (en 9a "le coup de YHWH" et en 12b "le malheur qui descend de chez YHWH"), et montrent cette catastrophe, touchant les portes mêmes de Jérusalem!ered[10]

Based on these observations, he outlines the structure of 1:8–16 as follows:

---

[7] See Rudolph, *Micha*, pp. 39, 42–43. Rudolph's first unit for comment is 1:2–16. However, he also breaks this down further into vv 2–7 ("Das Gericht über Samaria"), 8–9 ("Überleitung"), and 10–16 ("Das Unheil über Juda und Jerusalem"). Sellin (*Hosea-Micha*, pp. 309–14), however, divides between vv 8 and 9.

[8] Renaud, *Formation*, p. 37. For a discussion of the stylistic device of inclusion, see n. 16 below.

[9] Ibid., pp. 36–37.

[10] Ibid., p. 36. Here Renaud follows van der Woude in part; they differ in that "van der Woude y voit une inclusion et regarde les v 8–12 comme une unité close sure elle-même." Note also with regard to the correspondence between vv 9 and 12b that Renaud takes מבותיה in v 9 as מבות יה construing the יה as an abbreviation for YHWH. (Mays [*Micah*, p. 48] does the same.) Now, this reading is certainly possible. However, the abbreviated form יה is quite rare outside the psalms. Another possibility has been suggested by Herbert Donner (*Israel unter den Völkern: Die Stellung der klassischen Propheten des 8. Jahrhunderts v. Chr. zur Aussenpolitik der Könige von Israel und Juda*, VTSup, vol. 11 [Leiden: E. J. Brill, 1964] 95; cf. Renaud, *Formation*, p. 45) according to which the feminine singular antecedent called for by מבותיה is Samaria. But in this case one searches in vain for a masculine singular antecedent for the verb in the following line (מבותיה would make sense but is of the wrong gender). My tendency is to follow Renaud and Mays. However, even if the יה is not taken in this way, there is still a clear correspondence between vv 9 and 12b. This text problem affects only one of the four corresponding elements noted by Renaud. (For yet another possibility concerning the masculine singular subject of נגר, see Edward Pococke, *A Commentary on the Prophecy of Micah*, 2d impression [Oxford: printed at the THEATER, 1692] 6.)

Ouverture: v 8

Première strophe (v 9–12a)

—v 9: première justification introduite par *ky* avec pour centre le thème du "coup de YHWH" qui frappe "à la porte de mon peuple," c'est-à-dire "Jérusalem."

—v 10–12a: première série de 6 villes

Seconde strophe (v 12b–15)

—v 12b: seconde justification introduite par *ky* avec pour centre le thème du malheure qui vient de YHWH et descend "jusqu'aux portes de Jérusalem";

—v 13–15: seconde série de 5 villes.

Conclusion: v 16[11]

The lament is thus composed of two strophes which display parallel structure. Following this analysis, the main division of chap. 1 falls between vv 7 and 8. However, now that the כי clause of v 9 is seen as the beginning of the lament proper, it is clear that v 9 is not the referent of על זאת in v 8. Rather, as Renaud insists, על זאת refers back to vv 3–7 serving as the literary link which connects vv 3–7 and 8–16.[12]

1:8–16/2:1–5. At this point the reader encounters a major break in linear continuity. There is neither thematic continuity nor a logical transition to clarify the shift which takes place at 2:1. Clearly, if chaps. 1–2 do form a coherent unit, linear continuity is not a sufficient criterion to display this unity.

Within 2:1–5, however, linear continuity is eminently clear. This unit begins with an accusation (vv 1–2), here introduced by the particle הוי; then follows the logical connective לכן, the formula כה אמר יהוה, and the announcement of judgment (vv 3–4).[13] Verse 5 then carries the logical sequence one step further by making explicit the implications of this judgment. Moreover, the accusation in vv 1–2 and the judgment in vv 3–4 are tied together in yet another way. Observe first that several key terms from vv 1–2 are repeated in vv 3–4, in particular: חשב, רע, נשא, and שדה![14] This repetition highlights the correspondence between the people's sin and the coming punishment according to the principle of *jus talionis*.[15] In sum, 2:1–5 is unified by means of logical connectives, coherent flow of thought, repetition of key terms, and the correspondence between sin and punishment.

---

[11] Renaud, *Formation*, p. 37.

[12] See n. 6 above.

[13] The term "announcement of judgment" is here employed simply to describe the function of vv 3–4, not to indicate a form-critical genre.

[14] Within the judgment section itself, note the repetition of מיש in 2:3, 4. Also, יום הזאת in 2:4 refers back to עת in 2:3.

[15] Cf. Renaud, *Formation*, pp. 69–70.

2:1-5/2:6-11. The nature of this articulation is not immediately evident. It will be helpful in this case to discuss first the matter of continuity within 2:6-11 before addressing the question of how 2:1-5 and 2:6-11 are linked.

2:6-11 depicts a controversy between the prophet and his opponents. It is set off quite clearly from its context by an inclusio marked by the verbal root נטף.[16] This root occurs nowhere else in Micah outside this unit. Here it occurs three times in v 6 and twice in v 11, thus framing the unit. To determine the movement within the unit is a complex matter, however, due to a number of textual problems in addition to its apparent dialogical character.[17]

> Il s'agit, en effet, d'une controverse où les paroles du prophète se mêlent à celles de ses adversaires; déterminer ce qui revient à Michée et ce qui revient à ses partenaires constitue, en l'occurrence une opération délicate.[18]

To begin this operation as regards vv 6a-7a it seems best to follow the MT, but to take 7a together with 6c as suggested by Renaud. One may then translate:

> "Do not preach," they preach;
> "one should not preach about these things.
> 'Disgrace will not depart'—
> Should this be said, O house of Jacob?"

---

[16] As defined by Mitchell Dahood (*Psalms I: 1-50*, Anchor Bible, vol 16 [Garden City, NY: Doubleday, 1966] 5), the term "inclusio" refers to "a rhetorical device also called 'cyclic composition', in which the author returns to the point where he began." That is, inclusion is a framing technique; the beginning and the end of a unit are connected in some fashion thereby creating a structure which—to some extent—gives order to the unit as a whole. These links are expressed chiefly by similarities in vocabulary and morphology (Anderson and Freedman, *Hosea,* p. 119). For examples of inclusios, see: Dahood, *Psalms I,* also *Psalms II: 51-100* and *Psalms III: 101-150* (Anchor Bible, vols. 17 & 17A [Garden City, NY: Doubleday, 1968 & 1970])—refer to indices s.v. "inclusio(n)" for page references; Holladay, *Architecture of Jeremiah 1-20*, pp. 18, 33; Anderson and Freedman, *Hosea,* pp. 128, 134, 139, 174, 331, 161, 470, 473.

The inclusio should be distinguished from simple repetition. Repetition may arise from different sources and function in various ways; for example: 1) Repetition may arise coincidentally or as the result of a common topic of discourse; 2) it may be due to the recurrence of a motif; 3) repetition may function to link neighboring units (Anderson and Freedman, *Hosea,* p. 320); or 4) it may indeed be the primary signal of an inclusio (ibid.).

[17] For a full discussion of the textual problems in vv 6-8 as well as a survey of the solutions proffered regarding the speaker(s) in the text, see John T. Willis, "Micah 2:6-8 and the 'People of God' in Micah," *Biblische Zeitschrift* 14 (1970) 72-87. More generally, on such problems in 2:6-11, see: Renaud, *Formation,* pp. 81-103; A. S. van der Woude, "Micha II 7a und der Bund Jahwes mit Israel," *VT* 18 (1968) 388-91; and idem, "Micah in Dispute with the Pseudo-prophets," *VT* 19 (1969) 244-60.

[18] Renaud, *Formation,* p. 81.

In vv 6a–7a the prophet thus quotes his adversaries who forcibly refute his message of judgment; within this quote, v 6c is to be taken as a word of the prophet himself cited by his adversaries![19] The adversaries' speech is continued in v 7b–e wherein they justify their refutation of Micah's message.[20] Then, in vv 8–11, the prophet replies. He refutes his adversaries' claim to uprightness (vv 8–9),[21] announces judgment upon them for their oppression of the poor (v 10),[22] and closes with a sarcastic caricature of the kind of preacher to whom they would listen (v 11).

To return to the question of the articulation between 2:1–5 and 2:6–11, these units are linked in two ways. First, both 2:1–5 and 2:6–11 display the motif of dispossessing persons of their homes (note בית in 2:2, 9) and property (note שדה in 2:2, 4; and נחלה in 2:2, חלק עמי in 2:4, and הדרי in 2:9). So also Renaud observes:

> . . . on ne peut méconnaître qu'un lien thématique commun relie ces deux formes littéraires; dans les deux cas, le prophète s'adresse à des personnages qui par violence (v 2b cf. 10a), s'emparent des propriétés et des champs des pauvres (v 2a; cf. v 9a).[23]

Renaud continues by calling attention to "la parenté entre 'l'heritage' due v 2b et la 'splendeur' du v 9b, qui désigne la portion de terre Sainte, allouée à chacun des membres du peuple élu."[24] Secondly, the words of judgment in 2:3–5 appear

---

[19] Ibid., pp. 86–87.

[20] In v 7d read דבריו; cf. LXX. The MT's first person singular suffix is probably the result of confusion regarding the speaker (so Mays, *Micah*, p. 66) or haplography due to the sequence of three י's (so Willis, "Micah 2:6–8," p. 80).

[21] The general function of vv 8–9 as an accusation which refutes any claim to uprightness on the part of its addressees is clear, although the precise rendering of the text is of necessity conjectural. The MT of v 8 does not make sense and requires emendation. To begin, it seems best to follow Elliger's note a-a in *BHS* and redivide the consonants at the beginning of the verse: (על עמי ואתם לעמי). This solution has been adopted by numerous scholars; see J. M. P. Smith, *Micah, Zephaniah and Nahum*, p. 55. Due to this confusion it would appear that the verb תקומו (emended text) was corrupted in order to agree with the apparent subject עמי; see Mays, *Micah*, p. 67. The MT of v 8c ("From before a garment . . .") is also enigmatic. Emendation of ממול to מֵעָל clarifies the meaning. Taking the final ה of שלמה as article for the following word and restoring a final ת lost by haplography allows the translation:

> From the peaceful you strip the garment—
> from those who pass by trustingly, who turn away from war.

More radical emendation of v 9 seems unnecessary; these clauses may be rendered—as above—in apposition as further characterization of the victims.

[22] Redivide MT's תחבל וחבל and read תְּחַבְּלוּ חֶבֶל following LXX; cf. BDB, p. 287; Mays, *Micah*, p. 67; and J. M. P. Smith, *Micah, Zephaniah and Nahum*, p. 56. See the comment in Mays, *Micah*, pp. 71–72.

[23] Renaud, *Formation*, p. 116.

[24] Ibid. (Here Renaud refers to an earlier discussion beginning on p. 96.)

to be the referent of לאלה in v 6—the things to which "they," the prophet's opponents, object. That is, the prophetic oracle in 2:1-5 occasions the following controversy.[25]

2:6-11/2:12-13. The articulation between 2:6-11 and 2:12-13 appears quite harsh. As Renaud puts it:

> La presque totalité des critiques renonce à trouver un lien quelconque entre les versets 2,12-13 et ceux qui les précèdent. Nous ne pouvons que dire notre accord entier avec cette position. Le contenu de l'oracle de 2,12-13 diffère complètement des morceaux precédénts, qui formulent menaces ou reproches. Ceux-ci ne contiennent d'ailleurs ni mot d'appel ni élément thématique, fût-iul contrastant, qui amorce le développement des derniers versets. . . . Enfin le passage brutal de 11 à 12 se mesure au fait qu'en 2,11 c'est les prophète qui parle; en 2,12 YHWH. . . . aucune formule n'avertit que YHWH va parler, et le thème de l'oracle de salut n'a rien à voir avec le reproche de Michée lancé à ses adversaires au v 11.[26]

Nevertheless, after discussing some of the problems encountered in interpreting these verses, I shall consider those features which serve to unify Micah 1-2 and, in so doing, shall demonstrate that 2:12-13 is indeed an integral part of Micah 1-2.

Excursus: The Problem of Micah 2:12-13.

2:12-13 is certainly a crux for the interpretation of the book of Micah. Briefly, the problem is that when read as an oracle of salvation—as it almost invariably is—2:12-13 introduces an element of hope into a section (chaps. 1-3) which otherwise consists entirely of oracles of judgment. Moreover, 2:12-13 is commonly regarded as exilic in origin whereas the rest of Micah 1-3 is accepted almost *in toto* as authentic Mican material. Viewed from the standpoint of either of the two common critical partitionings of the book,[27] 2:12-13 is simply an intrusion. For this reason scholars have indeed tended to neglect it—as Smend (erroneously) charges Rudolph with doing.[28] Perhaps George Adam Smith provides the most blatant example: he translates 2:12-13 in a footnote and omits it from consideration in the commentary *per se.*[29]

Another option, rather than eliminating this passage as a secondary interpolation, has been to move it to a more suitable context.[30] Indeed, based upon

---

[25] To suggest that 2:1-5 provides the literary occasion for 2:6-11 is by no means to suggest that they reflect the same historical *Sitz-im-Leben,* the position of Willis ("Micah 2:6-8," p. 85) to which Renaud (*Formation,* pp. 116-17] objects. Cf. Mays, *Micah,* p. 68.

[26] Renaud, *Formation,* p. 115.

[27] I.e., chaps. 1-3/4-5/6-7 or 1-3/4-5/6:1-7:6/7:7-20. See pp. 22-30 above.

[28] Smend, *Entstehung des Alten Testaments, p. 179. Cf. Rudolph, Micha,* pp. 24, 63-65.

[29] G. A. Smith, *Amos, Hosea, and Micah,* p. 420.

[30] For a survey of the various transpositions proposed, see Willis, Dissertation, p. 119 n. 1.

an analysis of the compositional history of Micah 4–5, Renaud presents a strong argument in favor of transposing 2:12–13 to a position after 4:7.[31] Yet, this proposal generates several new problems; for example: "Why would a redactor break up an original coherent unit (i.e., 4:6–7; 2:12–13; 4:8)?" and "Why leave behind fragments with no clear progression of thought between them, as Renaud's analysis would suggest,[32] rather than moving the entire unit?" Despite these problems, Renaud's analysis of the compositional history of this unit may well be correct.[33] What is more important from the standpoint of this study is that Renaud's proposal would alter the present form of the book of Micah, whereas the purpose of this study is to present an analysis of the coherence of the book of Micah in its final form.

Attempting to deal with the text as it stands, regardless of its history of formation, Childs argues in favor of partitioning the book 1–2/3–5/6–7: a thrice repeated pattern of alternating judgment and salvation.[34] So too Willis, who analyzed the present structure of the book as a prelude to further redactional study, arrived at the same conclusion.[35] There remain, however, at least two serious problems with this reading. First, Micah 1–3 (less 2:12–13) does present itself as a unit with a clear progression of thought evident still in the "canonical form" of the book, though interrupted by 2:12–13. Again, it is true that as commonly interpreted 2:12–13 does add an element of hope to 1:1–2:13; yet it is hard to see these two verses as constituting a section of the book on a par with chaps. 4–5 and 7:7–20. Willis outlines the book as follows:[36]

  I) Extensive doom (1:1–2:11) + brief hope (2:12–13) [27 + 2]
 II) Brief doom (3:1–12) + extensive hope (4:1–5:14) [12 + 28]
III) Extensive doom (6:1–7:6) + brief hope (7:7–20) [22 + 14]

But even the adjective "brief" applied to 2:12–13 seems to belie its size in relation to the other sections when one compares the actual number of verses involved (given above in brackets).

---

[31] Renaud, *Structure,* pp. 20–25; idem, *Formation,* pp. 404–8. Renaud builds upon the work of Albert Condamin ("Interpolations ou Transpositions Accidentelles?," *Revue Biblique* 11 [1902] 379–86).

[32] Renaud, *Structure,* pp. 23–24; see also idem, *Formation,* p. 184.

[33] Should Renaud's analysis in *Structure* be correct, that would not alter the present study given my intent to work with the final form of the book. According to Renaud, the present position of 2:12–13 is not accidental but rather reflects the editorial activity of a post-exilic priestly school (*Structure,* p. 21). Moreover, based on Mays's redactional analysis, it seems likely that if indeed 2:12–13 was transposed from another position, it was also revised so as to fit in its new location. (Cf. n. 39 below.) Cf. also Renaud's more recent redactional analysis (*Formation,* pp. 104–18, 404–8) in which he continues to maintain that the present position of 2:12–13 is not a result of scribal error (p. 115).

[34] Childs, *Introduction,* p. 431.

[35] Willis, Dissertation and "Structure."

[36] Willis, Dissertation, p. 136; idem, "Structure," p. 13.

J. L. Mays has offered another alternative: to read 2:12-13 as an oracle of judgment.[37] Then 2:12-13 fits into the larger unit of chaps. 1-3, an unbroken series of oracles of judgment. Moreover, 2:12-13 is now seen to be the final in a series of redactional sayings which refer to the exile (1:16; 2:10). Now, Mays arrived at this analysis largely by means of a study of the verb פרץ with YHWH as its subject. Following his interpretation, the otherwise enigmatic reference to YHWH as הפרץ does make sense. "YHWH is not 'the breaker' who breaks walls of captivity to rescue his flock, but the one who breaks down the fortified gate of Jerusalem and leads them out through it [into exile]."[38] In view of this analysis, it is noteworthy that in Renaud's study of the parallels between 2:12-13 and 4:6-8, the first two cola of 2:13 (in which the root פרץ is prominent) offer no support for Renaud's argument.[39]

As Brevard Childs sees it, Mays's interpretation of 2:12-13 is forced and artificial.[40] Indeed, viewed in the context of modern interpretation, this construal does appear idiosyncratic.[41] Mays's reading of 2:12-13 may appear more

---

[37] Mays, *Micah*, pp. 4-5, 28, 73-76. Though differing in particulars, Albin van Hoonacker (*Les douze petits prophètes*, Etudes Bibliques [Paris: Librairie Victor LeCoffre, J. Gabalda et Cie., 1908] 374-76) also interprets 2:12-13 as an oracle of judgment. According to van Hoonacker, 2:12-13 announces a future time of distress when the people, overwhelmed by their enemies, will gather together to flee in order to escape total destruction.

[38] Mays, *Micah*, p. 75. (Cf. Willis [Dissertation, p. 206; "Structure," p. 26] who differs regarding the significance of הפרץ.)

Van Hoonacker (*Douze petits prophètes*, p. 376) differs regarding the role of YHWH. He contends that although the mention of YHWH here may be meant to identify "their king," it must be a gloss. Supposing its authenticity, however, van Hoonacker suggests that the author's intention would be to signify that "la protection de Jahvé, au lieu d'assurer au peuple la victoire, se réduit à le guider dans sa fuite." According to Mays, the people do not escape at all; rather YHWH himself leads them into exile.

[39] Cf. Renaud, *Structure*, pp. 22-24. According to Mays (*Micah*, p. 76), an original salvation oracle has been expanded and thus reinterpreted so that in its present form 2:12-13 "functions as an announcement of punishment." The fact that the first two cola add no significant support to Renaud's analysis suggests the possibility that, if Renaud is correct that 2:12-13 was originally situated after 4:7 and functioned as an oracle of salvation, 2:13ab may represent editorial expansion designed to reinterpret the unit and fit it into its new context (i.e., after 2:11).

[40] Childs, *Introduction*, pp. 431-32.

[41] The closest recent interpretation is that of van Hoonacker (see nn. 38 and 39 above). However, that of Arvid Bruno (*Micha und der Herrscher aus der Vorzeit* [Leipzig: A. Deichertsche Verlagsbuchhandlung Dr. Werner Scholl, 1923] 60-63) should also be noted. According to Bruno, 2:12-13 represents an authentic Mican word of judgment which was reworked during the exile being reinterpreted as a promise of deliverance. The original oracle was part of 3:1-4 (coming before אך; but note his rearrangement and reconstruction of the text) which was originally addressed to priests who "cannibalize" the people. According to 2:12-13 they will be gathered as animals into the pen to await slaughter; then they will go out and come before the butcher (הפרץ)!

plausible, however, when one considers those before him who have reached a similar conclusion. Edward Pococke, in his 1692 commentary on Micah, offers this as one of three major readings of 2:12-13 in the history of interpretation.[42] Among those who interpret 2:12-13 in this way Pococke notes: R. David Kimchi (though Kimchi also interprets it messianically—the option preferred by Rashi), Calvin, Paraeus, Drusius, DeDieu, Tirinus, Grotius, Tarnovius, R. J. Kimchi, and R. Tanchum.[43] Moreover, to this list one may add the great Antiochene interpreter Theodore of Mopsuestia.[44]

The following analysis of unifying features within Micah 1-2 will support this reading proposed by Mays.[45] Moreover, the correctness of this interpretation of 2:12-13 as well as the function of this text in its present position will become clearer in the larger context of Micah 1-5.

Unifying Features within Micah 1-2

The above section of linear analysis emphasizes the role of articulations, especially logical sequences and connecting particles, in establishing continuity and thus contributing to coherence. Yet, a variety of other features also come into play. For example, I pointed out instances of verbal repetition and use of sustained imagery, such as the link between the theophany in 1:3-4 and the judgment of Samaria in 1:6-7. In addition, I mentioned the role of inclusios in framing 1:8-16 and 2:6-11, the role of a clear structure which gives order and

---

[42] Pococke, *Micah*, pp. 22-23. The third major reading, that 2:12-13 is a prophecy of salvation but spoken by false prophets in opposition to Micah, has been subscribed to by Ewald (*Prophets*, 2:306-9). More recently, van der Woude ("Micah in Dispute," pp. 256-57) has supported this interpretation.

[43] Pococke, *Micah*, pp. 22-23. John Calvin, *Commentaries on the Twelve Minor Prophets*, trans. John Owen, vol. 3: *Jonah, Micah, Nahum* (Edinburgh: The Calvin Translation Society, 1848 [written 1559]) 210-14.

[44] Jacques P. Migne, ed., *Patrologiae Cursus Completus,* Series Graeca Prior, vol. 66 (Paris: J. P. Migne, 1864) cols. 357-8.

[45] Mays (*Micah,* p. 73), as most modern commentators, emends the MT's enigmatic בְּצְרָה to בְּצִירָה (translating "in the fold") and הַדִּבְרֹת to הַדֹּבֶר ("the pasture")—the וֹ belonging to the next word (cf. Gesenius, *Hebrew Grammar,* p. 413 [§127i]). The emendation is necessary to make sense of the text and is probably correct, though consideration should also be given to the suggestion of van Hoonacker (*Douze petits prophètes,* p. 375) to read instead דָּבָר/בַּצָּרָה ("in distress"/in the midst of "calamity"). Finally, the verb תהימנה would appear to be a hiphil from the root הום (The hiphil of הום occurs only here and in Ps 55:3, both of which are contested) meaning "to shew disquietude" or "murmur" according to BDB, or "to make a commotion" according to Ges. Most commentators (including Mays, *Micah,* p. 73; J. M. P. Smith, *Micah, Zephaniah and Nahum,* p. 67 [who cites a number of others]; see also KB) read תְּהֵמֶינָה from המה, "to discomfit" (BDB). The emendation yields a well attested Hebrew form and should probably be accepted; the translation, however, remains unaffected.

coherence to the lament in 1:9-15, and the role of thematic elements or motifs in linking 2:1-5 and 2:6-11. But there are also features which contribute to the coherence of Micah 1-2 by forging links over somewhat greater distances.

First, a number of such elements remain to be exhibited within chap. 1. In particular, note the repeated word pair חטאת/פשע which occurs in 1:5, 13 establishing a continuity with regard to sin vocabulary. Note also the repetition of ירד in 1:3, 12. In 1:3, YHWH "descends" and treads upon the high places (במות) of the earth. In 1:12, evil "descends" from YHWH to the very gate of Jerusalem. (Recall the parallel ירושלם/במות יהודה in 1:5.) Thus, as Mays notes, "Verse 12b echoes a theme of the theophany from v. 3 and applies it to Jerusalem."[46]

On a broader scale, coherence within 1:2-16 is firmly established by its overall flow of thought and thematic continuity. 1:2 consists of a summons addressed to the whole earth to hear YHWH's witness against them. The theophany of YHWH in vv 3-4 serves as motivation for the audience to respond. Then in v 5 the reader learns the reason for YHWH's coming, i.e., to deal with the combined sin/transgression of Jacob/Israel which pertains in particular to the capital cities of Samaria and Jerusalem. Verses 6-7 then announce YHWH's intention to destroy Samaria; and in vv 8-16 the prophet laments a disaster which spreads across Judah, but which pertains most particularly to Jerusalem.

> . . . les versets 1,8-16 sont tout entiers centrés sur Juda, plus particulièrement sur les villes du Bas-Pays mais aussi sur Jérusalem, mentionnée au moins deux fois (1,9b et 12b) et peut-être trois si l'on restitue "Fille de Sion" en 1,16. La structure que nous avons dégagée renforce encore la place de Jérusalem: es deux occurrences certaines sont situées en début de strophe; par là, le prophète semble vouloir montrer qu'à travers son environnement, c'est la capitale elle-même qui est "touchée" (c'est le mot propre de 1,9). Si telle est l'intention réelle du poète, on comprend que la péricope s'achève sur l'évocation de la Fille de Sion (1,16).[47]

Moreover, these two phases of judgment are linked not only in v 5, but also in at least two and perhaps three other ways. First, as noted above (pp. 78-81, especially n. 6), על זאת in v 8 refers back to the previous verses. Secondly, if Donner is correct, then "das Suffix der 3. Pers. f. sg. an מכתה V9 [as he emends MT's מכותיה] kann . . . schwerlich anders als Wiederaufnahme von שמרון V6 verstanden werden,"[48] And thirdly, Renaud argues

> . . . en ce qui concerne la thématique, la remarque de Donner reste valable. A plusieurs reprises en effet et précisément dans ces versets-clés 9b et 12b, apparaît l'idée que le malheur atteint jusqu'à Jérusalem: trois fois en 9, on trouve la mention "Jusqu'à Juda; jusqu'à la porte de mon peuple . . . jusqu'à Jérusalem" avec la répétition significative de 'd; cette insistance fait écho en 12b l'expression ". . . à la porte

---

[46] Mays, *Micah*, p. 38.

[47] Renaud, *Formation*, p. 41.

[48] Donner, *Israel unter den Völkern*, p. 95; but see n. 10 above.

de Jérusalem". D'où vient ce malheur? Par où a-t-il commencé à frapper? Ne serait-ce pas de Samarie pour s'étendre progressivement jusqu'a là capitale judéene? Or en 12b le verbe *yrd* "descendre" fait référence sans doute à la théophanie des v 3–4 où YHWH "descend" (*yrd*) de son sanctuaire céleste. Michée voit donc le châtiment de Juda dans le prolongement de celui de Samarie.[49]

Further, the correspondence noted above (p. 46) between the theophany and the judgment of Samaria reinforces Renaud's conclusion; i.e., such links exist between the theophany and both vv 6–7 and 8–16 as to further the likelihood of a progression. In conclusion, "The thematic continuity of vv 3–16 is apparent. YHWH comes to punish Samaria and Jerusalem; the punishment of Samaria is described; punishing disaster stands at the gate of Jerusalem."[50]

The strongest breaks within chaps. 1–2 of Micah occur at 1:1/1:2; 1:16/2:1; and 2:11/2:12. This is clearly indicated in the linear analysis above. The coherence of the two large blocks indicated by these breaks, 1:2–16 and 2:1–11, has already been demonstrated. Moreover, despite the lack of clear articulations at the above-mentioned points which would show the logical relations between adjoining sections, there are other factors which serve to bind together the larger unit, Micah 1–2.

The "gate of Jerusalem" motif functions in just this manner. In recapitulation, recall that 1:6–7 announces YHWH's judgment on Samaria; v 8 functions transitionally and establishes the relation between 1:3–7 and 1:8–16; then in v 9 the lament begins. At this point the "gate of Jerusalem" motif is introduced. YHWH's "wound" has reached even to Jerusalem, the capital of Judah, the "gate of my people." The repetition of this motif in 2:13 harks back to 1:9 and forms another inclusio; it draws together the section 1:8–2:13 by relating the intervening material to the overarching theme that the judgment announced for Samaria (thus linking in 1:2–7 also) is about to be visited upon Jerusalem also. The "gate of Jerusalem" motif occurs three times within Micah 1–2 (1:9, 12; 2:13) forming a triad which points to the climax of the motif in 2:12–13. Destruction has already reached to the gate of Jerusalem; now, in 2:13, the people are led out through the gate to meet their fate. Thus, this motif contributes in a significant way to the coherence of Micah 1–2.

A second major motif also contributes to this coherence. The exile motif is introduced in 1:16. Occurrences of this motif also form a triad (1:16; 2:10, 13) leading to its focal point and convergence with the "gate of Jerusalem" motif: the people are led off to exile with "YHWH at their head!" This is the ironic climax of Micah 1–2 and, as shall soon be demonstrated, a semi-climax viewed in the scope of Micah 1–3.

Finally, two more integrating features may be noted. First, the binomination Jacob/Israel occurs twice in this section, in 1:5 and 2:12, effectively framing the unit. Between these two occurrences of the pair, the terms are employed

[49] Renaud, *Formation*, p. 46.
[50] Mays, *Micah*, p. 38.

individually (Israel in 1:13, 14, 15; and Jacob in 1:5 — a second time — and in 2:7) thus establishing a thread of continuity which runs throughout the unit. Secondly, the designation "my people" is used for the people of Jacob/Israel both in 1:9 and in 2:4, 8, and 9.

The Coherence of Micah 3: A Summary

The following features were identified in chapter 3 (pp. 39–41) as contributing to the coherence of Micah 3. 1) The three units of which Micah 3 is composed all deal with the topic of wicked leaders. 2) All three units are parallel with respect to structure. 3) The chapter as a whole displays a continuity with respect to its major theme, that being the speaker's concern for justice. 4) Two motifs were noted as common to vv 1-4 and 5-8; a third motif links vv 5-8 and 9-12. 5) As regards vocabulary, eleven terms are common to two or more of these units. 6) Finally, I also appealed to a broader feature, "rhetorical form": i.e., the overall mode or style employed in structuring and presenting the argument of Micah 3 as a whole.

Relations between Micah 1-2 and Micah 3

The articulation between these two units, Micah 1-2 and Micah 3, will serve as a convenient focal point with which to begin this examination. The term ויאמר in 3:1 has long puzzled interpreters.[51] As I see it, the conjunction functions as a logical connective which leads the reader on to the next stage of the argument; for as the book is structured 2:13 is not the real climax of the first section. Rather, the tension continues to build — reaching its true climax at 3:12. The verb אמר with first common singular subject functions as a global quotation marker which extends the force of the speaking voice and underscores the irony engendered first by couching a judgment oracle in salvation language and now by setting a series of announcements of judgment in direct sequence with 2:12-13.[52] That is, the prophet concludes Micah 1-2 with a subtle oracle of judgment which employs salvation language coupled with a shift in its semantic function. Then follows a full frontal attack: the prophet lets loose a salvo of three announcements of judgment leading directly to the ultimate word of doom:[53] Jerusalem

---

[51] For a summary of the various positions taken, see Willis, "ויאמר in Micah 3:1."

[52] For the sake of accurate functional description, it is helpful to follow the usage of O'Connor (*Hebrew Verse Structure*, p. 410) and refer to ויאמר as a "global" quotation marker. O'Connor distinguishes between "actual quotations" — "quotations which the speaking voice of the poem identifies as proper to someone else's voice and which it uses as heterogeneous to itself" — and "global quotations" — "quotations which the speaking voice allows to extend the force of its own reach, to enrich its own intrinsic homogeneity."

[53] I am using the term "announcement of judgment" here in a functional sense. However, from a form-critical perspective, one might also seek to relate Micah 1-2 and Micah 3 by a generic comparison of their component parts. Micah 3 consists of three "announcements of judgment" (now indicating the genre). The same genre may be observed

itself shall be destroyed. Finally, the repetition of the term ראש (2:13; 3:1) reinforces this articulation by means of a phonetic link.[54]

Micah 1–3 is framed by an inclusio extending from 1:5 to 3:12 which establishes its governing theme: the same judgment will befall both Samaria and Jerusalem.[55] (Note the terms עי, במה, ירושלם, and שדה which occur in 1:5–7, are lacking in 1:8–3:11, and recur in 3:12.) Micah 1:6 announces YHWH's intention to make Samaria a heap (עי); then the intervening material in chaps. 1–3 moves toward the climax in 3:12 where the same fate is announced for Jerusalem.

The summons "Hear" highlights both the structure of and the movement within Micah 1–3. The summons in 1:2 opens the unit. After the semi-climax at 2:12–13, where the gate and exile motifs converge, the second summons resumes the rising tension and focuses attention on the leaders of Israel—those who bear the greater responsibility. Thus, in terms of the movement of Micah 1–3, this articulation introduces both a sharper focus to and an intensification of the accusation. Finally, the resumption of the summons in 3:9 completes another triad and signals the climactic oracle of Micah 1–3.

The principle of *jus talionis* is exhibited clearly in Micah 2:1–5; the רע, or טוב/רע, motif extends this principle throughout chaps. 1–3. The term רע is connected with YHWH as well as with certain groups of the people; note the symmetry in its occurrences:

1:12		רע comes down from YHWH (versus טוב awaited in v 12a)
	2:1	the wicked work רע
2:3		YHWH devises רע
	3:2	Israel's leaders love רע (and hate טוב)
3:11		While Israel's leaders expect not רע because YHWH is in their midst, the reader knows otherwise, in fact, YHWH himself is working רע.

The alternation here displayed underscores the correspondence between sin and punishment. Moreover, this correspondence is further reinforced by the implicit comparison between YHWH's deeds and those of Isael's leaders. In 2:7 the reader encounters the following rhetorical questions posed by the prophets adversaries:

---

in 2:1–5 and 1:5–7. Note the characteristic use of לכן in 3:6; in 3:12; and—in connection with the messenger formula—in 2:3. (In 1:6 and 3:2b the conjunction ו is employed with the same logical force.)

[54] According to Willis (Dissertation, p. 292; "Structure," pp. 39–40), they are linked according to the "catchword principle."

[55] Cf. Mays (*Micah*, pp. 4, 38) with regard to the "Samaria-Jerusalem programme."

Are these [i e., the events announced in 2:4-5] his [YHWH's] doings?
(מעלל)
Do not his words do good to the one who walks uprightly?"

The expected answer to the first question is "No," to the second "Yes." The questions boil down to this: "Are YHWH's deeds good (טוב) or evil (רע)?"[56] The expected answer is that YHWH does good, not evil. But it is clear to the reader from 2:3 that YHWH is in fact devising evil (רע). Similarly, one learns in 3:4 that Israel's leaders have made their deeds evil (רע, מעלל). Of course, this should come as no surprise in light of 2:1-2, 8-9. The clarity of the situation with respect to YHWH's workings in 3:11 is enhanced for the reader by comparing the use of the term ישר in 2:7 and 3:9. The question in 2:7de, "Do not my words do good to the one who walks uprightly?" (ישר), clearly expects a positive answer. But according to 3:9, Israel's leaders in fact "pervert all uprightness" (ישר). Given this situation, it is clear to the reader that the proper expectation in 3:11 is not good, but evil.

By now a second important motif has been mentioned several times, the motif of the people's misunderstanding. That the people lack true understanding of what YHWH is doing is evident in 2:7; 2:12-13; and 3:11. In 2:7, if the people truly understood YHWH's workings, the rhetorical question "Are these his doings?" would bring the rejoinder: "Yes, the judgment announced is indeed consistent with YHWH's character." Again, 2:12-13 reflects the people's expectation that YHWH will gather (קבץ/אסף) his people for good and will work salvation on behalf of his remnant (שארית). But YHWH is in fact gathering them for evil, to lead them off into exile. Finally, 3:11 presents the ironic climax of this motif. Israel's leaders depend upon YHWH for safety, whereas—as the reader is well aware—YHWH is about to unleash evil against them. Thus, one observes another triad of passages in which a motif is developed which climaxes in the final oracle of Micah 1-3. Here (in 3:9-12) the רע motif, the misunderstanding motif, and the main theme of chaps. 1-3 all converge, reach their climax, and thereby confirm the unity of this first judgment section of the book of Micah.

Finally, three more features remain to be noted. The binomination Jacob/Israel was noted earlier as framing Micah 1-2; in chap. 3 it occurs in all three oracles (3:1, 8, 9). Again, the appellation עמי recurs in 3:3, 5 serving as another link between the sections. Thirdly, the pair חטאת/פשע, noted earlier in 1:5, 13, is again employed in 3:8—this time in a specific description of the prophet's vocation: "to declare to Jacob his transgression and to Israel his sin."

II. THE COHERENCE OF MICAH 4-5

Linear Analysis of Micah 4-5

Continuity within 4:1-4 is clearly evidenced by syntax, as well as by a clear flow of thought and continuity of subject matter. 4:1 begins with an important

---

[56] The contrast of רע and טוב is implicit here, but explicit in 1:12 and 3:2.

transition to the future expressed by means of a temporal clause introduced by
והיה. והיה is resumed by an imperfect and a participle specifying the future event
prophesied.[57] The verbal sequence is then continued and the description
elaborated upon by a string of eight consecutive perfects interrupted by two
subordinate sequences:[58] 1) a quote in v 2b-g following ואמרו, and 2) an aside
concerning the nations in v 3ef. In the first case, resumption of the main verbal
sequence is signalled by ושפט (v 3a). The second time the main sequence is again
continued by a consecutive perfect, וישבו in v 4a; note also that the subject is
here expressed for clarity. The prophetic oracle is rounded out by the כי clause
which expresses its authority.

4:1-4/4:5

A transition is here signalled by a shift of speaker. For the first time the
audience intrudes into the prophet's discourse.[59] This community responds to
the oracle of YHWH's future reign by a confession of faithfulness to YHWH
in the present — or imminent future. (As one might expect, there is no change of
verb form which would definitely indicate a shift in time frame from the future
in vv 1-4 to the present in v 5.) The introductory כי links v 5 very closely to the
preceding oracle and indicates that it is to be construed as a response to that
oracle. Moreover, the double use of הלך in v 5 harks back to v 2 drawing both
a contrast and a comparison: in the latter days the peoples will walk in the paths
of YHWH (v 2); now, however, (contrast) they follow their own gods whereas
(comparison) we confess faithfulness to YHWH (v 5). Finally, the future orientation signalled in 4:1-4 by באחרית הימים (v 1a) and עוד (v 3f) is picked up in 4:5
by לעולם ועד.

4://1:6-7

Both the temporal clause ביום ההוא and the formula נאם יהוה serve as
introductory elements marking the beginning of a new oracle. Yet, they also
maintain an element of continuity: for the temporal clause points back to v 1a;
and, by correspondence to v 4c, נאם יהוה establishes the authority of 4:6-7 as
identical to that of 4:1-4. There is also a basic continuity of theme; vv 6-7
continue to relate the results of YHWH's reign on Mount Zion.[60] In a manner

---

[57] Samuel R. Driver, *A Treatise on the Use of the Tenses in Hebrew* (Oxford: Clarendon
Press, 174) §121 (pp. 159-60).

[58] Thomas O. Lambdin, *Introduction to Biblical Hebrew* (New York: Charles Scribner's
Sons, 1971) §197 (pp. 279-82).

[59] I.e., reading this unit in its literary context — as is the intention of the present study,
its first person common plural speaker is best understood as comprising the assumed
audience of the book including the present reader. (Of course, the unit might also be read
against a presumed liturgical context in ancient Israel, the speakers then being understood
as the worshiping community of Israel.)

[60] Note the references to "Zion," a "strong nation," and YHWH reigning as king.

similar to 4:5, the end of the present unit is indicated by the phrase מעתה ועד עולם. Again, this phrase displays continuity with the preceding material. מעתה points back to the temporal designations in vv 6a and 1a. Finally, ועד עולם harks back to vv 3f and 5e. A basic linear continuity has thus been observed extending throughout 4:1-7. After the communal response in 4:5, 4:6-7 resumes the main stream of prophetic discourse introduced in 4:1-4,

4:6-7/4:8

At v 8 the reader encounters a significant transition.[61] While Zion does remain the central topic of concern thus linking 4:8 to the preceding verses,[62] the verse begins with a disjunctive sequence accompanied by a shift of addressee; the next several oracles are addressed to a "you" identified as the "daughter of Zion." Moreover, as Renaud notes, there is a drastic thematic shift: "Mi 4,6-7 envisage le royaume de YHWH; Mi 4,8, en termes plus voilés, mais faciles à interpréter, de la royauté de David et de sa capitale, perspective plus étroitement nationaliste et monarchique."[63]

4:8/4:9-10

Repetition in v 10 of the phrase "daughter of Zion" displays one element of continuity between v 8 and vv 9-10, i.e., continuity of addressee.[64] The opening adverbial, עתה, in v 9 reveals an element of discontinuity. The articulation is a temporal shift: the focus shifts from the future to the present. Moreover, a contrastive relationship is set up between the two time periods.

Together with syntactical clues, its coherent flow of thought serves to establish linear continuity within 4:9-10. To begin, three questions addressed to an unnamed second person singular addressee are followed by two imperatives addressed to the "daughter of Zion." Proximity, continuity of theme, and continuation of direct address prompt the reader to identify the addressees and

---

[61] Willis (Dissertation, p. 191) and Allen (*Books of Joel . . .* , pp. 29-60, 329), however, consider 4:6-8 to constitute a single unit.

As regards the text of 4:8, the consecutive perfect ובאה should be eliminated; it represents either a variant reading (see Mays, *Micah*, p. 102) or an attempt to clarify a less familiar verb (תאתה), i.e., a gloss. For other opinions, see J. M. P. Smith, *Micah, Zephaniah and Nahum*, p. 90.

[62] Renaud (*Formation*, p. 272) would also observe a continuity with respect to imagery: "En évoquant le bercail de Jérusalem 'Tour du troupeau,' le verset rédactionnel 4,8 prolonge l'image du troupeau, exquissé en Mi 4,6-7 à travers l'image de la boiteuse et de la brebis maltraitée."

[63] Ibid., p. 184.

[64] It may be—as some have suggested—that ממלכת בת is a late addition to 4:8; nevertheless, its presence in the final form of the text reinforces the bond between 4:8 and 4:9-14 already established by this phrase בת ציון.

construe the two series together. By its repetition of the adverbial עתה, the כי clause in v 10cd confirms this bond between vv 9 and 10. Moreover, this כי clause serves as a key to the interpretation of the imperatives in v 10ab by disclosing the logical relation between the distress evident in vv 9a–10e and the deliverance of v 10f–h:

> ... l'image de la femme qui enfante va lui permettre de donner à ce cri de souffrance un signification d'espérance. *Parce qu*'il s'agit d'un cri d'accouchée, ce cri de souffrance se transformera en cri de de délivrance. La suite du morceau (v 10bc [10c–h]) va en effet découvrir le sens de la métaphore en donnant la justification des appels du prophète.[65]

There are also stylistic clues which preserve the distinction between the exile to Babylon which the prophet announces as belonging to the imminent future and the (more distant) future deliverance from Babylon.[66] For example, in this case, שם functions almost as a temporal adverbial in that by specifying the place whence they should be rescued it also reveals that such deliverance is subsequent to the events of v 10cd. Thus, by referring back to בבל in v 10e, שם functions as a transition which ties together vv 9a–10e and 10f–h.

4:9–10/4:11–13

Once again, the transition is marked by the adverbial עתה pointing the reader back to the present distressful situation. Further, vv 11–13 display an overall structure strikingly parallel to that of vv 9–10: עתה+description of present distressful situation+two imperatives+specification of addressee, the daughter of Zion+explanatory כי clause + promise of deliverance/victory.[67]

Opening v 12, והמה introduces a disjunctive sequence which marks the contrastive relation obtaining between vv 11 and 12. Although v 11 depicts the nations as assembling against and taunting Zion, the two negative clauses which follow disclose their ignorance regarding the plans of YHWH (which are specified by the כי clause in v 12d). Finally, in v 13 the focus again moves to the future: YHWH will act to bring glory to his people. Continuity with vv 11–12 is here maintained with respect to theme, YHWH's plans for the nations, and imagery (gathered as sheaves to be threshed). Moreover, by repetition of the phrase "daughter of Zion," the reader is led to make a connection back to vv 9–10.

4:11–13/4:14

The articulation here, signalled by the adverbial עתה, indicates another shift of scene back to the present. Continuity with the two previous units is maintained not only by the introductory עתה, but also by the sequence of two

---

[65] Renaud, *Formation*, p. 200.
[66] Ibid., p. 201.
[67] Ibid., pp. 200–201. Cf idem, *Structure*, p. 33.

feminine singular imperatives followed by an addressee of the form XXXX-בַּת. Its literary context would lead the reader to interpret the appellation here employed, בַּת גְּדוּד, as a variant of בַּת צִיּוֹן emphasizing the city's present situation as under siege.[68]

4:14/5:1

In 5:1 the reader encounters a shift of both time frame, from the present time of distress to the age of Israel's coming ruler, and central figure, from the impotent שֹׁפֵט of 4:14 to the powerful מוֹשֵׁל of 5:1-3. The articulation presents a striking contrast: "A l'humiliation du *sōphét* de Jérusalem, l'hagiographe oppose le glorieus destin du souverain de l'avenir à naître de la souche d'Isaï à Bethléem."[69] So too, Willis notes three such contrasts: (1) "the present 'judge of Israel' who is smitten" versus "the coming 'ruler of Israel' who will deliver;" (2) "the great city of Jerusalem" versus the "little town of Bethlehem;" and (3) "the reliance of the present king on military power and his subsequent defeat" versus "the reliance of the coming ruler on Yahweh and his subsequent success."[70] This contrast displays both the logical connection between 4:14 and 5:1 and an element of continuity with 4:9-10 and 4:11-13 in which this present distress/future salvation sequence is paralleled.[71]

Moreover, this enables one also to recognize a larger unit and to discern more clearly the continuity between 4:8 and the verses which follow it. A very strong link between 4:8 and 5:1 is established by (a) their common beginnings with מ + vocative specifying city addressed and (b) the correspondence between the coming of "the former dominion" (4:8) and the coming ruler whose "origin is from of old, of ancient days" (5:1). Together these features form an inclusio which ties together the section 4:8-5:3.[72]

---

[68] As regards this identification of בַּת גְּדוּד (4:14) with בַּת צִיּוֹן (4:8, 10, 13) and also בַּת יְרוּשָׁלַם (4:8), see: Renaud, *Formation,* pp. 200-202; John T. Willis, "Micah IV 14-V 5: A Unit," *VT* 18 (1968) 534; idem, Dissertation, pp. 234-35, and Mays, *Micah,* p. 112.

As to the significance of בַּת גְּדוּד, J. Coppens ("Le Cadre littéraire de Michée V:1-5," in *Near Eastern Studies in Honor of William Foxwell Albright,* ed. Hans Goedicke [Baltimore: Johns Hopkins Press, 1971] 61) translates it as "Fille habituée à être assiégée" and notes: "Nous avons déjà noté qu'aucune version n'est réellement suffisante. Pour 'habituée à être assiégée,' cfr. E. König, *Hebräisches und aramäisches Wörterbuch zum Alten Testament,* 2e et 3e éd., Leipzig, 1922, p. 55a: 'du angriffsgewöhnte . . .' " Note also Mays, *Micah,* p. 114; and Willis, "Micah IV 14-V 5," pp. 533-34.

[69] Coppens, "Michée V:1-5," p. 57. Cf. H. S. Pelzer, "Some Remarks Concerning the Contrast in Micah 5:1 and 2," OTWSA, p. 35.

[70] Willis, "Micah IV 14-V 5," pp. 532-35.

[71] Cf. Renaud, *Formation,* p. 273.

[72] W. Emery Barnes, "A Messianic Prophecy: Micah iv.8-v.6," *The Expositor,* 6th ser., 10 (1904) 383. See also Renaud, *Formation,* p. 185 (who also empasizes this correspondence, but draws another conclusion); and Theodor Lescow, "Das Geburtsmotif in den messianischen Weissagungen bei Jesaja und Micha," *ZAW* 79 (1967) 204-5.

5:1/5:2-3

Certainly Micah 5:1-3 is to be held together as one unit. Verses 1 and 3 have to do quite cleary with the coming ruler and his reign. Moreover, עתה in v 3c harks back to עד in v 2 tying together vv 2-3.[73] Nevertheless, the significance of v 2 and especially that of the adverbial לכן is not immediately evident. Willis contends that there is a logical flow of thought throughout 4:14-5:3.

> As a matter of fact, vs. 2 seems to fit into its present context very well. The present situation looks very dark (iv 14). But the prophet announces that a new ruler will arise in Israel (v 1). "Therefore", the present dismal situation is temporary, i.e , it will continue "only" until the "birth" (arrival or enthronement) of the coming ruler (vs. 2), a ruler who (unlike the present monarch) will depend wholly on Yahweh for strength and victory (vs. 3).[74]

This popular interpretation probably reflects the influence of Isaiah 9:6 and 7:14.[75] However, the literary context in Micah supplies the referent of יולדה and, by so doing, invalidates the above interpretation; יולדה in 5:2 refers back to the same word in 4:10 used in reference to בת ציון.[76] Further, as Mays notes:

As another feature which serves to bind 4:8 and 5:1 (and perhaps even 4:9-14), note the strong roots in the Davidic tradition observed by Renaud (*Formation*, p. 273).

[73] As further instances of עתה used with respect to the future, Mays (*Micah*, p. 111) notes: Mic 7:10; Isa 29:22; and Isa 49:19.

[74] Willis, "Micah IV 14-V 5," p. 536. In fact, Willis contends (pp. 537-47 that this logical sequence extends through Mic 5:5.

[75] However, as Coppens ("Michée V:1-5," p. 60) rightly observes (citing also the concurrence of Lescow, "Geburtsmotif;" cf. also Joseph Coppens, *Le Messianisme royal: ses origines, son développement, son accomplissement* [Paris: Editions du Cerf, 1968] 23-31): ". . . *yôlēdāh* n'est pas à interpréter en fonction d'Is.VII:14. Elle ne viserait ni la mère du roi idéal, ni la ville d'où il sera originaire, ni sa tribu ou sa souche." Mays (*Micah*, p. 116) concurs.

Eduard Nielsen (*Oral Tradition: A Modern Problem in Old Testament Introduction*, Studies in Biblical Theology, no. 1/11 [London: SCM Press, 1954] 87), however, holds a contrary opinion and cites three ways in which Mic 5:1-5 is related to Isaiah's "Immanuel prophecy."

[76] Cf. Coppens ("Michée V:1-5," pp. 60-61), who writes: "L'expression concerne plutôt la *yôlēdāh* dont il est explicitement question dans un context relativement proche, à savoir Jérusalem (IV:10). Entendue de Jérusalem, l'epression peut signifier soit le temps de détresse que la ville aura à subir et à traverser, soit le temps qui suivra la période de malheur . . ." Later, after arguing that 5:2 is not part of the original unit, Coppens concludes: "Pour le glossateur, il allait de soi qu'il s'agissait de 'Dieu' livrant les 'enfants d'Israël' à la détresse jusqu'à la venue du Sauveur."

Cf. also Lescow, "Geburtsmotif," pp. 204-5.

In 4.9f., and generally in the Old Testament, *yōlēdāh* is used as a figure for the distress brought on by the attack of enemies; the image is concerned only with the writhing of labour, not an expected birth. . . . Verse 3 applies the metaphor to the whole period of exile and dispersion. The "birth" is the end of that term of "labour" when all the remaining dispersion return to Israel.[77]

In this way, the deliverance in v 10f-h corresponds with the return in 5:3cd. Thus, read in context לכן serves not only to link 5:1/5:2-3, but also to link 5:2-3 back to the entire sequence from 4:8; 5:2-3 then function to explain the why behind the present distressful situation and to establish when the future kingdom is to be expected.

5:1-3/5:4-5

This articulation displays characteristics of both continuity and discontinuity. First, vv 4-5 are connected to vv 1-3, albeit loosely, by means of the verb והיה. According to Willis:

> . . . the most natural explanation of ו, "and", at the beginning of vs. 4 is that the final redactor intended for vss. 4-5 to be understood as the continuation of that which precedes. It is possible to interpret vss. 4-5 as an elaboration of the way in which the success of the coming ruler promised in v. 1ff. was to be realized.[78]

Now, while his interpretation of the connection between 4:4-5 and that which precedes it may well be correct, Willis overplays the significance of והיה in this regard. Gesenius notes: 1) והיה is frequently employed to attach announcements of future events and 2) in such cases, the perfect consecutive may carry "a kind of independent force" and "depend [only] loosely on sentences to which it stood only in a wider sense in the relation of a logical or temporal sequence."[79] Moreover, the reader encounters in 5:4-14 a string of units each beginning with והיה; but והיה does not seem to indicate such continuity as used in vv 6, 7, or 9 (nor in 4:1).

---

[77] Mays, *Micah*, p. 116; see also p. 105 and the passages there cited as examples.

Renaud (*Formation*, pp. 273-74; see also pp. 281-83) also makes the connection between 5:2 and 4:9-10, yet still insists that 5:2 has to do with the birth of the Messiah: "En effet, ce v 2 contient un rappel du temps d'épreuve (cf. Mi 4,9.11.14) qui doit précéder les temps messianiques: aux trois *'th* de ce morceau fait écho le *'d— 't* 'jusqu'au temps où' du v 5,2. La *Yôlēdāh* qui doit enfanter le Messie s'identifie avec la *Yôlēdāh*, Fille de Sion, qui souffre certes présentement, mais dont le cri de douleur doit se transformer en cri de délivrance. Ici encore, perce une volonté de donner une certaine épaisseur au temps qui prélude à l'ère eschatologique probablement en vue d'expliquer le retard apporté à l'accomplissement des promesses de salut."

Cf. also Samuel Sellery, "The Book of Micah," *Canadian Methodist Quarterly* 5 (1893) 21.

[78] Willis, "Micah IV 14-V 5," p. 538.

[79] Gesenius, *Hebrew Grammar*, §112x-z (pp. 334-35).

Again, Willis claims that a logical sequence extends from 4:14–5:5. In particular,

> iv 14 describes the present disastrous situation. Jerusalem is under siege (possibly Assyrian). The present leadership is inadequate because it depends on its military power rather than on Yahweh. But in v 1–3 the prophet announces the coming of a "David redivivus" who will trust in Yahweh and let Yahweh rule through him, and thus deliver Israel from her plight. Then in v 4–5 he summarizes: when Assyria attacks the "new regime" will be adequate to the task of successfully repelling and defeating her.[80]

This interpretation is incorrect, however. First, no mention is made in vv 1–3 of the coming ruler "delivering" Israel. Secondly, the people are to be given up until the return; i.e., the events of v 3 are subsequent to YHWH delivering his people from Babylon. Thus, vv 4–5 do not function as a summary of 4:14–5:3. Rather, they describe another situation entirely, though perhaps an example or result of the security expressed in v 3.

Further, an element of discontinuity between 5:4–5 and 5:1–3 is signalled by the occurrence in vv 4–5 of singular thematic elements (the seven shepherds, eight princes, and mention of Assyria) which do not carry over from vv 1–3. Part of this argument may be reversed, however; for the mention of shepherds (רעים) in v 4 and the use of רעה in v 5 hark back to the use of the same root in v 3 with regard to the coming ruler.

Further continuity is witnessed to by the similar tone of 5:1–3 and 5:4–5; both present a hopeful view of the future. Moreover, it seems most probable that both זה in v 4 and the third person masculine singular subject of the verb in v 5c refer back to the ruler of vv 1–3.[81] Within the unit, coherence is clearly manifest both in terms of linear flow and a clear symmetrical (ABA) strucure.[82]

The shift in 5:4 to the first person plural form of address helps somewhat to clarify the articulation. This change of speaker along with the elements of continuity with 5:1–3 already observed would seem to indicate that 5:4–5

---

[80] Willis, "Micah IV 14–V 5," p. 542.

[81] Cf. Kevin J. Cathcart, "Notes on Micah 5,4–5," *Biblica* 49 (1968) 512, 514; Willis, "Micah IV 14–V 5," p. 544; Renaud, *Formation*, p. 274; Mays, *Micah*, p. 118. Greater continuity with 5:1–3 could be achieved by emending "we shall raise" to "he will raise" in v 4. Then 5:4–5 would clearly be construed as a result of 5:1–3; i.e., the deliverance would be a direct result of the initiative of the מושל—a link that is made in v 5b of the text as it stands. (As the text stands, this is another element of tension between 5:1–3 and 5:4–5. In vv 1–3 the people simply enjoy the protection of the מושל, in vv 4–5 they also take military initiative themselves.) However, to emend the text to remove this tension would be highly questionable (especially in view of Renaud's redactional analysis [*Formation*, p. 274] which explains the origin of the text in its present state).

[82] Willis, "Micah IV 14–V 5," pp. 543–44. Renaud (*Formation*, pp. 234–39), after emending the text to remove the redactional elements, offers a very different analysis of the structure of 5:4–5.

functions as a communal response to 5:1-3.[83] In conclusion then, this unit is linked to 5:1-3 both as a communal response and as a result of the dominion of the ruler of 5:1-3.

5:4-5/5:6-8

Again והיה provides the transition at the beginning of v 6. The major theme of revenge over one's enemies is continued; especially compare vv 7-8 with v 5a. However, 5:6-8 does appear to be more inclusive than 5:4-5; whereas the latter refers to Assyria alone, 5:6-8 describes Israel's relation to "many nations." Discontinuity is also evident with respect to certain thematic elements: neither Assyria nor the shepherds/princes of vv 4-5 are referred to in vv 6-8; and the remnant motif, prominent in 5:6-8, is lacking in 5:4-5.

Within 5:6-8 there is a striking contrast between v 6 and vv 7-8. Nevertheless, despite the fact that v 6 appears to present a peaceful picture of the future and v 7 a warlike view, their parallel structure demands that they be read as functioning together.[84] The shift to the imperfect in v 8 introduces a summary of the picture presented in v 7—a summary which, however, by means of its use of the divine passive brings out the role of YHWH in this exaltation of the remnant over the nations.

5:6-8/5:9-14

Once more a new segment is introduced by והיה And once more the articulation is characterized by elements of both continuity and discontinuity. As noted by Renaud, v 8 functions to some extent as a transition between these units:

> Le v 8 assure la transition entre 5,7 et le dernier oracle. Le v 5,7 évoquait l'écrasement des nations par le petit reste. Le v 8 rappelle opportunément que c'est YHWH seul qui mène le jeu. Nous retrouvons ici le même souci, relevé plus haut, de réserver en dernier lieu à Dieu la haute main sur l'organisation des temps messianiques.[85]

Nevertheless, there is a strong tension between 5:6-8 and 5:9-14. The first declares that Israel will destroy her enemies, the second that YHWH will destroy Israel's weapons of war, her fortifications, and her idols. Note the contrasting objects of כרת in vv 8, 9-12. Ladame observes in this regard:

---

[83] See p. 104 n. 59 above.

[84] See the excellent discussion of this contrast in Renaud, *Structure,* pp. 15-16.

[85] Renaud, *Formation,* p. 275. In his earlier book (*Structure,* pp. 13-14), Renaud argued in favor of dividing between 5:7 and 5:8 and taking 5:8-14 as one unit. (See Willis [Dissertation, p. 279] for a summary of Renaud's argument—though he neglects mention of Renaud's appeal to the second person suffixes in 5:8—along with Willis's rebuttal.) Renaud defers to Willis and presents a revised position in *Formation* (p. 259).

Le verb כרת, dont l'object dans le verset 8, n'est pas le même que dans les versets 9–13, fait ressortir davantage la divergence des deux passages. Nous ne saurions croire, en effet, que les versets 7 et 8 soient du même auteur que ceux qui terminent le chapitre: là, Jacob doit dètruire ses adversaires, ici, il sera dépouillé par l'Eternel de tout ce qui rendrait cette destruction possible[86]

Again, 5:9–14 is also set off by the introductory נאם יהוה together with the radical shift to the first person singular verbs. The beginning of this unit immediately raises the question: "What is the antecedent for ביום ההוא?" Given the contrast noted above, it seems unlikely that ביום ההוא refers back to 5:6–8. Rather, both this temporal clause and the following phrase נאם יהוה appear to refer back to 4:1–7.

The main verbal sequence in 5:9–14 (composed of first person common singular converted perfects) portrays YHWH's action in that future day; two subordinated inverted verbal clauses (employing second person singular verb forms) describe some results of that action. Finally, the last verse continues the verbal sequence, but refers to the nations as the object of YHWH's punishment. Thus, this unit proclaims future hope for Israel in spite of YHWH's destruction of her own weapons.[87] Her deliverance will be wrought by YHWH, not by her own strength.

Thus, the section 5:4–14 falls easily into three units. All three of these deal with the future, present a hopeful picture, and begin with והיה. Within each of these, linear continuity is clearly maintained. Their articulations, however, are characterized by strong tension more so than by continuity.

Unifying Features within Micah 4–5

In the above section, I paid close attention to stylistic clues such as articulations, connectives, sustained imagery, and continuity of theme which contribute to the coherence of the text by establishing linear continuity. I sought to follow such linear continuity wherever it was apparent and, in addition, to note greater and lesser breaks of continuity. Having identified those features which contribute to linear continuity within Micah 4–5, the present task is to discern features which operate over some expanse of text—i.e., in a non-linear fashion—to link together various parts of chaps. 4–5 and thus further contribute to their coherence. At least two such features, similar beginnings and a pattern of alternating time frames, have already been mentioned in passing.

Similar Beginnings

One important feature which contributes significantly to the coherence of Micah 4–5 is the linking of several oracles in series by means of similar

---

[86] François Ladame, "Les Chapitres IV et V du Livre de Michée," *Revue de Théologie et de Philosophie* 35 (1902).

[87] Renaud (*Formation,* p. 278) differs.

beginnings. Within this section, one may note two such series. The repetition of the adverbial עתה in 4:9, 11, and 14 marks one series. In addition, this series is framed by two oracles beginning with אתה (4:8; 5:1) which, in effect, extend the series by means of phonetic link. Each oracle of the second series opens with the introductory והיה (see 5:4, 6, 7, & 9).[88]

Temporal Shifts

References to time are very pronounced throughout Micah 4-5.[89] Especially prominent, however, is the pattern of alternating time frame exhibited in 4:9-5:3. Within this passage, the temporal frame of reference moves back and forth three times between the present and the future. In 4:9-5:3 the sequence "description of the present introduced by עתה + announcement of future events" is repeated three times. (By contrast, a future orientation is retained in the preceding and following sections — with the possible exception of the confessional response in 4:5.) This alternation gives rise to the first of several motifs which run through these chapters.

Major Motifs

One important motif in Micah 4-5 is the contrast between the present and the future. In an abrupt temporal shift from chap. 3, chap. 4 begins with a reference to the "latter days." After the brief interlude in 4:5, which is best construed as referring to the present or imminent future, the temporal reference "that day" in 4:6 harks back to the "latter days" of 4:1-4. The pictures of this future time in both 4:1-4 and 4:6-7 depict the future as a time of salvation. 5:9-14 also presents a picture of the future prefaced by the temporal referent ביום ההוא, "in that day." Again, the picture presents a time of salvation.[90] In sharp contrast to this future time of salvation, the present is presented in chaps. 4-5 as a time of distress. This may be seen quite clearly in 4:9-5:3 in which descriptions of the present time of distress introduced by "Now" are alternated with announcements of the future time of salvation.

A second major motif is concerned with "many nations" or "many peoples"[91] This designation occurs in 4 2, 3, 11, 13; 5:6, 7. Moreover, the plural form עמים occurs also in 4:1 and 4:5 — in 4:1 parallel with "many peoples;" in 4:5, in the phrase "all the peoples." Two brief observations should be made with regard to this motif. First, the motif occurs in very disparate pictures. For example, the motif occurs several times within 4:1-4 which presents a picture of a

---

[88] Its incorporation into this series is one more reason for not splitting off 5:9-14 as beginning a new major section of the book. (Cf. p. 16 above.)

[89] See Renaud, *Structure*, p. 31.

[90] Cf. Willis, Dissertation, pp. 114-16. Cf. also Renaud's rebuttal (*Formation*, pp. 286-87) of Willis's argument.

[91] Note also Renaud's discussion (*Structure*, p. 28) of this motif.

peaceful relationsip between Israel and the nations; to this, contrast the militant spirit of 4:11-13. Again, 5:6 presents a peaceful picture; 5:7 is militant. And 5:14 depicts vengeance against the nations albeit accomplished by the hand of YHWH rather than Israel.[92] So too, the attitude of the nations toward Israel varies greatly; contrast their words and intentions expressed in 4:2 versus 4:11. Secondly, note that in 4:7 the future announced for the remnant of Israel is that YHWH will form them into a עצום גוי. In 4:3 the designation "strong nations" (עצמים גוים) occurs in parallelism with "many peoples." In this way it is announced that the future remnant of Israel will be powerful like the "many peoples"/"many nations."

Thirdly, note the multiple references to Zion in Micah 4.[93] Among these, two motifs may be distinguished. First, beginning in 4:8 there is a series of oracles addressed to the "daughter of Zion" (4:8, 10, 13). The parallel phrase "daughter of Jerusalem" employed in 4:8 belongs also to this motif. Moreover, the phrase גדוד בת in 4:14 also refers back to this series and continues the motif. Also, in 4:11 the designation Zion is used in combination with the daughter of Zion motif. Secondly, while the name "Mount Zion" in 4:7 does prepare the way for the designation "hill of the daughter of Zion" in 4:8 which introduces the daughter of Zion motif, it also links back to the "mountain of YHWH" in 4:2, and Zion/Jerusalem also in 4:2. Thus, one might say that the Zion motif is divisible into two distinguishable, but interrelated, submotifs — related to the terms "daughter of Zion" and "Mount Zion."

A fourth motif has to do with the word of YHWH. Three oracles within Micah 4-5 explicitly refer to YHWH as their origin and source of authority. This is expressed by the formula יהוה נאם in 4:6 and 5:9 and in 4:4 by the phrase דבר צבאות יהוה פי. Moreover, 4:2 declares that in the latter days the "word of YHWH" will come forth from Jerusalem.

The remnant motif appears first in this section in 4:6-7. Here the reader encounters YHWH's promise to form the lame, outcast ones whom he as afflicted into a remnant, into a strong nation over which he himself will reign. The remnant motif occurs again in 5:6 & 7, though some tension is evidenced within the motif by the varying pictures which accompany it. Both 5:6 and 5:7 depict the relation between the remnant of Israel and the nations. However, 5:6 appears to present a peaceful picture, 5:7 a militant one. One may also note allusions to this motif in 4:10 and 5:2.[94]

---

[92] As Renaud has aptly observed (*Formation*, p. 275), 5:14 sheds light on 5:6-7. "It introduces a criterion which allows one to resolve the apparent contradiction between 5:6 and 5:7; the chastisement will be exercised with respect to the nations who will not obey" (my translation).

[93] ציון occurs in 4:2, 7, 8, 10, 11, 13. For Renaud's discussion of this motif, see *Structure*, p. 31. Renaud observes that the Messiah depicted as a new David is prominent in Micah 5, but not in chap. 4, corresponding to the Zion motif which is prominent in chap. 4, but lacking in chap. 5.

[94] Cf. Renaud's discussion (ibid.).

This same tension between peaceful and militant pictures may be noted with respect to another motif within Micah 4-5, the weapons of war motif. In 4:3 the reader learns that in the latter days the nations will "beat their swords [חרב] into ploughshares and their spears into pruning hooks." But 5:4-5 presents a contrasting picture: peace (שלום) will be expressed when the leaders of Israel rule בחרב and בפתיחה.[95] Finally, 5:9-14 declares an end to Israel's weapons of war enforced by YHWH.

Other Linking Relations and Motifs

Micah 4-5 presents a clear contrast between the outcomes of human versus divine rule. Compare the picture of human rule in 4:9, 14 with that of YHWH as judge in 4:3, YHWH as king in 4:7, and the ruler in 5:1-3 who comes forth "for YHWH" and rules "in the strength of YHWH, in the majesty of the name of YHWH his God."

This last phrase, "the name of YHWH his God," is repeated as a motif in Micah 4-5. The respondents in 4:5 promise to walk "in the name of YHWH our God." Similarly, the ruler of 5:1-3 will rule "in the name of YHWH his God."

The depiction of YHWH in these chapters and that of the coming ruler are clearly linked. For example, a link may be seen with respect to the scope of their rule. 4:13 refers to YHWH as אדון כל הארץ, "Lord of all the earth." So also, the מושל of 5:1-3 who comes forth for YHWH and rules by his power will be great עד אספי ארץ. And again, Renaud observes:

> De son côté l'ajout de 'jusque dans le lointain' (4:3) tend à donner à la royauté de YHWH la même amplitude qu'à celle du Messie qui doit 'grandir jusqu'aux extrémités de la terre' (5,3).[96]

Again, a result of YHWH's rule in 4:1-4 is that war shall be no more and the people may thus sit (ישב) under their fig trees with no need for fear. So too, according to 5:3, as a result of the rule of the coming מושל the people will be able to dwell securely (again ישב with the same implication of security as in 4:4).[97]

Now, notice the relationship between Israel and her enemies. According to 4:10, YHWH will redeem (נצל) the daughter of Zion from the hand of her enemies (איביך), that is, from Babylon. So too the coming מושל, together with

---

[95] The MT's reading בפתחיה ("in her gates") in v 5b is enigmatic in context. To be preferred is the emendation בפתיחה ("with the drawn sword"), suggested in *BHS*, which provides a clear parallelism with בחרב in v 5a.

[96] Renaud, *Formation*, p. 272.

[97] Cf. ibid. According to Renaud, ישב in 5:3 echoes 4:4; moreover, he adds ". . . l'insertion du v 4 dans le prolongement de la paix entre les nations, dont parle 4,3, donne à l'oracle une résonance salomonienne qui se retrouve aussi en Mi 5,3. Le même rédacteur aurait aussi ajouté au début de 5,3b un 'ils s'établiront (demeuront)' qui rappelle discrètement le 'ils demeureront chacun sous sa vigne et sous son figuier' de Mi 4,4."

"seven shepherds and eight human princes,"[98] will deliver (נצל) Israel from
Assyria. But then in 5:7-8 the situation is reversed. Now the remnant of Jacob
has the ascendancy and there shall be none to deliver (נצל) her foes; rather, the
remnant will prevail over her enemies (איביך) and they will be destroyed.

Note also the following repeated images or motifs. The image of a woman
in labor is employed in 4:9-10 and in 5:2. Pastoral imagery may be noted in 4:8
(עדר), 5:3, 4-5 (ורעה ,רעים ,ורעו), and 5:7 (בעדרי צאן).

Finally, note the similar use of קום in 4:13 and 5:4. In 4:13 the daughter of
Zion is to "arise" and be victorious over many peoples. In 5:14 the מושל will
"stand" and rule in the strength of YHWH.

In addition, Renaud notes the theme of the flock, the theme of royalty
which gives place to that of a shepherd, and the theme of the assembly. From
the multiplicity of diverse and overlapping literary motifs, Renaud once concluded that Micah 4-5 is an original work, the product of a single author rather
than that of an editorial linking of independent oracles. He has since altered this
position.[99] These features clearly do, however, lend support to the thesis that
Micah 4-5 exhibits a certain type of literary coherence.

Excursus: A Critique of Proposals regarding the Structure of Micah 4-5

While it has not been a primary concern of this study to present a precise
sructural outline of each section of the book of Micah, but rather to examine
1) the linear flow of that section as the reader encounters it and 2) interrelations
within the section which contribute further to its coherence, the structure of
Micah 4-5 has been an issue of some import in recent scholarly debate, an issue
which in light of that debate I feel constrained to address. Therefore, I shall
review several major contributions to that discussion, offer a critique of their
strengths and weaknesses, and finally offer a proposal of my own which reflects
the results of the foregoing analysis.

Nielsen

According to a traditio-historical analysis of Micah 4-5 published by
Eduard Nielsen in 1954, these two chapters constitute a literary unit with a
discernible structure. In particular, Micah 4-5 consists of a nucleus of both
positive and negative elements together with two surrounding layers of tradition.
That is, it displays a concentric structure. Micah 4:1-4 and 5:9-14 form the outer
layer. They are related by two similarities with regard to their content. First,
whereas 4:1-4 depicts the exaltation of Zion as the center of worship for the
whole world, 5:9-14 is concerned with the abolition of false worship. Secondly,
5:9-14 speaks of the "extirpation of the entire military power" while 4:1-4 speaks

---

[98] See Willis ("Micah IV 14-V 5," pp. 539-42) for a summary of the various views
regarding the identity of these shepherds/princes.
[99] Renaud, *Structure*, pp. 28-32; idem, *Formation*, pp. 271-72, 279.

of the conversion of swords into ploughshares and spears into pruning hooks. The next layer consists of 4:6-8 and 5:6-8, both consisting of promises to the "remnant." Finally, the center, 4:9-5:5, consists of a negative part (4:9-14) and a positive part (5:1-5). The negative part may be broken down further into three oracles, 4:9-10/11-13/14, all concerned with a situation of immediate distress to the "daughter of Zion." The positive part promises the birth of a descendant of David together with deliverance from Assyria.[100]

Nielsen further contends that each of the two outer layers are connected to the nucleus in such a way as to explain why they were attracted as literary deposits around it. He locates the key to the remnant deposit in 5:1-2 which, according to his interpretation, mentions YHWH giving the people up until the time when "the *remnant his* [the people's] *brethren shall return unto the children of Israel.*"[101] Further, 5:3 suplies a link to the outer layer, i.e., 4:1-4 and 5:9-14; for a new David reigning in the strength of YHWH surely implies a new exaltation of Zion.[102]

The chief contribution of Nielsen's study has been to point out the existence of certain correspondences between the various oracles which make up Micah 4-5, also to note the basic symmetry of this unit — an aspect which has been developed further and given greater emphasis in subsequent studies by Renaud, Willis, and Allen. Nevertheless, there are certain problems with Nielsen's analysis. Its chief weakness is that it is based solely on the content of the oracles. According to Renaud, "Ce critere legitime est employe d'une façon trop exclusive." Renaud contends, and I concur, that it is necessary also to pay attention to the literary form of the piece, especially the verbal joints which mark the articulations between sections.[103] Moreover, the link which Nielsen posits between the nucleus and the outer layer is insufficient even if one grants that 5:3 carries implicitly a promise of new glory for Zion thereby linking it with 4:1-4, such new glory for Zion is not a theme to be found in 5:9-14; nor can either of the major themes of 5:9-14, the extirpation of military power and the abolition of false worship, be found in 5:3. Thirdly, as Allen points out, Nielsens proposal fails to do justice to the fact that 4:9-14 "contains a strong element of promise."[104] Fourthly, I would also debate whether the division suggested by Nielsen is the most appropriate partitioning of Micah 4-5![105] For instance, this

---

[100] Nielsen, *Oral Tradition,* pp. 85-89. I have altered Nielsen's text references so as to correspond with the numbering in *BHS.*

[101] Ibid., p. 88 (his emphasis and brackets). Note also that, according to Nielsen (pp. 88-89), this "return" in 5:2 refers to a return of the Northern Kingdom from apostasy. (Coppens [Michée V:1-5," p. 60] cites van Hoonacker as advocating this view.)

[102] Nielsen, *Oral Tradition,* pp. 90-91.

[103] Renaud, *Structure,* p. 11.

[104] Allen, *Books of Joel . . . ,* p. 258.

[105] Cf. the analysis on pp. 59-68 above, which focuses on breaks and/or transitions in the linear flow of the text, as well as the summary of my conclusions regarding the structure of Micah 4-5 on pp. 82-84 below.

partitioning ignores entirely both the very strong ties between 4:8 and 5:1 and the daughter of Zion motif which binds 4:8 to 4:9–14. Finally, the historical argument Nielsen offers regarding the relation of 4:6–8 and 5:6–8,[106] is speculative in the highest degree and carries little weight with regard to the literary relation between these texts.

Renaud

The most extensive study devoted solely to Micah 4–5 is Renaud's monograph *Structure et attaches littéraires de Michée IV–V.* As noted above, Renaud criticizes Nielsen for depending too heavily on content as a criterion for structure. Moreover, Renaud also contests a number of Nielsen's conclusions. Yet, Renaud does commend Nielsen's analysis of the structure of Micah 4–5 as both original and fruitful and makes use of a number of Nielsen's insights as a starting point for his own analysis.

Seeking to improve upon Nielsen's analysis of Micah 4–5, Renaud contends that these chapters display a chiastic structure: A B C C' B' A'.[107] The weight of his argument falls on his demonstration of the parallels between sections A and A', etc. (although the partitioning of the unit will also be a matter of concern). To begin, Renaud presents three arguments for the correspondence of 4:1–4 and 5:8–14. Following Willis's translation, these are:

> . . . (a) they have the same theme—the destiny of the nations in the eschatological age; (b) they form a striking detailed contrast according to the principle of antithetical parallelism:
>
> A Salvation of the subject nations. 4:1–4
>   a Exaltation and blessing of Zion. v. 1.
>   b Pilgrimage to the Temple. v. 2a.
>   c In order to seek the law and word there. v. 2b.
>   d Transformation of weapons into tools for agricultural work. v. 3.
>   e Happiness of the nations. v. 4.
> A' Chastisement of the unsubdued nations. 5:8–14.
>   e' Unhappiness of the nations. v. 8.
>   d' Destruction of weapons of war and fortified cities. vv. 9–10.
>   c' Destruction of sorcerers and diviners. v. 11.
>   b' Suppression of idols and the ungodly cult. vv. 12–13.
>   a' Curse against the nations v. 14.
> and (c) the with the same verbal joint *wĕhāyāh* (4:1; 5:9).[108]

---

[106] Nielsen, *Oral Tradition*, p. 89. With respect to the referent of שארית in 4:6–8 and 5:6–8 Nielsen proposes the "working hypothesis, either that the 'remnant' passages originally referred to the Northern Israelites after the fall of Samaria, or that the circles which have transmitted the Micah prophecies to us and are responsible for Mic. 4–5 in its present form understood the 'remnant prophecies' as referring to the Northern Israelites."

[107] Renaud, *Structure*, p. 14 (see also the detailed diagram on p. 26).

[108] Willis, Dissertation, pp. 277–78 (translating Renaud, *Structure*, p. 13).

In response, Willis argues—rightly, in my opinion—that Renaud claims too much in saying that the theme of each is the "destiny of the nations in the eschatological age." As Willis notes, "5:9ff is devoted primarily to a description of the chastisement of Israel, not of the nations. The nations appear for the first time in v. 14 (assuming that v. 8 belongs together with vv. 6–7)." Willis also argues that "it is a mistake to separate 4:1ff from 3:9–12" and "the major concern of the pericope is Israel and not the nations."[109] Here I must part ways with both. Certainly 4:1–5 does deal with "the destiny of the nations in the eschatological age;" but this is too narrow to be taken as the theme of 4:1–5. The destiny of the nations is an outworking of the exaltation of Zion; this is the prime focus of the oracle (as underscored by the contrast with 3:9–12). Willis, on the other hand, confuses the issue by taking 3:9–4:5 as one pericope. He apparently presumes his conclusion that Micah 4–5 is formed of seven parallel pericopes each with doom + hope. Certainly 3:9–12 and 4:1–5 are to be interpreted together; the contrast between them is striking in its precise detail![110] But they need not be taken as inseparable. However, rather than arguing regarding the themes of 4:1–5 and 5:8–14, I think that Nielsen provides the better description of the correspondence between these two sections by describing their content.

Furthermore, while ingenious in its conception, the detailed contrast between these sections displayed by Renaud seems overdrawn. First of all, 5:8 should be taken with 5:6–7 not 5:9ff. which eliminates the contrast labelled e/e'.[111] Again, "a" deals with Zion, "a' " with the nations. Of the others listed, only d/d' is a clear correspondence. Moreover, the title given to 4:1–4, "Salvation of the Subject Nations," is not well-founded; nowhere in this section is it hinted that it is limited to "subject" nations in the way that 5:14 is restricted to the nations "that will not obey." Nor is "Chastisement of the Unsubdued Nations" an adequate description of 4:9–14, most of which is actually addressed to Israel![112] Finally, the articulation וְהָיָה does not support Renaud's analysis, but would rather suggest drawing the break between 5:8 and 5:9![113] That there is some correspondence between 4:1–5 and 5:9–14 seems clear in light of Nielsen's analysis. However, this correspondence is not so detailed as Renaud would lead

109 Willis, Dissertation, pp. 278–79.

110 See pp. 84–85 below, especially n. 156.

111 See above pp. 116–18 Cf. Willis, Dissertation, p. 279; idem, "Micah IV 14–V 5," p. 532.

112 Cf. Allen, Books of Joel . . ., p. 258.

113 See pp. 65–68 above. Although Renaud criticizes Nielsen for focusing too much on content to the exclusion of elements of literary form, especially those verbal joints which mark articulations, it seems that Renaud falls into the same trap. Micah 5:4–5, 6–8, and 9–14 are linked in series by their identical introductory articulations, וְהָיָה. Yet Renaud (Structure, pp. 11, 35) takes 5:4–5 with 5:1–3 rather than with the series; emphasizes that וְהָיָה in 5:9 parallels 4:1 (and also echoes 5:4, 6), rather than its more clear function of binding 5:9ff. in series with 5:4–5 and 5:6–8; and divides between 5:7 and 5:8 completely missing the significance of וְהָיָה as an introduction.

one to believe. It may be taken into account even with a much different analysis of the structure of Micah 4-5.

Next, Renaud seeks to show that 4:6-7 corresponds to 5:6-7. To this end, he presents only one argument: "Both deal with the theme of the 'remnant' in the messianic era: B with regard to its assembly and triumph; B' with regard to its role in the midst of the nations."[114] This argument is similar to that of Nielsen, though phrased in terms of theme rather than simply their common content (i.e., promises to the "remnant"). Willis's critique of this correspondence is quite weak. That "the concept of the 'remnant' is assumed in all of the pericopes in chaps. 4-5" is of little consequence (if indeed it be true, which Willis does not bother to demonstrate); the "remnant" is mentioned explicitly and is of prime concern in these two sections. Nor does the presence of the remnant theme in 5:2 defeat this correspondence,[115] though it may indeed suggest some caution as to one's interpretation of it. Thus, I am again compelled to acknowledge that a correspondence does exist. Yet I hesitate to interpret its significance too quickly.

Finally, with regard to the correspondence between 4:8-14 and 5:1-5, Renaud suggests a number of arguments. (1) "Both pericopes describe the appearance of the eschatological era, howbeit in strongly contrasting pictures. Whereas 4:8-14 depicts the savage and violent final combat, 5:1-5 announces the advent of the essentially peaceful messianic era."[116] Micah 5:1 functions as a transition point or watershed within chaps. 4-5.[117] Two problems present themselves immediately as to this argument. First, 4:8-14 and 5:1-3 are not simply contrasting pictures. Rather, they together present one interrelated picture. Contrary to Renaud, 5:2 does not begin a description of the benefits of the messianic era,[118] but rather explains the reason for the present delay in the accomplishment of salvation; the term ילדה in 5:2 is dependent on 4:9-10 for its interpretation.[119] Moreover, the pictures in 4:8 and 5:1-3 are striking in their similarity—not contrasting pictures. Indeed, the announcement in 5:1 of the coming מושל does present a major transition. But it does so first within the coherent section 4:8-5:3; in turn 4:8-5:3 plays a transitional role within the larger

---

[114] Renaud, *Structure*, p. 14 (my translation). On pp. 20-25, Renaud presents an excellent argument in favor of transposing 2:12-13 to a position between 4:7 and 4:8. This transposition would significantly strengthen the parallelism between 4:6-7(+ 2:12-13) and 5:6-7 and thus tend to make his overall analysis more attractive. However, Renaud contends that his results stand [i.e., that Micah 4-5 displays an A B C C' B' A' structure) even if one rejects this transposition.

[115] Willis, Dissertation, p. 280. Renaud (*Structure*, p. 32) does indeed recognize the presence of the remnant theme in 5:2. One may still consider the differing vocabulary— שארית in these verses versus יתר in 5:2—to be of some significance.

[116] Renaud, *Structure*, p. 16 (my translation).

[117] Ibid., pp. 32, 34.

[118] Ibid., p. 34.

[119] See pp. 64-65 above.

unit of Micah 4-5. Secondly, I would also argue that 5:4-5 be taken as a separate oracle, linked to 5:1-3 but tied more closely within the series 5:4-14. (2) Renaud also argues that both pericopes are introduced by a reference to a city, the same verbal joint (ואתה), and the same sequence of ideas![20] Now, these correspondences certainly are striking. However, I would contend that their significance is somewhat different. 4:8 and 5:1 do not introduce two contrasting pictures; rather, 4:8 and 5:1-3 form an inclusio around 4:9-14, framing one picture and providing the key to the interpretation of 4:9-14![21] (3) Renaud notes a parallel development in the two pericopes marked by a series of contrasts between 4:9 and 5:2; 4:10-13 and 5:5; and 4:14 and 5:4-5. Though Renaud admits these correspondences to be less striking, Willis demonstrates them to be nevertheless overdrawn![22] (4) Renaud further contends that this contrast is emphasized by the repetition or echoing of certain words from 4:8-14 in 5:1-5. In particular, he notes: הממשלה in 4:8 and מושל in 5:1; ואתה in 4:8 and 5:1; ילדה in 4:9 and 5:2; כי עתה in 4:10 and 5:3; and כל הארץ in 4:13 and אפסי ארץ in 5:3![23] Certainly this "echoing" is significant; these words do provide links within the unit. Notice, however, that none of these repetitions involve 5:4-5. This evidence thus tends to support my contention that 4:8-5:3 should be taken as one unit and a partition drawn between 5:3 and 5:4.

Willis

Willis also emphasizes the symmetry of Micah 4-5, but a much different type of symmetry than that perceived by Nielsen or Renaud. Willis argues that Micah 4-5, or to be precise 3:9-5:14, consists of seven parallel pericopes. Moreover,

> each of the seven pericopes in these two chapters is composed of two parts: a description of the present hopeless situation, and an announcement of divine deliverance, involving giving Israel victory over her enemies or restoring her former status or both. . . . Each pericope begins with a description of or a reference to the disastrous nature of the present situation. Then it announces the glorious future![24]

There are a number of problems with this proposal. To begin, how to divide the pericopes of Micah 4-5 is an important issue. Willis does acknowledge this

---

[120] Renaud, *Structure*, pp. 18-19. The ideas of YHWH's royalty and of the "days of old" continue this sequence. Renaud also reinforces this parallel between 4:8 and 5:1 by arguing that the idea of a flock, explicit in the appellation מגדל עדר, is also present implicitly in the reference to Bethlehem, "la ville de David qui y faisait paître son troupeau quand Dieu le choisit pour être le pasteur d'Israël."

[121] See above pp. 61-65.

[122] Renaud, *Structure*, p. 19. Willis, Dissertation, pp. 282-83.

[123] Renaud, *Structure*, p. 19.

[124] Willis, Dissertation, p. 213.

problem; nevertheless, he simply asserts his own partitioning without defense![125] I would contest his division at at least two points; these changes would make a significant difference in his analysis of the overall structure of the unit![126]

The most significant area of difficulty with Willis's proposal has to do with the parallels which Willis draws between these seven pericopes. First of all, he contends that they all begin with a description of the present distressful situation![127] But is this the case? To begin, neither of the two "remnant" pericopes describe a present disastrous situation. Moreover, Renaud argues, even if one were to accept the references to the lame in 4:6 as involving implicitly such a situation, there is not even such an allusion in 5:6–8. But Renaud is highly critical of Willis for his frequent reliance on this kind of implicit evidence![128] As another example of such implicit reasoning, consider Willis's statement: "each of the seven parallel pericopes in chaps. 4–5 assumes or states that Israel's leadership is impotent and/or that Zion is hopelessly doomed or is about to be destroyed."[129] Now, one can find evidence to this effect in three pericopes: 4:9–10; 4:11–13; and 4:14–5:5 (using Willis's partitioning). As to what the other pericopes assume, that is a matter of speculation. Of course, Willis also insists that 3:9–4:5 be taken as one pericope. But, as Renaud aptly demonstrates, this raises several problems of its own. First, 3:9–12 is inseparably linked within chap. 3. Secondly, 3:9–12 does not only picture a distressful situation; it also announces sins. No other oracle in Micah 4–5 speaks of Israel's infidelity; rather, all promise salvation. Moreover, the distress mentioned in 3:9–12 is not present but future. Finally, the contrast between 3:12 and 4:1 should not be taken as interior to the unit Micah 4–5, but rather as providing a guide to the relationship between chaps. 1–3 and 4–5![130]

Willis also contends that each of these seven pericopes involves a contrast between the present and the future. This is surely the case within 4:8–5:3. Willis is correct in picking up on these time shifts, but not in universalizing them. That is, such present/future shifts are limited to 4:8–5:3, whereas Willis insists that all seven pericopes set forth this contrast![131] Consider 5:6–8 for example: this oracle is oriented toward the future; the present is not in view. As for 5:9–14, Renaud responds:

---

[125] Ibid , p. 191. Here Willis divides Micah 4–5 as follows: 4:1–5, 6–8, 9–10, 11–13; 4:14–5:5; 5:6–8, 9–14. Then in a footnote, he remarks: "There is no division of chaps. 4–5 which has enjoyed what may be called 'general' acceptance. The above division is based on the present writer's own impressions and interpretations."

[126] In particular, I would draw two additional partitions: between 4:7 & 8 and between 5:3 & 4. See pp. 61 and 65–67 above and pp. 82–84 below. Renaud (*Formation*, p. 286) also differs with Willis as to the proper partitioning of Micah 4–5.

[127] Willis, Dissertation, pp. 216–30.

[128] Renaud, *Formation*, pp. 280, 287.

[129] Willis, Dissertation, p. 231.

[130] Renaud, *Formation*, p. 286. See also pp. 84–85 below.

[131] Willis, Dissertation, pp. 289–90. Cf. pp. 61–65 above.

Même dans l'hypothèse, tenue par Willis, mais que nous récusons, selon laquelle Mi 5,9-14 viserait Israël, on ne peut pas dire que l'auteur sacré décrit un présent de détresse à proprement parler. Le présent qu'il dépeint est un présent de péché. La détresse apparaît comme la conséquence de ce péché, comme une réalité *d'avenir*, comme le montre le futur "je supprimerai."[132]

In a similar fashion, Allen contends that 5:9-11 "is more naturally viewed as a reference to God's future punishment of Israel than as a description of present distress."[133] I would also argue that 4:15, 4:6-7, 4:8 and 5:4-5 also have the future in view and do not present such a present/future contrast.

Finally, Willis contends that each pericope announces "divine deliverance, involving giving Israel victory over her enemies or restoring her to her former status or both."[134] This does seem to be the case, although Renaud is bothered by Willis's assumption with regard to 5:9-14 that YHWH's punishment of the nations involves deliverance for Israel. He responds: "Peut-être, mais on ne peut faire porter le poids du contraste sur un tel non-dit, car l'hypothèse repose alors sur des bases bien fragiles."[135] One might also note that whereas 4:8 and 5:1 do mention the "former dominion" and a ruler whose origin is "from of old, from ancient days," 4:1-5 and 4:6-7 refer not to a restoration of Zion's former status, but to a conferring upon Zion of a status it never had.

In conclusion, the evidence does not adequately substantiate Willis's claim of a present distress/future deliverance pattern in each of the pericopes of Micah 4-5. Rather, this pattern appears forced and breaks down in a number of particular instances. Moreover, Willis's qualification that this contrast is set forth in three different ways (and these not following a pattern) appears to show a lack of symmetry![136] Finally, Renaud argues:

Qui dit promesse dans la Bible, dit souvent regard jeté sur l'avenir à partir d'un présent douloureux. En ce sens, on pourrait parler de contraste, mais cela vaut pour à peut près toutes le prophéties de salut contenues dans les livres prophétiques. Cette idée est trop générale pour qu'elle servir de principe d'explication à une structure aussi caractérisée que celle ce Mi 4-5![137]

Two other problems are worthy of brief mention with regard to Willis's thesis. First, Renaud observes quite correctly that Willis's thesis is unable to account for the order of the pericopes![138] In fact, Willis is quite leary of "sequential explanations."[139] But as I shall demonstrate, while linear continuity

---

[132] Renaud, *Formation,* p. 287.
[133] Allen, *Books of Joel . . . ,* p. 259.
[134] Willis, Dissertation p. 213.
[135] Renaud, *Formation,* p. 287.
[136] See Willis, Dissertation, pp. 289-90.
[137] Renaud, *Formation,* p. 287.
[138] Ibid.
[139] Willis, "Micah IV 14-V 5," p. 532.

is not unbroken in Micah 4–5, there is a basic flow of thought which does link
the oracles in a sequential fashion. Moreover, according to Willis, although each
pericope contrasts present distress to a glorious future, *"there is no logical transition between these two contrasting pictures!"*[140] This is certainly not the case as
has been shown above (pp. 61–65). Secondly, Willis appeals to the presence of
"catchwords" within Micah 4–5 as "incidental" evidence for the coherence of the
final form of this unit. While agreeing that these repetitions do contribute to the
coherence of Micah 4–5, I would argue that they are more significant than the
word "incidental" would indicate. For that matter, "catchword" is also an inadequate description from a literary standpoint. When viewed as part of the literary
fabric and not simply a factor in the compositional history of the text, these
features serve as keys to literary structure![141]

Allen

Allen finds certain helpful insight in each of the previous studies. And,
while he admits to depending heavily on Willis, he also considers it "questionable . . . whether he [Willis] has done justice to certain elements discerned by
both Nielsen and Renaud." After giving a brief critique of each of the above
studies, Allen attempts to arrive at a synthesis deriving elements from all of
them. He concludes that Micah 3–5 displays a concentric structure with a three
part nucleus: A. 3:1–4:5; B. 4:6–8; C (1). 4:9–10; C (2). 4:11–13; C (3). 4:14–5:5;
B'. 5:6–8; A'. 5:9–14. Allen indeed displays an impressive synthesis, but a
synthesis which falls prey to many of the same problems which pertain to the
above studies. In general, he tends to overdraw elements of symmetry. (1) I am
in basic agreement with Allen regarding the parallelism of 4:6–8 and 5:6–8;
however, I am hard pressed to find "allusions to present distress" in 5:6–8![142]
(2) As for the parallelism of 3:1–4:5 and 5:9–14, while it may be superficially true
that each can be described as presenting doom + hope, this correspondence is
nevertheless problematic. First, chap. 3 presents indictments and announcements
of punishment; 5:9–13 only announces YHWH's coming acts. Secondly, in
contrast to the themes of 5:9–13 — reliance on armament and false worship —
chap. 3 deals with wicked leaders. Thirdly, whereas 4:1–5 presents a promise of
peace; 5:14 rather depicts YHWH's wrath. (3) Finally, several problems arise
concerning Allen's description of the so-called nucleus. First, 4:8 is linked to the
following oracles by the "daughter of Zion" motif; Allen apparently misses this.
Again, there are a number of parallels between 4:8 and 5:1 of which he does not
take account. And he also overlooks the verbal repetitions which tie together
4:8–5:3; the articulation והיה which binds 5:4–5 into a series with 5:6–8 and

---

[140] Idem, *Dissertation*, pp. 213–14 (his emphasis).

[141] Ibid., pp. 290–92. In fact, the links listed by Willis, with the exception of that
between שארית in 5:6–7 and יתר in 5:2, favor my division of Micah 4–5 into three sections.
See pp. 82–84 below.

[142] Allen, *Books of Joel . . .* , pp. 259–60 (references altered to correspond with *BHS*).

5:9-14; and the logical relation between 4:9-10 and 5:2 signalled by the word
ילדה.

Renaud

In his more recent book, *La Formation du Livre de Michée,* Renaud has reconsidered the problem of the structure of Micah 4-5 in light of a redactional analysis. Although Renaud modifies his analysis in a number of ways, the basic chiastic pattern, A B C C' B' A', remains![143] The first main correspondence for which Renaud argues is between 4:1-4 and 5:9-14. (1) Renaud furthers his argument for a link between והיה in 5:9 and 4:1. Yet I still find this link rather tenuous; surely והיה links 5:9 more closely into the series 5:4-14 in which it introduces all three oracles. (2) Renaud's more recent argument for antithetical parallelism between 4:1-4 and 5:9-14 shows admirable restraint in comparison to his earlier work; the two oracles are compared in a very reasonable fashion. (3) Renaud still insists that 5:9-13 and 5:14 have the nations in view throughout, not Israel. With this I disagree; the "you" addressed in vv 9-13 is most likely the "you" addressed in v 8, which is the remnant of Jacob. (4) Renaud gives a much better analysis of the theme of 4:1-4, earlier described as "salvation of the subject nations;" now he writes: "ce morceau développe un double thème complémentaire: l'exaltation de Sion et, d'autre part, la conséquence qui en résulte: l'attraction des nations qui se rendent à la ville sainte 'pour y entendre la parole et la torah de YHWH.' " (5) Finally, Renaud has reversed his earlier position that 5:8 was to be taken with 5:9-14. Though maintaining that it also functions as a transition between 5:6-7 and 5:9-14, he cedes to Willis the case that 5:8 is indeed more closely tied to 5:6-7![144]

The "remnant" theme ties together 4:6-7 and 5:6-7. Renaud's position here is little changed, though better expressed. In response to Willis's criticisms, Renaud replies: 1) if indeed the theme of the remnant is present in 5:2, it is certainly not central; 2) moreover, it remains doubtful that 5:2 is really an allusion to the remnant theme at all; and 3) we categorically deny Willis's contention that all seven pericopes allude to the remnant theme. In particular: 4:1-4 does not; 5:9-13 does not; and, properly speaking, 4:9-14 does not![145]

Finally, Renaud still argues for the parallelism of 4:8-14 and 5:1-5, though in a modified sort of way. After drawing out very well the parallelism of 4:8 and 5:1, he draws the implication that they open two parallel sections. With this conclusion I disagree as described above. Departing somewhat from his earlier position, Renaud now urges that one not force the correspondence between these units; he considers their relation as more on the order of a temporal sequence. This is a marked improvement; for, as has been shown, there is inded a logical interrelationship within 4:8-5:3, not merely a correspondence. Finally, although

---

[143] Renaud, *Formation,* pp. 276-87; note especially the diagram on p. 281.
[144] Ibid., pp. 277-79 (quote from p. 278).
[145] Ibid , pp. 279-80.

Renaud now does perceive a relationship between the occurrences of ילדה in 4:9–10 and 5:2, his construal of this relation differs from that advocated in this study![146]

Conclusions

One of the key problems with regard to the structure of Micah 4–5 is simply "What are the units?" Table 4 displays areas of both consensus and lack thereof with regard to partitioning Micah 4–5. Among the most pressing questions revealed are: Is there to be a division at 4:7/8? Should one divide at 5:3/4? Should 4:8–5:5 be taken as one unit, split in two, in five?

TABLE 4
PROPOSED PARTITIONINGS OF MICAH 4–5[147]

Eissfeldt	Fohrer	Mays	Nielsen	Renaud	Willis	Allen
4:1–5	4:1–5	4:1–5	4:1–4(5)	4:1–4(5)	4:1–5	4:1–5
4:6–7	4:6–7,8	4:6–7	4:6–8	4:6–7*	4:6–8	4:6–8
4:8–14		4:8		4:8–14		
	4:9–12	4:9–10	4:9–5:5		4:9–10	4:9–10
	4:13–14	4:11–13			4:11–13	4:11–13
5:1–5	5:1–3	4:14–5:3		5:1–5	4:14–5:5	4:14–5:5
	5:4–5	5:4–5				
5:6–8	5:6–8	5:6–8	5:6–8	5:6–7**	5:6–8	5:6–8
5:9–14	5:9–14	5:9–14	5:9–14	5:8–14**	5:9–14	5:9–14

*Here Renaud transposed 2:12–13 to follow 4:6–7.
**This is Renaud's earlier partitioning. In his more recent book, he divides between 5:8 and 5:9 as do the others.

Such issues have been discussed in the above section "Linear Analysis of Micah 4–5" (pp. 59–68). To sum up, however, this examination noted overall continuity within Micah 4–5, but with greater breaks at 4:7/8 and 5:3/4. Thus, although some connections were also observed between 4:6–7 & 8 and between 5:1–3 & 4–5, it appears best to divide chaps. 4–5 into three main sections: 4:1–7; 4:8–5:3; and 5:4–14. In turn, lesser breaks within the sections lead to the following partitioning:[148]

[146] See the discussion of this relation on pp. 64–65 above; as regards Renaud's interpretation, see n. 77.

[147] Eissfeldt, *Introduction*, p. 408; Fohrer, *Introduction*, p. 446; Mays, *Micah*, pp. 6–7 (cf. pp. vii–viii, 121–22); Nielsen, *Oral Tradition*, pp. 85–89; Renaud, *Structure*, pp. 11–19, 26; idem, *Formation*, pp. 276–81; Willis, Dissertation, p. 191; Allen, *Books of Joel . . .* , p. 260.

[148] As is clear from the above analysis, these units may be broken down yet further. For example, one may note the transition between 4:1–4 & 4:5 and subdivide 4:1–5 into units on a lower level still.

$$
4:1-7 \quad
\begin{cases}
4:1-5 \\
4:6-7
\end{cases}
$$

$$
4:8-5:3 \quad
\begin{cases}
4:8 \\
4:9-10 \\
4:11-13 \\
4:14-5:3
\end{cases}
$$

$$
5:4-14 \quad
\begin{cases}
5:4-5 \\
5:6-8 \\
5:9-14
\end{cases}
$$

It may be noted that this partitioning is consonant with that in table 4 proposed by Mays. The discussion which follows will summarize those features which mark off the three major sections of Micah 4-5 and briefly describe the interrelation of these sections.

To begin, 4:1-7 is bound together by its continuity of theme (YHWH's future reign on Mt. Zion), a consistent orientation toward the future, and a number of linking words, phrases, and motifs. Secondly, the component units of 4:8-5:3 all pertain to the daughter of Zion. Within this section, the repetition of עתה in 4:9, 11, & 14 serves to tie together 4:9-14. Moreover, 4:8 and 5:1 each begin with אתה thus extending the series by phonetic link. Several additional similarities also bind 4:8 and 5:1 with the effect that they serve as an inclusio. In contrast to the first, this second major section is characterized by shifts in time frame. By a series of alternating descriptions, the future time of salvation is set in sharp contrast to the present time of distress. Functioning together, 4:9-10 and 5:2 reveal the logical relation between the present distress and the future time of salvation. Finally, the third section, 5:4-14, again displays a future orientation throughout. Its three oracles each begin with והיה and present results of the coming of the messianic era, i.e., of the rule of the מושל whose coming is announced in the preceding section.

Thus, 4:1-7 presents a vision of future glory when YHWH reigns on Zion; then peoples come streaming to Zion to hear Torah, war is forgotten, and the remnant is established as a strong nation. 4:8-5:3 depicts the appearing of the messianic era, explains the delay in its coming, and reveals when it is to be expected. 5:4-14 describes the results of the coming of the messianic era![149]

The pictures here portrayed are not entirely consistent; one may note elements of both continuity and tension. There is a great deal of continuity with respect to motifs. (See pp. 69-72 above.) There is also a marked symmetry or balance between the first and third sections![150] Yet, elements of dissonance warn

---

[149] Cf. Barnes, "A Messianic Prophecy."

[150] In this respect note the contributions of Nielsen, Renaud, and Allen (see pp. 72-77 & 80-92 above). See also Ladame, "Chapitres IV et V," p. 459.

against facile harmonization which does not do justice to the creative tension maintained in the text.

III. RELATIONS BETWEEN MICAH 1-3 AND MICAH 4-5

Up to this point I have discussed Micah 1-3 and 4-5 independently seeking to demonstrate the coherence of each. I shall now address the question of their relationship. In particular, I shall argue that these two units are not merely juxtaposed (though even such juxtaposition need not be without significance); rather, the two units are so bonded together by concrete, literary features as to form one larger, coherent, literary unit. Moreover, they are not to be construed as merely contradictory pictures which by their proximity nullify each other[151] but as complementary parts of a whole which together present a meaningful contrast.

To begin, the stylistic technique of inclusion may be observed also with respect to the larger unit of Micah 1-5. Recall from 1:2 the summons "Hear" (שמע) addressed to עמים כלם. Now, the only other place in Micah 1-5 where עם occurs in its plural form is in chaps. 4-5 as part of the "many peoples/many nations" motif. This suggests the possibility of a link. Moreover, in 5:14 the term גוים, used in parallel with עמים throughout chaps. 4-5, appears in conjunction with the verb שמע. Micah 1-5 is thus framed by a summons adjuring the nations to hear/obey and a warning of judgment upon those nations which do not hear/obey.[152] 1:2 introduces the "many peoples/many nations" motif which is later developed in chaps. 4-5; and conversely, the warning in 5:14 calls back to mind the court setting introduced in 1:2.

The two interrelated Zion motifs of chaps. 4-5 point to two more points of contact with chaps. 1-3. First, Micah 1 introduces not only the "many peoples/many nations" motif, but also in 1:13 the "daughter of Zion" motif.[153] Secondly, the word "Zion" is used elsewhere in chaps. 1-3 only in 3:9-12. There Zion occurs twice (3:10, 12), both times in parallel with Jerusalem. Zion and Jerusalem are used again as parallel terms in 4:2. Moreover, the phrase "mountain of the house," used in parallel with Zion and Jerusalem in 3:12, is also repeated with variations in 4:1 (twice), 2, and 7. These, and other connections between 3:9-1 and 4:1-5, provide a strong bond between chaps. 1-3 and 4-5 at their point of articulation.[154] 3:9-12 and 4:1-5 are in direct contrast;[155] the first announces that Zion will be leveled, the second that it will be established as the highest of the mountains. In fact, the two oracles are directly contrasting in

---

[151] Cf. Willis, Dissertation, p. 214.

[152] Cf. Mays, *Micah,* p. 6.

[153] See Mic 4:8, 10, 13.

[154] For instance, common vocabulary between 3:9-12 and 4:1-5 includes: הר, בית, אמר, ראש, ציון, כל, ירושלם, ירה, יעקב, יהוה, and שפט.

[155] Cf. Childs, *Introduction,* p. 331. Sharp alternations of judgment and salvation occur throughout Isaiah 2-11; note especially 2:1-5/2:6ff.; 3:1ff.; 4:2ff.; 9:8ff.; and 11:1ff.

several ways — to the extent that some scholars have suggested that one oracle was formulated in direct response to the other![156] It should be noted, however, that this abrupt transition is not made without explanation; thus Barnes observes:

> . . . a great gap in thought is left between the two passages, for we are not told how disaster is to issue in triumph. The explanation follows, however, in chapter iv. 8 – v. 6, in which the Person is introduced through whom the transition is made from present distress to the great Restoration![157]

2:12-13, the semi-climax of chaps. 1-3, is another point at which the continuity with Micah 4-5 is particularly clear. In carrying out a comparison between 2:12-13 and chaps. 4-5, similarity of vocabulary leads immediately to 4:6-7 where the following terms are all repeated: שארית, קבץ, אסף, and מלך![158] But how does this square with the interpretation of 2:12-13 suggested above (pp. 51-59 passim)? Note that in 4:6 the people are gathered (קבץ/אסף) for salvation; however, in 4:11-12 the nations are gathered (קבץ/אסף) for destruction. Which then is the case in 2:12-13? In my opinion, the latter is most likely. By use of what is commonly employed as salvation language, 2:12-13 embodies supreme irony. Israel in 2:12-13, just as the nations in 4:11-12, does not understand what YHWH is doing; YHWH is working רע when the people expect otherwise![159] Thus, the misunderstanding motif noted in chaps. 1-3 is present also in 4-5![160]

Moreover, the convergence of the gate and exile motifs in 2:12-13 provides a major link with chaps. 4-5; for with the climax of the exile motif the remnant

---

[156] Cf. Willis, "Structure of Micah 3-5," p. 196 n. 24 (or idem, Dissertation, pp. 121-22 n. 1), wherein he lists the contrasts between these two units and cites several other scholars on this topic (including, among others, Beck, Ackroyd, and Weiser). According to Willis, "Even Ed. Nielsen, Oral Tradition 1954, 92, is probably not too radical when he says: 'the thought forces itself upon us that these passages (i.e., 3:9-12 and 4:1-5) cannot even have originated independently of each other.' "
According to Nielsen (Oral Tradition, p. 92), "the contrast is carried out in detail. The ploughing of Zion and the exaltation of Zion, Zion as a jungle sanctuary and Zion exalted above the hills; Zion built in violence and bloodshed and Zion as the place from which YHWH's word and teaching goes forth, from which the nations shall be judged; Zion shall become heaps and the nations shall come to Zion with peaceful intentions."
[157] Barnes, "A Messianic Prophecy," p. 376.
[158] Willis (Dissertation, p. 119 n. 1) sums up positions taken with regard to the original position of Mic 2:12-13. Though a number of suggestions have been made, Willis contends that "among those scholars that maintain that 2:12-13 must be transferred, the most widely held view is that this passage belongs after 4:7." In support of this, he cites Condamin, Sellin, Lippl, Deden, and Renaud.
[159] See my discussion of the רע motif in Micah 1-3 on pp. 58-59 above. רעע in 4:6, "those whom YHWH has afflicted," harks back to the רע motif in Micah 1-3 (especially to רעע in 3:4 and to YHWH's action in 1:12; 2:3). So also מחשבת in 4:12 relates to the same motif (note חשב in 2:3).
[160] Cf. Mic 2:7; 2:12-13; and 3:11. See also the discussion on p. 59 above.

motif is introduced. Now, the term remnant (שארית) might appear to pose a problem for this construal of 2:12-13 in that, except for 2:12, שארית always occurs in salvation contexts![161] In 2:12-13, however, the people are led *out* of Jerusalem; this parallels 4:10. (Note יצא in both.) In 4:10 they are led to Babylon; this is also their destination, I would suggest, in 2:12-13. How then does the remnant motif fit in? Note the articulations: 2:12-13 follows immediately on v 11 without any transition; but at 4:1 there is an articulation with respect to time. In "that day" or "the latter days" YHWH will gather the remnant for salvation; in 2:12-13 they are gathered for judgment. Thus, 2:12-13 and 4:6-7 present the converse sides of YHWH's grand scheme. This is confirmed by the explicit statement of this plan in 4:10.

The times of distress described in the "Now" passages in chaps. 4-5 provide another link between chaps. 1-3 and 4-5. Accordin to 1:9, YHWH's wound (מכות יה) has come to Judah![162] In 4:14, "they strike" (נכה) the ruler of Israel. Not only is the root נכה repeated, but it also occurs in the proximity of יהודה (1:9; 5:1) neither of which appear elsewhere in Micah 1-5. Again, רעע in 4:6 (in the phrase "those whom I [YHWH] have afflicted") certainly harks back to the רע motif in chaps. 1-3 (and the usage of רעע in 3:4).

These features contribute significantly to the coherence of Micah 1-5. In addition, one may point to a variety of other features which, though of lesser individual weight, nevertheless add to the cumulative force of the argument. For example, according to Eybers, the theme of "divine punishment according to the *ius talionis*" occurs repeatedly in the book of Micah. In particular, he draws attention to "the corresponding words used in connection with the sin and the punishment in Mic. 1:7 (*'etnan*); 2:1-4 (*hoseb* and *śade*); 3:6-7 (the roots *ḥzh* and *qsm*)." To these he suggests comparing also 4:11-12![163] Given the transposition suggested above, this theme may be noted also in 3:1-4. Or consider the use of הלך. According to 2:7 & 11, one may "walk uprightly" or "walk about uttering wind and lies." Chapter 4 presents a similar dichotomy: the option of "walking in YHWH's paths" or "walking in the name of YHWH" is contrasted to "walking in the name of other gods" (4:2, 5). Note also the following motifs: (1) The "word of YHWH" motif occurs in both chaps. 1-3 and 4-5. Compare 1:1 and 2:7 with 4:2; 2:3 and 3:5 with 4:4 and 4:6 (cf. also 4:12). (2) The amplitude of YHWH's lordship is underscored in both sections also. Thus, the summons in 1:2 is addressed to עמים כלם and ארץ ומלאה. This same motif may be observed in 4:3, 13; 5:3. (3) The motif of YHWH's sovereignty may also be observed in both chaps. 1-3 and 4-5. Note that in 1:15 it is YHWH who brings a conqueror upon Israel. Moreover, while the nations are assembled against Zion in 4:12, in actuality it is YHWH who has assembled them for his own purposes.

---

[161] Cf. Mic 4:7; 5:6, 7; 7:18.

[162] Regarding the emendation of the text to מכות יה, see p. 47 n. 10.

[163] I. H. Eybers, "Micah, the Morasthite: the man and his message," OTWSA, pp. 14, 22 n. 58.

(4) The motif of the destruction of idols frames chaps. 1-5 occurring in both 1:7 and 5:12 (note פסיל in both). (5) Another common motif has to do with horses and chariots (מרכבה in 1:13 and 5:9; רכש in 1:13; סוס in 5:9). The instruction "Harness the steeds to the chariots" is given to Lachish, the city referred to as "the beginning of sin to the daughter of Zion." According to 5:9 the future day of salvation will nevertheless include judgment upon such armaments. (6) According to Allen, the sheep and shepherd motif is employed in 2:12 and 4:6-8 "to describe the covenant relationship between Yahweh and his people." Moreover, in 5:4 it is "applied to his [YHWH's] royal representative."[164]

Finally, Willis observes that the doom oracles in Micah 3 (especially vv 1-2, 5, 9, 11-12) "present a suitable background" for the emphasis in chaps. 4-5 of "restoring Israel to her former status as Yahweh's covenant people" by "showing the lack of responsible leadership in Israel and by announcing the destruction of Zion."[165] Note the lack of good leadership in chaps. 1-3 and the "Now" sections of 4-5 versus the descriptions of YHWH's leadership. Compare the human judges in 3:11 and 4:14 to YHWH in 4:3.

---

[164] Allen, *Books of Joel* . . . , p. 252.
[165] Willis, Dissertation, p. 231.

5
The Coherence of Micah 6-7

Having described the coherence of Micah 1-5, it remains to do the same for Micah 6-7. My procedure will be basically the same in this chapter as in the last. However, as shall be seen, the literary style of Micah 6-7 is drastically different from that of chaps. 1-5. Micah 6-7 is dialogical in character. For this reason, the linear analysis of Micah 6-7 will emphasize elements of continuity within speeches, breaks between speeches, and relations between successive speeches and groups of speeches — including the interchange of speakers and addressees.

I. LINEAR ANALYSIS OF MICAH 6-7

Micah 6:1-8

6:1-2

Micah 6 begins with a three-fold summons (vv 1a, 1bc, 2). However, whether this summons is spoken by one person or several is not immediately clear. The first and third parts of the summons refer to YHWH in the third person; thus, while YHWH may be the speaker of the second part, he is probably not that of the first or third. Again, only the third summons specifies its addressee; the first and second leave this question open. I shall examine these issues more closely in order to determine their most probable resolution.

The speaker of v 1a is commonly taken to be the prophet. Moreover, v 1a appears to identify the speaker of v 1b as being YHWH. Now, according to both Renaud and Huffmon, v 1b is addressed to the prophet.[1] Watson takes the addressees as being YHWH and the people, in the roles of plaintiff and defendant.[2] And Mays thinks that it is addressed to the people of YHWH.[3] The latter two possibilities, however, appear as unlikely in view of the fact that v 1b employs masculine singular imperatives. Nevertheless, the option offered by Mays must not be ruled out in view of the masculine singular suffixes used in vv 3-5 in reference to עמי. I shall return to this question of the addressee in v 1 after discussing further that regarding the speaker(s) in vv 1-2.

---

[1] Renaud, *Formation,* p. 302; Herbert B. Huffmon, "The Covenant Lawsuit in the Prophets," *JBL* 78 (1959) 287.

[2] Watson, "Form Criticism," p. 64.

[3] Mays, *Micah,* p. 128.

Assuming that the above suggestions are correct in regarding YHWH to be the speaker of v 1b, there would appear to be another change of speaker in v 2 given that v 2 refers to YHWH in the third person.[4] Renaud concludes: "la mention de YHWH à la troisième personne en 2a comme en 2b doit nous faire supposer que c'est encore le prophète qui parle ici," but he then observes that such a double introduction placed in the mouth of the prophet is quite unusual.[5] It is also awkward; the speech of YHWH in v 1b interrupts the prophet's introduction and the words of the prophet in v 2 interrupt YHWH's own speech. Thus, it seems more likely that the prophet is speaking throughout vv 1-2 and that vv 1-2 function together to introduce the words of YHWH which follow. That is, the change of speaker anticipated in v 1a is delayed until the completion of the three-fold summons.

Verse 2 is addressed to the mountains. The addressees of vv 1a and 1b have yet to be identified. In this regard, note that the parties clearly involved in 6:1ff. are the prophet, YHWH, the mountains, and the defendant on trial—identified in v 2 as Israel. The imperative in v 1a is singular, those in 1b are plural. From these data it seems most likely that v 1a is addressed to Israel and v 1b to YHWH.[6]

To sum up: as I read it, the summons is spoken by one person: the prophet acting as an official of the court. It is addressed, in its three parts, to: the people

---

[4] Cf. ibid. Despite these third person references, Mays considers YHWH to be the speaker in v 2 on the basis of the introduction in v 1a.

[5] Renaud, *Formation*, p. 302. This leads Renaud (pp. 303-4) to suspect the presence of a gloss. Upon further examination, he argues that v 1bc and v 2 are contradictory: ". . . les éléments cosmiques concernés ne remplissent pas la même fonction dans les deux introductions: au v 1, les montagnes et les collines sont citées comme accusées au tribunal de Dieu, mais, au v 2, les montagnes et les fondements de la terre le sont au titre de témoins. Bien plus, au v 2, le Jeu des relations est complément inversé par rapport au v 1. En 6,1, le prophète s'adresse au peuple pour lui annoncer qu'il a reçu mission d'ouvrir un procès contre les montagnes. En 6,2, en revanche, il convoque les montagnes au procès de YHWH contre son peuple." Based on these observations, Renaud concludes that 6:1 is secondary—an addition and not part of the orignal unit.

Whether or not Renaud is correct regarding the presence of an editorial addition, the purpose of the present study is to make sense of the resultant text. Renaud states correctly that the phrase רִיב אֶת most often indicates a process engaged against someone. However, the phrase need not be so construed in this case for אֵת may also signify "before" or "in the presence of" (BDB, p. 86 [§1c]). Given these possible translations, the latter option is clearly preferable from a literary standpoint to that advocated by Renaud. (Cf. Mays, *Micah*, p. 131; Willis, Dissertation, pp. 338-39 n. 4.)

[6] As Mays (*Micah*, p. 128) suggests, v 1a may be taken as simply addressed to a general audience; and the singular imperative of v 1b could be addressed to עַמִּי. However, that YHWH has a case against his people, not vice versa, is clear in vv 3-5 (though v 1b may be ironic, as v 3).

of Israel, the defendants on trial; YHWH, the plaintiff; and the mountains which function as learning witnesses.[7]

6:3-5

A disjunctive relation obtains between vv 2 and 3; the latter begins with the vocative עמי, rather than the verb, signalling a change of speaker. And, while the question as to the speaker(s) and addressee(s) of vv 1-2 remains open to debate, with v 3 YHWH's opening argument in his case with his people clearly begins.[8]

Verses 3 and 4 are connected syntactically. In v 3, two parallel questions beginning with מה and connected by the conjunction ו are followed by an imperative demanding a response. Then v 4 describing YHWH's past action with respect to his people is set in relationship to v 3 by the connective כי.[9]

Verse 5 begins with the repetition of the vocative עמי. Despite the displacement of the verb from first position, which would ordinarily create a disjunction, the use of the vocative here relates back to v 3 and thus establishes continuity within the speech. The vocative עמי, as a reference to the people of YHWH, serves to structure the address in vv 3-5. Moreover, it also links this address to the summons above which stated "YHWH has a controversy with his people" (עמו). This vocative introduces an injunction for Israel to remember her past—in continuity with v 4—and culminates in a purpose clause.[10]

---

[7] Regarding the function of the mountains as learning witnesses, see above, pp. 24 n. 44 and pp. 25-26 n. 47. Cf. Watson, "Form Criticism," pp. 64-65.

[8] Cf. Driver, *Introduction,* p. 331; Mays, *Micah,* p. 128; J. M. P. Smith, *Micah, Zephaniah and Nahum,* p. 120; Watson, "Form Criticism," p. 64; and Renaud, *Formation,* p. 302.

[9] In vv 3-4 note the word-play between the opposites העלתיך and הלאתיך. See Conrad von Orelli, *The Twelve Minor Prophets,* trans. J. S. Banks (Edinburgh: T. & T. Clark, 1893) 213; Renaud, *Formation,* p. 302.

[10] Excepting the apparent lacuna in v 5, the text of 6:1-8 presents little difficulty. A number of emendations have been suggested to improve grammar (e.g., the addition of הדבר in v 1), parallelism (e.g., changing והאתנים in v 2 to והאזינו), meter (e.g., shifting עמי at the beginning of v 5 to עמו at the end of v 4; deletions of the phrases מלך מואב and בן בעור in v 5), or style (e.g., emending צדקות יהוה to צדקותי in v 5). None of these, however, are truly necessary. Consider, for example, the emendation of והאתנים to והאזינו in v 2. This emendation, accepted by most commentators since Wellhausen (see Willis, Dissertation, pp. 339-40, Mays, *Micah,* p. 128; J. M. P. Smith, *Micah, Zephaniah and Nahum,* p. 119), does provide better parallelsm. Moreover, as Smith notes, the confusion of ו and נ would be relatively easy in the old script. Yet, the MT makes perfect sense translated as "enduring ones," set in apposition to the following construct phrase. Cf. D. K. Innes, "Some Notes on Micah," *Evangelical Quarterly* 41 (1969) 216; Renaud, *Formation,* pp. 91-92.

Nevertheless, the lacuna in v 5 presents the interpreter with a real difficulty. As regards the existence of a lacuna there is a general consensus. A number of solutions to the problem have been offered. For example, Weiser and Robinson have suggested that one read בעברך in place of בן בעור (Mays, *Micah,* p. 128). The editors of the *NEB* chose to

6:6-7

The interrogative במה opens v 6, creating another disjunction signalling change of speaker. Now YHWH is spoken of in the third person while the speaker employs the first person. In context, the function of these verses is clear; vv 6-7 is the response called for in v 3. Speaking to Israel, YHWH demands: ענה בי. To this demand, a voice speaking in the first person singular now responds with a series of parallel questions. The speaker may be taken as either a representative of or a personification of Israel. The vocative "O man" in v 8, referring back to the speaker of vv 6-7, may favor the former option. Yet 6:6-7 might also be read as reflecting a sense of corporate identity; that is, Israel is personified so that the "I" of vv 6-7 is the עמי of vv 3-5![11]

6:8

In v 8 the speaker changes again. The verse does begin with the verb; but now the verb is in the third person singular rather than the first person. Moreover, v 8 presents an answer to the questions asked in vv 6-7 regarding how properly to worship YHWH. Verse 8 appears to be spoken by the prophet in response to the questions of the people voiced by their representative.[12]

Verse 9 is introduced by another disjunctive sequence beginning with the noun קול. While this first phrase may be spoken by the prophet who speaks in

---

retain בן בעור and insert בין עברך (L. H. Brockington, *The Hebrew Text of the Old Testament: The Readings Adopted by the Translators of the New English Bible* [Oxford: Oxford University Press, 1973] 256). And Paul Haupt ("Critical Notes on Micah," *American Journal of Semitic Languages and Literatures* 26 [1909-10] 222, 248), in a characteristically radical manner, suggests the addition of זכר נא מה הפליאו להעזר. For a catalog of other suggestions, see Willis (Dissertation, pp. 340-41 n. 4). Though one cannot reconstruct the text with certainty, the suggestion of Weiser and Robinson may well reflect an earlier state of the text. Regarding the sense of the present text, however, there is general consensus. The phrase . . . מן is to be construed as an object of the verb זכר in v 5a. The general sense is thus: "Remember [what happened] from Shittim to Gilgal . . ." (So RSV; cf. Willis, Dissertation, p. 341). Thus Renaud (*Formation*, pp. 95-96) writes: "La difficulté du texte s'explique, sans doute, par chute d'un mot; mais le sens général de la proposition n'en est nullement affecté: la préposition *mn* exprime à elle seule cette idée de passage que le terme perdu devait comporter."

[11] So also much "I" language in the Psalms was read corporately in a later situation. Morcover, in support of this option one might also appeal to the personification of the city in the following cycle of dialogue.

[12] YHWH is mentioned in the third person in v 8. The verse is spoken in response to the voice of the people in vv 6-7. The prophet is the remaining known interlocutor in the dialogue. That the prophet speaks here is also the general consensus of commentators; see, for example, Driver, *Introduction*, p. 331; Renaud, *Formation*, p. 303; Ewald, *Prophets*, 2:327 (though Mays [*Micah*, p. 136] and J. M. P. Smith [*Micah, Zephaniah and Nahum*, pp. 123-28] leave the speaker unidentified).

v 8, the logical relation between the prophetic oracle of v 8 and the speech which begins in v 9 is not immediately clear. Moreover, the cycle of dialogue begun in vv 1-2 reaches a resolution in v 8.[13] A break is thus noted at this point. I shall later return to this articulation and seek to discover the relationship between 6:1-8 and 6:9ff.

Micah 6:9-16

The text of 6:9-16 is quite difficult, requiring emendation at several points![14]

---

[13] One feature which both contributes to the coherence of 6:1-8 and sets it off from its context is the repetition of the interrogative particle מה. This particle occurs seven times within 6:3-8 (twice each in vv 3, 5, & 8; and once in v 6 – thus in all three speeches [vv 3-5, 6-7, 8]), but nowhere else in the book of Micah.

[14] a) יראה in v 9 should most likely be repointed as from ירא following LXX, Vg, Syr (see J. M. P. Smith, *Micah, Zephaniah and Nahum,* p. 130; Willis, Dissertation, p. 343 n. 2), though Mays (*Micah,* p. 143) retains the Masoretic reading and translates "to heed."

b) For ומי יעדה עד in vv 9-10 read ומועד עיר: see p. 26 n. 49 above. So RSV, *NEB* (see Brockington, *Hebrew Text,* p. 256); Renaud, *Formation,* p. 328; Willis, Dissertation, p. 344 n. 2 (wherein he catalogs scholarly opinions); Mays, *Micah,* p. 143; J. M. P. Smith, *Micah, Zephaniah and Nahum,* p. 130.

c) For האש in v 10, read האשה (from נשה) "Can I forget . . . ?" See Mays, *Micah,* p. 143, J. M. P. Smith, *Micah, Zephaniah and Nahum,* p. 130; Willis, Dissertation, p. 345 n. 1 (wherein he lists the opinions of others). So RSV, *NEB,* JPS.

d) Repoint האוכה in v 11 as piel (note Vg:*justificabo*) versus qal in Masoretic tradition. See *BHS;* Renaud, *Formation,* p. 330; so also *NEB.* See Willis (Dissertation, pp. 345-46 n. 2) for a catalog of opinion.

e) In v 12 one encounters the problem of determining the antecedent of אשר and the feminine singular suffixes which follow. This problem leads most interpreters to transpose v 12 to a position after v 9 or after v 9a. Yet neither of these suggestions is wholly satisfactory. Taking v 12 after v 9a, the prophet introduces YHWH's speech and then intervenes with an indictment of his own before YHWH's speech begins in v 9b (Cf. Willis, Dissertation, p. 343 n. 3, following Marti). Taking v 12 after v 9, v 12 is part of YHWH's own speech. This option is preferable to that which precedes. Yet one would expect masculine singular suffixes in agreement with מטה and מועד, rather than feminine singular pointing to עיר. (See Mays, *Micah,* p. 143; J. M. P. Smith, *Micah, Zephaniah and Nahum,* p. 130; Haupt, "Critical Notes on Micah," p. 221, and others cited by Willis.) The benefits seem insufficient to justify this radical solution.

It seems preferable simply to delete אשר as a result of dittography due to following עשיריה (see Renaud [*Formation,* pp. 330-31] for discussion; cf. Allen, *Books of Joel . . . ,* p. 376) and maintain v 12 in its present position. While the suffixes then have no immediate antecedent, Renaud (p. 331) notes: "Les suffixes féminins renvoient clairement à la ville par-dessus les v 10-11: construction *ad sensum* qui dans le cas présent n'offre guère d'ambiguïté." Moreover, an analysis of the structure of vv 10-15 confirms the retention of v 12 in its present position (see Renaud, *Formation,* pp. 335-36).

f) In v 13, instead of החליתי (hiphil from חלה), read החלותי (hiphil from חלל) following *BHS* which cites the support of LXX, Vg, Syr, Aquila, and Theodotion. According to J. M. P. Smith (*Micah, Zephaniah and Nahum,* p. 130) eleven codices in Kennicott read

Nevertheless, the overall flow of the text is clear. Verse 9a is either spoken by the prophet (as v 8) or simply a literary device; in either case it functions to identify the speaker to follow. After this introduction and a short parenthetic statement, YHWH's speech begins with the summons "Hear, O tribe and assembly of the city." This summons is followed by an accusation in vv 10-12 which serves as the basis for the judgment which follows (vv 13-15). As Renaud has observed, vv 10-12 and 13-15 are related by means of a structural parallel in addition to the logical relation of accusation and judgment.

> La correspondance entre les reproches et la condamnation est ici particulièrement soignée: les deux sections commencent par l'intervention directe de Dieu (v 10-11 et v 13), elles continuent par une présentation plus neutre soit des reproches (v 12) soit des menaces (v 14-15), où YHWH ne se met plus direcrement en cause![5]

Moreover, the second person masculine singular suffixes in vv 13-15 establish another link within vv 9-16 by referring back to the addressees of the speech: מטה and מועד (both masculine singular) in v 9. Verse 16 functions as a recapitulation; it summarizes the evil deeds of the people by comparison to the deeds of Omri and Ahab and, once again, pronounces judgment upon them.

While the reference to Omri and Ahab in v 16 may appear a departure from the content of vv 9b-15, several factors indicate that v 16 is to be included as part of this speech. First, the reference in v 16 to בית אחאב, "the house of Ahab" — the paradimatic wicked ruler, harks back to בית רשע, "the house of the wicked," in v 10. Moreover, v 16 refers to both the inhabitants of the city (ישבת+third person feminine singular suffix) as in v 12 and the tribe/assembly to which the speech is addressed (second person masculine singular suffixes; cf. vv 9b, 13-15). Thirdly, v 16 is tied back to v 14; by a parallel expression of judgment. According to v 14, even what the people are able to rescue, YHWH will give to (נתן ל-) the sword; similarly, in v 16, YHWH pronounces that as a result of their sins he will give them (נתן ל-) to destruction (or, as BDB suggests, "appalment, horror").

The Relation of 6:1-8 & 6:9-16

Micah 6:16 is followed by a disjunction and a new speaker in 7:1. This break provides a convenient point at which to pause and consider the relationship between 6:1-8 and 6:9-16.

החלתי (a defective spelling of the suggested reading). See also Mays, *Micah,* p. 143; Willis, Dissertation, p. 346 n. 2 (see for citations of other scholars); Renaud, *Formation,* p. 331. So also RSV.

g) In v 16, emend וישתמר to ותשמר following the versions (see *BHS;* J. M. P. Smith, *Micah, Zephaniah and Nahum,* p. 131). So RSV, *NEB,* but not JPS. See also Mays, *Micah,* p. 143; Willis, Dissertation, p. 348 n. 1.

h) For עמי in v 16, read עמים following LXX (see *BHS*). So RSV, *NEB,* JPS; Mays, *Micah,* p. 144; J. M. P. Smith, *Micah, Zephaniah and Nahum,* p. 131, but not Willis, Dissertaton, p. 49 n. 1. See Smith and Willis and note almost unanimous scholarly consensus that עמי is inappropriate in context.

[15] Renaud, *Formation,* pp. 335-36.

As noted earlier, the speaker of v 8 may also be the speaker of v 9a, the introduction to YHWH's speech. Secondly, שמע in v 9, a significant structural word in the book of Micah, harks back to v 1. The word קול referring to the voice of YHWH is also repeated from v 1 in v 9. Thus, the beginnings of 6:1-8 and 6:9-16 are related. The summons in 6:9 functions not only to set off what follows as a new speech, but also to set that speech in relation to 6:1-8, and—as in 3:1—to introduce a more narrow focus with regard to the circle of addressees (see pp. 25-27 above), now the "tribe and assembly of the city" as opposed to the whole people of Israel. Thirdly, not only do 6:1-8 and 6:9-16 begin in the same fashion, but both speeches of YHWH also end in the same way (vv 5, 16), i.e., with a למען clause (probably expressing purpose, though result is also possible in v 16).[16] In v 5 the people are urged to call to mind certain events to the end that they might know YHWH's saving acts. The למען clause at the end of v 16 stands in sharp contrast to the above purpose stated in v 5. Rather than calling to mind the events of their history with YHWH, the people have in fact followed the sinful practices of the Northern Kingdom represented by Omri and Ahab with the stated purpose that YHWH would make them a desolation and they would bear the scorn of the peoples![17] Of course, it seems unlikely that the people acted with the express intention of bringing about this judgment. As J. M. P. Smith explains: "In accordance with a common Hebrew usage, the prophet ironically attributes what was an inevitable but undesigned consequence of a course of action to the deliberate purpose of the actor."[18] Yet, the contrast with v 5 remains striking. In conclusion, these several formal characteristics all serve to link vv 1-8 and 9-16.

Beyond this, Willis contends that the whole of Micah 6 functions as a unit. He observes that the "covenant lawsuit" pattern introduced in the beginning of chap. 6 leads one to expect a verdict. Thus, interpreters have suggested a variety of explanations as to why 6:1-8 contains no sentence. According to Willis, however, "the lawsuit in Micah 6 only seems to lack the sentence." That is, following the indictment in vv 3-5, the lawsuit is interrupted; the people ask what sacrifices YHWH requires (vv 6-7) and the prophet responds to the question (v 8). But the lawsuit is not over, for the new summons in v 9 signals the resumption of YHWH's controversy. Finally, in vv 13-15 the expected word of judgment is pronounced. This "logical sequence of events" binds the whole of chap. 6 into a single functional unit. So Willis argues![19]

---

[16] See Williams, *Hebrew Syntax,* pp. 61-62 & 86-87 (§§ 367-68, 520-21, & 526). From a syntactic standpoint, it seems best to render the למען clause in v 16 also as expressing purpose; למען clauses expressing result are rare, but this is also a possibility. Note the explanation offered by J. M. P. Smith (see below).

[17] Note also the contrast between "walking humbly with God" (v 8) and "walking in the counsels of Omri and Ahab" (v 16). More generally, Mays (*Micah,* p. 145) points to a contrast between God's requirements expressed in v 8 and the style of life described in vv 10-12, 16. Cf. Willis, Dissertation, p. 264.

[18] J. M. P. Smith, *Micah, Zephaniah and Nahum,* p. 135.

[19] Willis, Dissertation, pp. 259-64.

However, this construal of the chapter violates its literary shape in favor of an expectation that it conform to a particular form-critical genre, the covenant lawsuit (or "*rīb*-pattern"). The summons in v 9 signals the beginning of a new discourse (note the change of addressees), not simply the resumption of the lawsuit introduced in 6:1. The climax of 6:1ff. is to be found in 6:8, not in some expected word of judgment.[20] Verse 9 presents a major transition; YHWH now enters into controversy with a new interlocutor. Thus, while 6:1-8 and 6:9-16 are indeed related in the ways noted above, there is also a distinct break between them.[21]

Micah 7:1-10

7:1-6

The interjection אַלְלַי which opens 7:1 sets it off quite sharply from the verses which precede. Moreover, there is also a radical change in tone at this juncture. In 6:13-15, 16d-f the reader encounters a pronouncement of judgment. Now, in 7:1ff the tone is one of lamentation. Although 7:1 still employs the first person singular form of address in continuity with the previous speech, YHWH is no longer the one speaking.[22] However, the identity of this new speaker is not immediately evident.[23]

Employing a rather enigmatic metaphor, the speaker gives the reason for his/her lament. He/she has become as that period after the harvest of summer fruit; there is no good fruit to be found. The connection between vv 1 and 2 seems to be that the חָסִיד and יָשָׁר are no more to be found than the ripe fruit. Now, if v 2 is to be taken as a continuation of the speaker's self-description begun in v 1b, this would favor a collective interpretation of this "I". Such a reading would also be supported by the context of 6:9-16 which is addressed to the tribe/assembly of the city and also makes mention of the city's inhabitants. Then 7:1ff. could function as a reply to the preceding speech, i.e., as a lament of the tribe/assembly of the city (if the speaker is masculine in gender) or of the city itself (if feminine) over its lack of godly/upright inhabitants.

Having stated the lack of godly/upright inhabitants in v 2ab, the speaker introduces a description of the actual state of the inhabitants (vv 2c-4b) beginning with כֻּלָּם. Moving from general to particular, 3b-4b focuses on the

---

[20] As repeatedly stated, my concern in this study is for the literary shape of the text in its final form. With respect to the compositional history of the text, it remains possible that an editor may have juxtaposed these units with the intention of supplying the sentence lacking in 6:1-8. Cf. Renaud, *Formation*, pp. 343-44.

[21] Cf. ibid., p. 289.

[22] Cf. Mic 6:10-11, 13a, 14d, & 16d. Cf. ibid., p. 345.

[23] Among the possibilities suggested by interpreters as to the identity of this speaker are: the prophet, the community, the Church, the city (Zion or Jerusalem), the true Israel, and the ideal Church. For the opinions of a few particular interpreters, refer to table 5 on pp. 108-9 below.

leaders and best citizens and declares that even they are corrupt. The last part
of v 4 announces that their punishment is imminent.[24]

At this point the speech shifts from description in the third person to direct
address. Moreover, the focus of attention moves from "the public sphere and its
officials" to "the personal private sphere." The reader is warned in v 5 to trust
no one. As Mays observes, "The list of those who cannot be trusted moves
through structures of increasing intimacy: neighbor, close friend, wife."[25]
Finally, the reason for this degree of caution is given in v 6 beginning with כי.

Despite the shifts in forms of address (from first person to third to second
to third), vv 1-6 form a connected speech. Continuity is preserved with regard
to both speaker (the [collective?] "I") and topic—the widespread corruption
which pervades both public and private spheres.

7:7

Micah 7:7 is both set off from and set in relation to vv 1-6 by the strong
disjunction ואני.[26] Accompanied by an abrupt change of mood from lamentation to confident hope, this juncture represents a radical turning point in the flow
of thought. Yet, linear continuity remains unbroken; for the opening ואני
underscores the contrastive relation between vv 1-6 and v 7 revealing this
contrast as that underlying element of continuity which binds them together.
Though vv 5-6 warn against trusting in even one's friends and close relations,
the speaker of v 7 boldly confesses his/her trust in God.[27] So also Mays suggests
that in contrast to the claim of v 2 that the faithful (חסיד) have perished from
the earth, the speaker of v 7 identifies with the way of the חסיד.[28]

With respect to the speaker in v 7, two possibilities present themselves. First,
v 7 may be a continuation of the speech in vv 1-6; if so, then here the collective

---

[24] Emend באה to בא in 7:4 to agree with its subject יום; it appears to have been
corrupted in order to agree with the word which immediately precedes it.

It also seems best to emend the second masculine singular suffixes in v 4c (which have
no antecedent) to third plural in line with v 4abd. See Mays, *Micah,* p. 149; J. M. P. Smith,
Micah, Zephaniah and Nahum, p. 140. This emendation must remain tentative, however;
for, as Willis (Dissertation, p. 354) notes: "the LXX and Vulgate support the MT, and
changes of persons similar to that which occurs here appear often in the Old Testament."
Cf. Renaud, *Formation,* p. 351.

[25] Mays, *Micah,* pp. 150, 152.

[26] Cf. ואולם אנכי in Mic 3:8. See p. 36 above. Some interpreters have treated 7:7 as the
opening line of 7:8ff., but, as Mays (*Micah,* p. 156) observes, "the *waw*-adversative which
begins the line never appears at the opening of a lament of an individual or a song of
confidence."

[27] As regards the relation beween בטח (v 5) and יחל (v 7), see B. J. van der Merwe,
"Micah 1:12 and Its Possible Parallels in Pre-exilic Prophetism," OTWSA, p. 46. Cf. Mays,
Micah, pp. 156-57.

[28] Mays, *Micah,* p. 157.

"I" (the tribe/assembly of the city or the city itself) — though characterized by a lack of righteous inhabitants — sets its self resolve in opposition to the behavior described above. Or, perhaps the prophet himself breaks in at v 7 contrasting his own trust in YHWH to the current state of affairs related in vv 2-6. So construed, this verse would function in a fashion similar to 3:8, the prophet's self-recommendation vis-à-vis the prophets described in 3:5-7. In either case, the contrast with vv 1-6, the speaker's stated intention to trust in YHWH, and his/her expectation of future salvation wrought by YHWH are clear.

7:8-10

As in v 7, the mood in vv 8-10 is that of confident expectation of deliverance. The first person singular form of address employed in vv 1-7 is also continued; here, however, the feminine gender of the speaker is revealed by the suffix ךְ: in v 10d. The inverted verbal sequence with which v 8 begins apparently signals a shift of addressee. This new addressee is given only as אֹיַבְתִּי, "my enemy"; her (feminine singular) precise identity is not stated. However, this shift of addressee is only apparent: "Though the poem opens with direct address to the enemy (v 8a), the style is rhetorical and dropped immediately (cf. v 10)."[29]

Within these verses the flow of thought is clear. The enemy is exhorted to refrain from her gloating since the speaker's vindication is imminent.[30] Even in the midst of darkness the speaker testifies to the light of YHWH's presence. Then, v 9 explains the state of affairs in greater detail. According to the speaker, she is presently bearing YHWH's זַעַף (RSV-"indignation"; BDB-"rage") as a result of her sins.[31] Nevertheless, she expects and waits for YHWH to plead her case, execute judgment in her favor, and bring her out of darkness (cf. v 8) into light; thus she will see YHWH's צְדָקָה. Verse 10a-d then describes the reaction of her enemy upon seeing the speaker's deliverance. Finally, the speaker looks forward to gloating over the destruction of her enemy (v 10e-g).[32]

Along with this clear flow of thought, internal references by means of suffixes contribute to the coherence of this unit, as does the usage of certain key terms. Thus, אוֹר in v 9 harks back to both אוֹר and חֹשֶׁךְ — the absence of אוֹר — in v 8. The term אֹיֵב is repeated in v 10 from v 8. And the verb רָאָה occurs three times in vv 9-10.

The Speaker(s) in 7:1-10

It will be helpful at this point to reconsider the question regarding the identity of the speaker(s) in 7:1-10. Note first the suggestion above that 7:1-6 is

[29] Ibid., p. 158.

[30] 7:8b-d states the basis for v 8a by means of two short sentences each beginning with כִּי.

[31] 7:9b is a כִּי clause expressing cause.

[32] The term עַתָּה is used in 7:10f. to introduce the final state of the enemy. This use to signal a summary within an oracle may also be observed in 7:4.

susceptible to construal in continuity with 6:9–16 by simple reversal of speaker and addressee; i.e., the first person singular speaker in vv 1–6 could very likely be either the tribe/assembly of the city (if masculine in gender) or the city itself (if feminine). Secondly, the first person singular form of address is continued throughout vv 1–10 despite two junctures (7:6/7 & 7:7/8 at which a shift of speakers is possible. Thirdly, the gender of the "I" in vv 8–10 is revealed as being feminine. Taken together, these data suggest the tentative conclusion that 1) the speaker is the same throughout 7:1–10 and 2) her identity is the city addressed in 6:9–16. A reconsideration of the function of 7:7 will confirm this analysis. Recall first that 7:7 is tied closely to 7:1–6 by the introductory וַאֲנִי which characterizes their relation as one of contrast, not a mere juxtaposition of unrelated units. Moreover, it is unlikely that *waw*-adversative would be used to open a new speech. Secondly, 7:7 is also bound closely to 7:8–10 by continuity of discourse style, mood, and theme. While the tone of vv 1–6, i.e. lamentation, differs radically from the confident expectation of deliverance which characterizes vv 8–10, v 7 provides a transition linking the two sections. These observations speak in favor of a continuity of speaker within 7:1–10. The change of mood then occurs when the speaker shifts her focus from her own internal corruption to YHWH her faithful deliverer. So also Mays concludes: "7:7 unites the lament (7.1–6) and the song of confidence (vv. 8–10) and identifies the speaker in the lament as the feminine personification of the city who speaks in the song."[33]

Micah 7:11–13

While the speaker does change at this juncture, linear continuity is maintained. The feminine singular speaker of vv 1–10 now becomes the addressee in vv 11–13.[34] Given both the preceding interchange (6:9–16/7:1–10) and the character of vv 11–13, it is clear that these verses are to be taken as the words of YHWH.[35] YHWH now confirms the hope expressed in vv 7–10 by assuring the city of a coming day when her walls shall be built, her borders extended, and

---

[33] Mays, *Micah*, p. 31; see also pp. 151, 153, 156. See table 5 on pp. 108–9 below for the opinions of a number of other interpreters.

[34] Cf. ibid., p. 161.

[35] So, for example, Mays (ibid., pp. 9, 11) regards vv 11–13 as the words of YHWH. Hermann Gunkel ("Der Micha-Schluss: Zur Einführung in die literaturgeschichtliche Arbeit am Alten Testament," *Zeitschrift für Semitistik und verwandte Gebiete* 2 [1924] 159–60. English translation: "The Close of Micah: A Prophetical Liturgy," in *What Remains of the Old Testament and Other Essays*, trans. A. K. Dallas [London: George Allen & Unwin, 1928] 130) notes that neither speaker nor addressee is stated explicitly, but considers it most probable that YHWH here addresses Zion. Alternately, some (e.g., Driver, *Introduction*, p. 331; Horton, *Minor Prophets*, p. 267) consider these verses as spoken by the prophet in reply to the preceding verses. Again, see table 5 on pp. 108–9 below.

people will come to her from all the earth.[36] However, in stark contrast to the city, the rest of the earth will be desolate (v 13a) due to the deeds of its inhabitants (v 13b).

Micah 7:14-20

7:14

In v 14 it again appears that the previous speaker becomes the present addressee. The verse opens "Shepherd thy sheep . . ." clearly addressed to YHWH—although YHWH is not named. The speaker(s) now address/es his (their) petitions to YHWH, the great shepherd, on behalf of YHWH's own people. Although the speaker(s) is/are not identified, either the prophet (if singular) or the community (if plural) would seem appropriate in context. Finally, no thematic link stands out as binding v 14 to vv 11-13,[37] although in broad terms vv 11-13 promise future salvation and v 14 petitions for the same (though expressed quite differently). The "city" which played a major role in 6:9-7:13 is notably absent from view in 7:14.

7:15

Linear continuity between vv 14 and 15 is immediately apparent. Verse 15 opens with the clause כימי צאתך מארץ מצרים which ties it back to the end of

---

[36] Although the sense of 7:11-13 is clear, the text does require emendation at several points: a) In v 11, emend מההוא to הוא (cf. v 12a); the article represents a corruption (see Gesenius, *Hebrew Grammar,* p. 409 [§126x]). It seems best also to restore the following copulative as in v 12a.

b) The meaning of MT's יֹרחק חק in v 11 is uncertain. (See Mays, *Micah,* p. 160.) It seems best to follow Elliger's suggestion in *BHS* to emend חק to חָקֵּךְ—a reading which makes clear sense in context, restores parallelism, and has the support of part of the LXX tradition. The final ך may have been lost by haplography facilitated by the consonantal sequence of repeated חק. See Renaud, *Formation,* p. 360. For a list of those who support this emendation together with a survey of other suggestions, see Willis, Dissertation, pp. 355-56 n. 5.

c) Repoint ועדיך as having a second feminine singular suffix to agree with v 11 and its apparent antecedent—the feminine singular speaker in v 1-10 (see above). So Elliger in *BHS.* Cf. Mays, *Micah,* p. 160; Willis, Dissertation, pp. 356-57 n. 2.

d) So also emend יבוא to יבואו as required by context and supported by LXX. See Mays, *Micah,* p. 160; Willis, Dissertation, p. 356 n. 1.

e) For MT's ועָרי, read ועָדי. So Mays, *Micah,* p. 160; Willis, Dissertation, p. 357 n. 1; and most commentators (see the list in Willis).

f) Finally, in v 12d the text is clearly confused as it stands although its meaning is clear. The most likely reading is that suggested by Elliger in *BHS,* מים עד הר. So מים עד ים ומהר עד הר. So Mays, *Micah,* p. 160. Cf. Willis, Dissertation, pp. 357-58 n. 3; Renaud, *Formation,* p. 361. Cf. J. M. P. Smith (*Micah, Zephaniah and Nahum,* p. 149) regarding any of the above.

[37] This slight break in the linear flow of Micah 6-7 is noted in passing by Mays (*Micah,* p. 164) when he observes with respect to 7:14-17 that its "continuity of content" with vv 8-10 and 11-13 "is not precise."

v 14, בִּימֵי עוֹלָם. Both expressions call to mind Israel's salvation history with YHWH (as does the following clause [v 15b]). However, while vv 14 and 15 are clearly related, the nature of this relation is debated. Mays states the problem quite succintly:

> The MT of v 15 says, "As in the days when *you* went forth from the land of Egypt *I* will show *him* wonders." The three pronouns seem inconsistent within the sentence and with the context. Something has brought disorder into the text.[38]

Interpretive tradition at one time favored retention of the MT despite its difficulties and understood v 15 as a divine response to the prayer in v 14.[39] On the other hand, an extensive scholarly tradition since Wellhausen prefers to resolve this problem by emending אַרְאֶנּוּ to הַרְאֵנוּ and translatihg v 15 as a petition: "let us see . . ."[40] In this way, v 15 continues the prayer begun in v 14. This emendation may indeed reflect a more "original" text; however, from a literary point of view, the former option seems preferable.[41] In response to the

---

[38] Ibid., p. 165 (his emphasis).

[39] So Pococke, *Micah*, p. 104; Edward B. Pusey, *The Minor Prophets* (New York: Funk & Wagnalls, 1885) 2:98; von Orelli, *Twelve Minor Prophets*, p. 219; Driver, *Introduction*, p. 332; Margolis, *Micah*, p. 77.

[40] Thus, for example, Mays (*Micah*, pp. 9, 11, 164, 166) takes vv 14-20 as a single prayer in two parts—petition (vv 14-17) and praise (vv 18-20)—addressed to YHWH by the congregational "we." (Note also his literary analysis of 7:7-20 on pp. 152-56 in which he also reviews the history of interpretation of this text since Stade's article of 1903.) J. M. P. Smith (*Micah, Zephaniah and Nahum*, p. 152) lists sixteen scholars in addition to himself who make this emendation (Gunkel varies regarding pointing). Cf. Gunkel "Micha-Schluss," pp. 163–64 (Eng. trans.: "Close of Micah," pp. 134–35), Horton, *Minor Prophets*, p. 269, Willis, Dissertation. p. 359 n. 2 (Willis lists a number of other scholars who make this same emendation). Allen (*Books of Joel* . . . , p. 392) repoints אַרְאֶנּוּ as an "imperative of an Aramaic-type Aphel conjugation."

[41] Approaching this problem from a literary-critical standpoint, two questions come to the fore: 1) Is the present text capable of meaningful construal? (If not, the mandate for emendation is clear.); and 2) If the present text is capable of meaningful construal despite the obvious difficulty, does this difficulty appear to be the result of an error in the transmission of the text and thus within the domain of textual criticism proper? Or is the difficulty to be considered part of the final form of the text and its resolution within the domain of source, form, or redaction criticism (and thus the text not to be emended within a strictly literary-critical analysis)?

As I see it, 7:15 is capable of meaningful construal in its present form. By its use of the first person, the tradition of the MT places this verse in the mouth of YHWH (Cf. Renaud, *Formation*, p. 366). The second masculine singular suffix in v 15a then refers to the speaker of v 14 now being addressed. Finally, though one would expect v 15b also to employ the second person form of address, its third masculine singular suffix may be taken as a referent to עַמְּךָ in v 14, just as masculine singular suffixes are employed in 6:3-5 in reference to עַמִּי. With respect to the second question, I agree with the analysis of Renaud (p. 362) according to whom: "Il est donc probable que cette correction [the emendation of אַרְאֶנּוּ to הַרְאֵנוּ in v 15] représente le text originel. Mais plus que par une faute de

prayer in v 14, YHWH now (v 15) gives voice to his word of assurance.

7:16-20

The form of address now changes to first person plural drawing the reader in as part of the audience (gathered by the summons in 6:1a) which now responds to YHWH's promise.[42] With respect to speaker, this first person plural form of address is maintained throughout vv 16-20; with respect to addressee, the style alternates between direct address — spoken to YHWH — and indirect address — spoken about YHWH. Verses 16-17 paint a vivid picture of how the nations will react when they see the wonders YHWH works on behalf of his people.[43] Verse 17e reveals the character of these verses as a response directed to YHWH. Then, in v 18 the tone of this response changes to praise. The audience (and the reader as part of that audience) now testifies to YHWH's grace: YHWH the God who forgives sins and shows חסר to his people.[44]

II. RELATIONS WITHIN MICAH 6-7

In the preceding section I followed the flow of the text through Micah 6-7 paying special attention to features of connectedness such as thematic continuity, transitions, flow of thought, and logical relations both within speeches and between successive speeches. In addition to such linear relations, however, there are other relations within chaps. 6-7 which extend over greater distances serving to bind this unit together yet more closely and thus greatly to enhance its overall coherence.

Structural Features

Participants in Dialogue

Micah 6-7 employs a dialogical style; that is, several voices speak in alternation. With regard to the characters who participate in the dialogue, chaps. 6-7 follow an ABA pattern. In 6:1-8, the participants are YHWH, a representative of his people Israel,[45] and the prophet; 6:9-7:13 involves YHWH and the city;

---

copiste, cette leçon du TM, s'explique par une intervention rédactionnelle." (See Renaud's analysis of the redactional history of 7:15 on pp. 366-68. Cf. the analysis suggested by Mays [*Micah*, p. 165].) For these reasons I retain the reading of the MT in 7:15 and construe the verse as YHWH's response to the prayer offered in v 14.

[42] Cf. Mays (*Micah*, p. 164), according to whom in vv 14-17 "the congregation speaks as a corporate body."

[43] In addition to the logical connection between vv 15 and 16-20, they are also linked by the repetition in close proximity of the verb ראה.

[44] As noted above, the reader is effectively drawn into the response in vv 16-20 as part of the audience. 7:14 might also be interpreted in this same fashion.

[45] Or, rather than a representative Israelite, this interlocutor might be taken as the עמי of 6:3-5, i.e., as YHWH's people personified. See p. 92 above.

and in 7:14-20 the people are reintroduced and participate along with YHWH and the prophet.

Dramatic Tension

The most immediately striking feature in reading Micah 6-7 is the abrupt change of mood from doom to hope which takes place at 7:7. This is a watershed point not only within the city's speech, but also within the section as a whole. As mentioned above (pp. 14-20 passim, 27), Micah 6-7 may be analyzed as following a two part eschatological schema (judgment + salvation). Put in terms of dramatic movement, tension rises in 6:1-7:6, reaches its climax in the dramatic reversal at 7:7, and is resolved in the remainder of the section.

Use of the Verb שמע

The significance of the imperative of שמע has been discussed above (pp. 22-28). This summons to hear occurs twice in Micah 6-7. First, in 6:1 it signals the beginning of the section, the opening of YHWH's controversy with his people. Secondly, the recurrence of this summons in 6:9 marks a major transition within YHWH's controversy and the beginning of the second cycle of dialogue.[46] Finally, the verb שמע appears once more in Micah 6-7 (though not in the imperative);[47] it occurs in 7:7 in the middle of the city's response to YHWH at which point her tone changes from lament to confident expectation. Furthermore, the confession "My God will hear (שמע) me" anticipates the prayers in vv 14, 16-20.

Israel/Jacob

These names, so common in Micah 1-5, occur only once each in Micah 6-7. Specifically, the name Israel occurs at the beginning of the unit (6:2) and Jacob at the end (7:20). This binomination for the people of YHWH may thus be read as an inclusio which frames the section.[48]

Theme: Covenant Faithfulness

The theme of YHWH's faithfulness to his chosen people runs through chaps. 6-7. Thus, YHWH's speech in 6:3-5 calls to mind YHWH's saving acts on behalf of his people; the confession in 7:7 presumes YHWH's faithfulness to his people; the prayer in 7:14 refers to Israel as YHWH's inheritance and calls

---

[46] As regards the character of this transition, see pp. 94-95 above. (See also pp. 22-28.)

[47] Thus the significance of ישמעני in 7:7 ought not be overplayed.

[48] When one reads chaps. 6-7 in isolation, this feature hardly stands out. Indeed, the arrangement may be fortuitous. Nevertheless, when one reads chaps. 6-7 in sequence with 1-5, the relative infrequency of these terms in 6-7 is striking. The binome ישראל/יעקב stands out by contrast—thus leading the reader to consider its location and literary function.

upon YHWH to act as their shepherd; YHWH's response (7:15) promises saving acts comparable to the Exodus; and the song of praise in 7:18–20 ties it all together: YHWH will have compassion upon his people, forgive their sins, display אמת and חסד to them just as he did to their forefathers.

Major Motifs

The יום Motif

The word יום occurs six times in Micah 6–7 and is used in three different ways. In 7:4 יום refers to a present or imminent "day" of punishment. By contrast, it designates a future "day" of salvation in 7:11 and 7:12. Finally, 7:14, 15, & 20 call to mind past "days" when YHWH acted on behalf of his people and look forward toward such times in the future. Thus, יום is used consistently through out Micah 6–7 to refer to specific times when YHWH's activity vis-à-vis his people is openly visible.

The Salvation History Motif

The יום and salvation history motifs meet at the point of YHWH's past activity on behalf of his people. The reference to "days of old" in 7:14 is interpreted in 7:15 as a reference to the Exodus; and, calling to mind YHWH's saving activity in that event, 7:15 looks forward to similar נפלאות in the future. YHWH's speech in 6:3–5 also recalls YHWH's past activity on behalf of his people and sums up such actions by the term צדקה יהוה (6:5). Using this term in the same sense, the speaker in 7:9 looks forward to seeing YHWH's צדקה in the future. The terms ארץ מצרים (7:15 & 6:4) and בית עבדים (6:4) refer explicitly to the Exodus. And YHWH's saving activity is also called to mind by the term קדם (BDB-"ancient time") in 7:20 along with the names Abraham and Jacob and the more general "our fathers."

The People of YHWH Motif

The speaker in 6:2 states that YHWH's ריב has to do specifically with עמו, "his people," i.e, with Israel. This designation for Israel recurs twice in YHWH's opening speech (6:3, 5). The city replaces Israel as YHWH's partner in dialogue in 6:9–7:13. But in 7:11 the people of YHWH are brought back into the inter-change as the prophet once again employs the term עמך.

The ריב Motif

YHWH's ריב with his people is introduced in 6:1. The verbal root ריב occurs in 6:1 and its nominal form appears twice in 6:2. These verses effectively invoke a juridical setting for Micah 6–7. Later, the speech of the city in 7:1–10 is linked back to chap. 6 by the introduction of another ריב, that of the city vis-à-vis her enemy.[49] The city waits hopefully, in anticipation that YHWH will plead

---

[49] As in 6:1–2, both nominal and verbal forms of ריב occur in 7:9.

her case. According to Mays: "The introduction of the *rīb* motif at beginning and centre [of Micah 6-7] provides a dramatic setting for the alternation of voices and interprets it as the verbal struggle in which YHWH brings Israel to justice and to justification."[50]

The Characteristics of YHWH Motif

Micah 6:5 introduces one characteristic of YHWH which recurs in 7:9, namely: YHWH works צדקה. Two more such characteristics are introduced in the prophetic oracle in 6:8. First, YHWH requires that his people עשה משפט; that doing מצפט is also a characteristic of YHWH is evidenced in 7:9. Secondly, YHWH requires that his people love חסד (6:8), another of his own characteristics as seen in 7:18, 20.

Repeated Patterns

A common pattern binds 7:9-10 and 7:15-16 together. Note the parallel sequence of terms:

	7:9	7:15	
יוציאני			צאתך
אראה			אראנו
צדקה			נפלאות
ותרא	7:10	7:16	יראו
איבתי			גוים
בושה			ויבשו

In 7:9-10, the city is brought out (יצא) of its distressful situation and sees (ראה) YHWH's activity on its behalf; then its enemy sees (ראה) and is ashamed (בוש). Similarly, in 7:15-16, the people comes out (יצא) of its distressful situation and sees (ראה) YHWH's wondrous works on its behalf; then the nations see (ראה) and are ashamed (בוש).[51]

Only three times in the book of Micah is the verb חטא or the noun חטאת used with reference to one's own sin (specifically in 6:7; 7:9; & 7:19). In two of these, a pattern may be observed: the acknowledgment of sin is connected with an expectation of forgiveness (7:9, 18-19).

A third pattern is noted in respect to the root שמם. In 6:13, YHWH declares that he is making the city desolate because of her sins. Similarly, according to 7:13, the earth will be desolate because of the doings of its inhabitants.[52]

Repetition and Internal References

Finally, a number of other verbal links contribute also to the coherence of Micah 6-7. Consider the following: 1) In 7:9 the city declares that it will bear

[50] Mays, *Micah,* p. 12.
[51] Cf. ibid., p. 153.
[52] See ibid., p. 33.

(נשא) the rage of YHWH (זעף יהוה). This harks back to YHWH's pronouncement in 6:16 that the city will bear (נשא) the scorn of the peoples (חרפת עמים). 2) In 7:13, YHWH declares that because of the deeds of its inhabitants (ישביה) the earth will be desolate. This calls to mind YHWH's mention of the inhabitants (ישביה) of the city in 6:12-13 & 16: They speak lies and YHWH has begun to punish them. 3) The term נחלה occurs as a designation for YHWH's people in 7:14 and 7:18. The former refers to Israel by the terms עמך and צאן נחלתך. The parallel expression in 7:18 is שארית נחלתו. 4) 7:2 declares that the godly have perished from the earth. According to 7:13, the earth will be desolate because of the deeds of its (ungodly) inhabitants. 5) In 6:7 a representative of Israel inquires as to how to atone for his transgression (פשע). In 7:18, collective Israel praises the God who forgives their transgression (פשע). 6) Finally, 6:12 and 7:3 both refer to sins of speech: the city's inhabitants speak lies; the great man utters his evil desire.

III. EXCURSUS: THE DIALOGICAL CHARACTER OF MICAH 6-7

Since the advent of the critical era the tendency in study of the prophetic literature has been in the direction of fragmentation; that is, toward viewing the literature primarily as collections of small discrete units. Until recently, this was certainly the case with regard to Micah.

However, within the limited scope of Micah 7:7-20, a movement counter to the above tendency began with Gunkel's article "Der Micha-Schluss" in which he suggested that this section might be read as a unit, a prophetic liturgy. Since Gunkel, a number of other scholars have written regarding the liturgical character of Micah 7:7-20.[53] Moreover, Reicke has extended Gunkel's evaluation of this text as a prophetic liturgy (or a prophetic imitation of a liturgical form) to encompass the whole of Micah 7.[54]

---

[53] See Mays (ibid., pp. 153-55) for a brief survey of the history of interpretation of this text since Stade. Following Gunkel in viewing Mic 7:7-20 as a prophetic liturgy, note: Otto Eissfeldt, "Ein Psalm aus Nord-Israel: Micha 7,7-20," *ZDMG* 112 (1962) 259-68; John Willis, "A Reapplied Prophetic Hope Oracle," in *Studies on Prophecy,* VTSup, vol. 26 (Leiden: E. J. Brill, 1974) 64-76. See also Jan Dus, "Weiteres zum nordisraelitischen Psalm Micha 7,7-20," *ZDMG* 115 (1965) 14-22.

[54] Bo Reicke, "Liturgical Traditions in Micah 7," *Harvard Theological Review* 60 (1967) 349-67. In extending the liturgical thesis to the whole of Micah 7, Reicke is followed by Arvid Kapelrud ("Eschatology in the Book of Micah," *VT* 11 [1961] 392-405). See Renaud (*Formation,* pp. 381-82) for an evaluation of their results.

Based on his analysis of its redactional history, Renaud (pp. 380-82) also affirms the coherence of the final form of Micah 7 as a prophetic imitation of a liturgy.

Finally, though working on a level prior to the final form of the book, Lescow ("Micha 6-7") extends the liturgical thesis yet further (encompassing 6:9-7:20). See Mays (*Micah,* p. 154) for a summary of his conclusions. Cf. Lucas Grollenberg, "Een Boete-Viering?," *Schrift* 17 (1971) 188-91.

Despite this tendency to view Micah 7:7-20, or even 7:1-20, as a prophetic liturgy, Mays's proposal that chaps. 6-7 display "interrelatedness and coherence as a whole" still seems quite radical. Mays contends that the entire section, Micah 6-7, presents a continuous dialogue, "an antiphonal interchange of voices."[55] The present study has confirmed Mays's analysis in this respect.

While this proposal indeed appears radical in the context of critical discussion of Micah, within the broader context of the history of the interpretation of Micah it is less surprising. Consider, for example, this statement from Kitto's *Cyclopedia:*

> The second part, from this to the end [i.e., Micah 6-7], consists of an elegant dialogue or contestation between the Lord and his people, in which the corruption of their morals is reproved, and their chastisement threatened; but they are consoled by the promise of a return from their captivity.[56]

In keeping with this basic view of the character of Micah 6-7, the earlier commentators paid careful attention to changes in speaker(s) and addressee(s). For example, with regard to 7:11-13, Pococke writes:

> That there is no small difficulty in this and the following verse, appears by the irreconcilably different expositions which are by Interpreters given of them, in respect both to the person spoken to, and the things which are spoken concerning that person. As to the person pointed to by the word or pronoun *thy,* on stating of which much depends the understanding of what is either promised, or threatened, some will have to be meant Jerusalem, or the Nation of the Jews, God's Church or People; Others, on the contrary, the insulting enemy before mentioned, who ever she be.[57]

Again, in his *Introduction to the Old Testament* of 1827, Jahn displays the same concern.

> Dialogue is a favourite style with Micah, and, agreeably to the usage of oriental writers, different interlocutors are introduced without apprizing the reader of the change of speakers. Unless, therefore, he pays strict attention, he will often become involved in darkness, where in reality all is perfectly clear.[58]

Finally, that this concern did not vanish immediately upon the dawning of historical criticism is evidenced by both Driver's *Introduction* of 1897 and Horton's commentary of 1904.[59]

---

[55] Mays, *Micah,* pp. 9-10.

[56] Wright, s.v. "Micah," p. 334. See also Sellery, "The Book of Micah," p. 25.

[57] Pococke, *Micah,* p. 97.

[58] Jahn, *Introduction,* p. 334. As examples of such dialogue, Jahn cites Mic 2:6-12 and 7:7-17. (Though it is not entirely clear, Jahn apparently intends to restrict the dialogical character of chap. 7 to vv 7-17.)

So also Ewald (*Prophets,* 2:336) writes: "The main thing here, as in every drama, is to catch the right voices and their right interpretation; and unless this is done an interpretation must be in the highest degree uncertain."

[59] Driver, *Introduction,* pp. 330-32; Horton, *Minor Prophets,* pp. 257-70.

TABLE 5

THE SPEAKERS IN MICAH 6-7 [60]

	Pococke	Ewald	Pusey	Orelli	Driver
6:1a	The prophet	The prophet	The prophet	— —	(Exordium)
6:1b	The Lord		God	God*	
6:2					
6:3-5		Yahvé			Jehovah
6:6-7	The people*	The people	The people	The nation*	The people
6:8	The prophet	The prophet	Micah	The prophet	The prophet
6:9-16	The Lord	Yahvé[63]	God/Micah	God*	Jehovah
7:1-4	The prophet or the Church	A godly man	Micah	Zion, the ideal Church	The prophet
7:5-6	(see n. 61)	a 2d godly man			············
7:7		The community			The community
7:8	The Church or the Nation of the Jews		The people*		
7:9-10			The penitent*		
7:11-13	(see n. 62)	Yahvé	God*		The prophet[64]
7:14	The prophet	The prophet	The prophet		The prophet[65]
7:15	God		God	God	Jehovah
7:16-17			Micah	--	The prophet
7:18-20	The prophet		All the redeemed	--	(see n. 66)

TABLE 5 continued

	Horton	Mays	Margolis	Renaud	The writer
6:1a	---	---	The prophet[71]	The prophet	The prophet
6:1b	Yahweh[67]	YHWH		God	The prophet
6:2	The prophet[68]			The prophet	YHWH
6:3–5				God	
6:6–7	Israel	an "I"[72]	The people	The people	a representative Israelite[74]
6:8	(the prophet?)	a voice	The prophet	The prophet	The prophet
6:9–16	Yahweh	YHWH	YHWH*	YHWH	YHWH
7:1–4a	(see n. 69)	The city	The community*	Zion	The city
7:4b–6				The prophet[73]	
7:7–10	Israel*		The remnant*	Zion	
7:11–13	The prophet[70]	YHWH	The prophet or the enemy	The prophet[73]	YHWH
7:14	Israel*	The congregation	The prophet	Zion	The prophet[75]
7:15			YHWH	YHWH	YHWH
7:16–17			The prophet		The audience (including the reader)
7:18–20			The remnant*	Zion	

* This notation indicates that the prophet is acting a mouthpiece for the party specified.[76]

[60] Pococke, *Micah,* pp. 67–68, 72–73, 76–77, 87, 94–97, 104–5; Ewald, *Prophets,* 2:326–31; Pusey, *Minor Prophets,* 2:79–102; Orelli, *Twelve Minor Prophets,* pp. 213–19; Driver, *Introduction,* pp. 330–32; Horton, *Minor Prophets,* pp. 257–70; Margolis, *Micah,* pp. 9, 61, 63, 65, 69, 73–78; Mays, *Micah,* pp. 9–10; Renaud, *Formation,* pp. 301–3, 335, 380–81.

[61] According to Pococke (*Micah,* p. 94 [his emphasis]), Mic 7:7 presents "The prophet speaking of himself, in the person of any godly and prudent man [noting Drusius and Grotius], of the true Israel [noting R. D. Kimchi], or Gods People, or *Jerusalem,* or in the person of that Nation in captivity [noting R. Tanchum], . . ."

[62] Regarding 7:11–13, Pococke (ibid., p. 97 [his emphasis]) writes: "As to the person pointed to by the word or pronoun *thy* . . . some will have to be meant *Jerusalem,* or the Nation of the Jews, Gods Church or People; Others, on the contrary, the insulting enemy before mentioned, who ever she be."

[63] Ewald (*Prophets,* 2:327) specifies that 6:9ab—the introduction to YHWH's speech—is pronounced by the prophet.

[64] Driver, *Introduction,* p. 331. In 7:11–13, the prophet speaks in reply to 7:7–10.

[65] Ibid., p. 332. In 7:14, the prophet addresses "Jehovah . . . in the name of the penitent people."

[66] Ibid. "The prophecy closes with a lyric passage."

[67] Horton (*Minor Prophets,* p. 257) writes: "Wellhausen says the prophet is addressed as Yahweh's plenipotentiary. He is to stand before the court and urge Yahweh's case against the erring people."

[68] Ibid. Regarding 6:2, Horton writes: "Yahweh has said to the prophet, Arise and state my case; immediately he obeys and addresses the hills."

[69] Ibid., p. 264. According to Horton, in 7:1–6 "Jerusalem, or the prophet, or the true Israel, the Israel within Israel (Cheyne)" speaks.

[70] Ibid., p. 267. "Suddenly the prophet turns [in 7:11–14] and addresses Israel (masculine, not feminine as before) who had been speaking." Then, in 7:14–20 "The prophet prays for his people."

[71] Margolis (*Micah,* p. 59) writes: "The prophet bids the people listen to the divine word just at this moment becoming audible to him. . . . In the ensuing controversy, the Lord, as it were, keeps in the background, the prophet appearing in His stead and on His behalf as prosecutor."

[72] According to Mays (*Micah,* p. 9), "An 'I' responds (vv. 6f.) and is answered in turn by a voice which uses the vocative 'man' to address the 'I' (v. 8)."

[73] Renaud (*Formation,* pp. 380–81) describes Micah 7 as dialogical in character: Zion speaks in vv 1–4a, 7–10, 14, & 18–20; vv 4b–6, 11–13, & 15–17 are three oracles of consolation of which the last is spoken by YHWH himself. Although Renaud does not state explicitly who the speaker is in vv 4b–6 and 16–17, what he does say would seem to imply that he considers the prophet to be speaking in these verses.

[74] Or, "the people" personified. See the discussion on p. 92 above.

[75] See p. 100 above.

[76] For example, Pococke (*Micah,* pp. 72–73) writes regarding 6:6–7 that the prophet puts this question "as in the person of the people." Again, according to Pusey (*Minor Prophets,* 2:93–94), the prophet speaks in 7:8 making "himself one with the people" and in 7:9–10 "in the name of those who were penitent." Similarly, Horton (*Minor Prophets,* p. 266) writes regarding 7:7–10: "The speaker is Israel; the mouth piece is the prophet."

Thus, in the above analysis of Micah 6-7, I have at points made reference not only to modern commentators, but also to the works of Pococke (1692), Ewald (1876), Pusey (1885), Orelli (1893), Driver (1897), Horton (1901), and Margolis (1908). For the sake of reference and comparison, the opinions of these scholars with regard to the speakers in Micah 6-7—along with the findings of Mays, Renaud, and present study—are summarized in table 5 on pages 108-9.

The Structure of Micah 6-7 in Relation to its Dialogical Character

The analysis presented above (note especially the summary of structural features on pp. 102-3) shall be seen to support two very different structural outlines of Micah 6-7 based on different criteria. Depending upon which set of criteria the reader focuses, Micah 6-7 will be seen to be composed of either three major sections (6:1-8 / 6:9-7:13 / 7:14-20) or two major sections (6:1-7:6 / 7:7-20).

The three part partitioning is based upon close attention to the dialogical style of Micah 6-7. In particular, the dialogue of Micah 6-7 consists of three cycles distinguishable on the basis of their participants: the prophet, YHWH, and a representative of the people in 6:1-8; YHWH and the city in 6:9-7:13; and the prophet, YHWH, and the people in 7:14-20. As Mays notes, the middle cycle stands out quite prominently:

> There is an inner block of material organized by the theme of "the city," 6.9-15; 7.1-12. The song of confidence sung against a particular enemy (7.8-10) and the oracle of salvation (vv. 11f.) both feature the feminine personification of the city. . . . The result is a sequence whose first and final units are messages from YHWH; . . . Between the divine speeches is a response of the city . . .[77]

Moreover, breaks may be discerned between these cycles, i.e., at 6:8/9 and 7:13/14. At 6:9ff. one may note a disjunctive sequence beginning with a noun, a new summons with a different addressee than that of 6:1-2—an addressee which played no role at all in 6:1-8, and a concern for social injustice that was not evident in the first cycle of dialogue.[78] The break at 7:13/14 is characterized first by another shift of speaker (but this happens within cycles also). In addition, while the city plays a major role in the second cycle of dialogue, it is notably absent in 7:14-20. Thirdly, there are no observable thematic links between 7:13 and 7:14.[79]

Nevertheless, while three cycles of dialogue may indeed be distinguished within Micah 6-7, the section is clearly one dialogue; for despite the breaks noted at 6:8/9 and 7:13/14, there are also unifying features within 6-7 which work across these breaks and bind the three cycles closely together—not only into a single unit, but indeed into a single dialogue. First, several features which

---

[77] Mays, *Micah,* pp. 31-32.
[78] See pp. 92-93, 94-96 above; Renaud, *Formation,* p. 289.
[79] See p. 100 above.

serve to link 6:1-8 and 6:9-16 have been noted above (pp. 94-95). It is important
to note that the summons in 6:9 functions as a major transition within the
dialogue. Thus, this articulation is characterized by conjunctive as well as
disunctive relations. In particular, this transition introduces a more narrow focus
with regard to the circle of addressees and an intensification of the indictment
against them.[80] Secondly, while no direct thematic links were noted between 7:13
and 7:14, by its announcement of judgment upon the whole earth 7:13 does
anticipate an important thematic element of the third cycle, i.e., the humiliation
of the nations in vv 16-17.[81] Moreover, the contrasting situations of Zion and
the rest of the world depicted in 7:11-13 and 7:16-17 hark back to 6:16 as a direct
reversal of the situation there portrayed.[82] Thirdly, a review of pp. 104-5 above
will reveal that all of the major motifs and repeated patterns there noted operate
across the boundaries between cycles of dialogue. Finally, while three cycles of
dialogue may be distinguished within Micah 6-7 on the basis of the different
interlocutors who participate in them, Mays correctly observes that "the alternation of voices can be read as a [single] dialogue between YHWH" and Israel,
wherein Israel "appears in a montage of identities (singular people, representative Israelite, city, corporate congregation)."[83]

Another way of outlining the structure of Micah 6-7 was suggested in table
2 (p. 27 above). According to this outline, based primarily on differences in
"mood and content,"[84] a section with a prevailing tone of judgment (6:1-7:6)
unfolds in two movements (6:1-8 & 6:9-7:6);[85] then, a section with a prevailing
tone of salvation follows in 7:7-20. The striking transition at 7:7 and its function
as the climax of the dramatic movement within chaps. 6-7 has been discussed
above (pp. 99 & 103).

---

[80] See pp. 25-27 & 94-95 above. As I, with respect to this articulation, speak of a
focusing of addressees, so in a similar manner Mays (*Micah*, p. 10) writes: "[6:9-16] is
addressed to 'the city,' a designation which shows . . . that the Israel with whom God
struggles is a population whose identity is focused in Jerusalem."

[81] As Mays (ibid., p. 31) notes: "7:13 expands the oracle of salvation to the city (vv. 11f.)
with an announcement of judgment upon the whole earth and makes the transition to the
congregational prayer for Yahweh to exalt himself against the nations." Note also his
comment on p. 161.

[82] Ibid., p. 162.

[83] Ibid., pp. 9-10.

[84] See ibid., pp. 3, 9. (Note also pp. 15-20 passim above.)

[85] Note Driver (*Introduction*, p. 331) who writes: "In their connexion with c. 6, the
verses 7:1-6 may be taken as exhibiting anew the necessity of the judgment held out in
6:13-16 against a people which will listen neither to the admonition of 6:8, nor to the
denunciation of 6:9-12."

While the prevailing tone of 6:1-7:6 is certainly one of judgment or doom, it may also
be noted that only 6:13 & 16d-f actually announce judgment, and only 6:10-12 & 16a-c
present a direct accusation. Cf. Mays, *Micah*, p. 9.

The watershed point within Micah 6-7 thus occurs in the middle of its second cycle of dialogue. With regard to this cycle, Mays observes that "it begins with judgment and ends with salvation." Moreover, its central speech is "a response of the personified city which begins with lament at its human helplessness and turns to reliance on the salvation of YHWH after she shall have undergone his punishment." In other words, "The organizing pattern of the movement which gives coherence to the final form of chs. 6-7 is already present in this first complex [i.e., within the central cycle of dialogue, 6:9-7:13]."[86]

In conclusion, attention to the dialogical style of Micah 6-7 leads to a three-part outline of its structure. Attention to its mood, content, and dramatic movement leads to a two-part outline (wherein the first part may itself be divided into two sections). The superimposition of these two different structures adds to the dramatic richness of the section; they complement rather than conflict with each other. Finally, whereas the three-part outline appears more prominent when one focuses on the dialogical style of Micah 6-7, the two-part outline—which breaks at the point where the dramatic movement of 6-7 climaxes—will be shown to be more prominent in relation to the structure of the book as a whole.

---

[86] Mays, *Micah,* p. 32.

6
Relations between Micah 1-5 and 6-7

Having examined and demonstrated the coherence of the two major sections of the book of Micah, the issue now arises: How do they fit together? What interrelations are to be found between them? Need one follow van der Woude and speak of a I and II Micah even with regard to literary form — historical questions aside?[1] Or, do these two sections correspond, interlock, and function together in such a way as to form a larger whole?

Recall first that the overall coherence of Micah 1-5 is established largely by means of syntactical continuity, logical connectives, and a clear progression of thought. Where these criteria fail, an overall coherence is nevertheless maintained by structural features (e.g., the summons שמעו and the use of inclusios), recurrence of certain motifs, and thematic continuity.

Though varying somewhat in degree of prominence, the same phenomena may be observed in chaps. 6-7. For example, although inclusios are a prominent feature in chaps. 1-5, I note only one instance of inclusion in this section.[2] Logical connectives are also somewhat less prominent than in chaps. 1-5; they are used within speeches, but not between them.[3] On the other hand, recurrence of motifs plays a major role in both sections.

One significant difference between these two sections is that chaps. 6-7 are dialogical in character, whereas 1-5 are not. To be sure, voices other than the prophet's may be heard in Micah 1-5; but aside from the brief responses from the audience/congregation in 4:5 and 5:4-5, these "other voices" are but quotes within the prophet's own speeches:[4] e.g., the mocking lament in 2:4, the words of Micah's opponents in 2:6-7 signalled by "thus they preach," the cry of the

---

[1] Van der Woude, "Deutero-Micha." For a summary of van der Woude's conclusions, see Jeppesen, "New Aspects of Micah Research," pp. 20-23. Cf. F. C. Burkitt, "Micah 6 and 7 a Northern Prophecy," *JBL* 45 (1926) 159-61.

[2] The binomination Israel/Jacob, split between 6:2 and 7:20, forms an inclusio framing the section. (See p. 117 below and also p. 103 above.) One might also apply the term inclusion to the ABA pattern which obtains with regard to the three cycles of dialogue in Micah 6-7; I would prefer, however, to use the term "ring composition" in this regard.

[3] See the "Linear Analysis of Micah 6-7" on pp. 89-102 above.

[4] One might, of course, attempt to distinguish between words of the prophet and words of YHWH in Micah 1-5. However, as I see it, these words are so melded in most of Micah 1-5 as to make such an attempt ill-advised.

false prophets in 3:5, and the words of the nations in 4:11.

Among other differences between chaps. 1-5 and 6-7, one may note that while the exile motif pervades chaps. 1-3 and recurs in 4:10, it is notably absent in chaps. 6-7. Again, the principle of *jus talionis* is a prominent motif in the first judgment section (chaps. 1-3), but not in the latter.[5]

I. STRUCTURAL PARALLELS

Nevertheless, despite such differences, it is clear that chaps. 1-5 and 6-7 do belong together. First of all, they correspond with respect to structure. Both begin with the summons "Hear,"[6] language which evokes a juridical setting, and the setting forth of a controversy with YHWH in the role of plaintiff. Both are characterized by a sharp transition which functions as a partition between words of judgment and words of salvation. Both judgment sections proclaim that YHWH himself will bring judgment upon the people,[7] in fact utter desolation,[8] as a result of their sins.[9] Moreover, in each case the judgment section falls into two parts, the beginning of the second being signalled by a repetition of the summons שמעו which introduces an intensification of the indictment, a greater degree of specificity with respect to the sins condemned, and a narrowing of the group addressed—focusing now on the leaders, those who bear the greater responsibility. The salvation sections in each case promise future deliverance and exaltation. In each of these sections the audience joins in in response to the promises (cf. 4:5; 5:4-5; 7:16-20). Moreover, the salvation sections follow logically upon those of judgment in that the punishment mentioned in the doom sections

---

[5] See Mays, *Micah,* p. 61. Willis and Eybers differ however. Willis (Dissertation, pp. 148-49, 157) sees this principle operative in 6:10-15 and 7:4, 9. Eybers ("Micah, the Morasthite," pp. 14, 22) cites 7:8-10, 13. Perhaps 7:8-10 does come close to exhibiting the principle of *jus talionis:* when "I" fall the enemy gloats; therefore the enemy will be trodden in the streets and "I" will gloat over her.

[6] See pp. 23-27 above wherein I display attendant features which show a clear correspondence between the summons in 1:2 and that in 6:1-2 and which distinguish them from 3:1, 9 and 6:9.

[7] As regards the punishment coming from YHWH himself, see Willis, Dissertation, pp. 174-75. Note the verbs with YHWH as subject in 1:6-7; (1:12); 1:15; 2:3; 2:12; 3:4; 6:13, 16; plus the additional examples cited by Willis in which "the passive voice [is employed] with Yahweh as the assumed motivating force."

[8] See ibid., p. 157. Cf. Mic 1:6-7; 2:1; 3:12; 6:13, 16.

[9] Regarding the link between sin and punishment, note Mic 1:5; the ו translated "therefore" in 1:6 and 3:2b (following the emendation proposed above [pp. 30-32]); the transition לכן in 2:3, 3:6, & 3:12; וגם in 6:13 relating the following punishment to the preceding list of sins; the למען relating sin and punishment in 6:16; and the causal clauses in 3:4d, 6:13, 7:9a, and 7:13. (Note also the close relation between the reasons for punishment in 3:4 and 7:13, i.e.: כאשר הרעו מעלליהם and על ישביה מפרי מעלליהם.)

is interpreted as prerequisite to the execution of the promises![10] Thus, clear structural parallels do exist between Micah 1-5 and 6-7 such as may lead the reader to construe them in conjunction with each other.

II. VERBAL LINKS AND TERMINOLOGICAL CORRESPONDENCES

A variety of features serve to connect Micah 1-5 and 6-7 in other ways. To begin, while there is no unambiguous signal of continuity at their articulation, the repetition of the verbal root שמע in 5:14 and 6:1 does provide a phonetic link between the sections.

One may also note a number of terminological correspondences between chaps. 1-5 and 6-7. The most common designation for God in both sections is יהוה (total: thirty-nine times). The term אלהים occurs eleven times: five times in chaps. 1-5, six times in chaps. 6-7. With two exceptions (3:7 & 4:5), אלהים is always used in combination with יהוה, either as a parallel expression or in the phrase "יהוה our/your אלהים."

The most common designations for the people of God in Micah 1-5 are ישראל and יעקב; they appear intechangeable and occur in combination roughly half the time. In chaps. 6-7, however, these names occur only once each. They are significant nonetheless in that they form an inclusio framing the section; ישראל occurs in 6:2, יעקב in 7:20![11]

In chaps. 6-7, Israel/Jacob is more often referred to as עמו (6:2), עמי (6:3, 5), or עמך (7:11) — that is, the people of YHWH. Corresponding to this, one may observe the frequent reference to "my people" in chaps. 1-5![12]

The sin vocabularies of chaps. 1-5 and 6-7 overlap to a large degree. In both the most common terms are פשע and חטאת;[13] moreover, these terms occur together in 1:5, 13; 3:8; and 6:7 (also, in close proximity, in 7:18-19). The terms רשע and עון occur twice each in chaps. 6-7, but not in 1-5.

There is also significant correspondence with regard to specific sins under indictment. Thus compare 3:5, 11 and 7:3 with regard to the bribery of officials. According to chaps. 1-5, YHWH does good to the upright (ישר), but the leaders pervert all equity (ישר) [2:7 & 3:9]. Lack of ישר is also the problem in 7:2, 4.

---

[10] This is especially clear in 4:10 and 7:9. Cf. Willis, Dissertation, p. 192; idem, "Structure," pp. 23-24.

[11] See p. 103 above. On the use of the name "Israel" and its referent see Gustav A. Danell, *Studies in the Name of Israel in the Old Testament* (Uppsala: Appelbergs Boktryckeri-A.-B., 1946) 189-202; Willis Dissertation, pp. 178-82.

[12] In 2:8, 9 this designation עמי clearly refers to the "people of YHWH." In 1:9; 3:3, 5 it appears to denote the people of Micah. (2:4 is less clear.) Nevertheless, in chaps. 1-5 one should avoid making too sharp a distinction between YHWH and the prophet as his spokesman. Cf. Mays, *Micah*, p. 55; Willis, Dissertation, pp. 182-87.

[13] פשע occurs four times in Micah 1-5, twice in 6-7. חטאת occurs three times in 1-5, four times in 6-7.

Note also the condemnation of violence and bloodshed in 3:10; 6:12; and 7:2. The leaders of Israel/Jacob are condemned in 3:10 for "building Zion with bloodshed and Jerusalem with 'violent deeds of injustice' (BDB)." Similarly, Micah 6-7 decries persons "full of violence" (6:12) and those who "lie in wait for blood" (7:2).

III. COMMON MOTIFS

Several motifs, common to Micah 1-5 and 6-7, also serve to link the two sections. The טוב/רע motif, for example, has been displayed as a prominent feature in chaps. 1-5;[14] it recurs in 6-7. Twice in chaps. 1-5, רע is set in opposition to טוב (1:12; 3:2). Though its parts are separated, the same opposition may be observed in chaps. 6-7; YHWH requires what is טוב (6:8), but the inhabitants of the city do what is רע (7:3) and they do it well (להיטיב)![15]

A second motif which spans the entire book has to do with Israel's relation to the "peoples" or "nations." As discussed above (pp. 69-70, 84), the "many peoples/many nations" motif is most prominent in Micah 4-5. However, it is introduced in 1:2 and thus spans chaps. 1-5. Altogether in Micah 1-5, the plurals of עם and גוי occur eleven times (1:2; 4:1, 2, 3, 11, 13; 5:6, 7, 7, 14); the adjective רב accompanies six of these. This motif encompasses a variety of very disparate pictures: 4:1-4 presents a picture of the nations coming to Israel in peace; in 4:11, the nations assemble against Zion; 4:13 and 5:7 depict Israel taking vengeance against the nations; and in 5:11 YHWH himself judges the nations. The situation is similar in Micah 6-7. First, as Mays observes, 6:16 "places Israel's punishment by God in the context of the peoples and describes it with motifs of the judgment which shall come upon the nations in the course of YHWH's future salvation of his people."[16] 7:16-17 presents the opposite picture: now the nations experience humiliation while YHWH delivers Israel and does marvelous works on her behalf. While the terms עמים and גוים occur in chaps. 6-7 only in the two above-mentioned verses, two other verses may be related to this motif. 7:12, "in that day they shall come to you," provides a striking parallel to the pilgrimage of the nations to Zion in the latter days described in 4:1-2.[17] And 7:10, in describing the judgment of the city's enemy (איבתי) employs the same term (רמס) as used in

---

[14] See pp. 58-59 above and also p. 85 n. 159.

[15] Note also that the term ישר, the occurrences of which in 2:7 and 3:9 were related to the טוב/רע motif, occurs also in 7:2, 4. These occurrences are employed in negative description of those who do רע according to 7:3. Again, note the opposition between 6:8 (YHWH requires love of חסד) and 3:2 (the leaders love רע).

[16] Mays, Micah, p. 33. Mays notes further: "This interest in the world setting of YHWH's history of judgment and salvation is a feature of the compilation of ch. 1-5, where the future of Jerusalem in the midst of the peoples is a major feature."

[17] Mays (ibid., p. 162) rejects this interpretation of 7:12 on the basis of parallel texts in Isaiah and Zechariah. Considered, however, within the literary conext of the book of Micah (alone) it remains a possibility.

5:7 to describe Israel's vengeance upon the nations/peoples who are also termed their enemies (אֹיְבַיִךְ) in 5:8.

The יוֹם motif is prominent in both sections. In each, the term יוֹם is used with three different referents: 1) the present time of distress (2:4; 3:6; & 7:4); 2) the future age of salvation (4:1, 6; 5:9[?]; & 7:11, 12); and 3) the "days of old" referring to the events of salvation history (יְמֵי עוֹלָם in 5:1 & 7:14; יְמֵי קֶדֶם in 7:20 [cf. קֶדֶם in 5:1]; and יְמֵי צֵאתְךָ מֵאֶרֶץ מִצְרַיִם in 7:15).

In both sections the verb הָלַךְ is used predominantly with regard to behavior.[18] Moreover, each section delineates a clear behavioral dichotomy.[19] One's options are:

to walk haughtily (2:3)	*or*	to walk uprightly (2:7)
to walk about uttering wind and lies (2:11)		to walk in YHWH's paths (4:2)
to walk in the name of other gods (4:5)		to walk in the name of YHWH (4:5)
to walk in the counsels of Omri and Ahab (6:16)		to walk humbly with your God (6:8)

Another motif employs the imagery of a flock and its shepherd to describe the relationship between Israel and YHWH. This may be noted first in 2:12-13. The remnant of Israel is to be gathered כַּצֹּאן בָּצִירָה כְּעֵדֶר בְּתוֹךְ הַדֹּבֶר,[20] "like a flock in the fold, like a herd in the midst of the pasture." Although the term רָעָה is not here employed with regard to YHWH, the description of his action clearly portrays him in the role of shepherd. The motif appears next in 4:8, where Zion is addressed as מִגְדַּל עֵדֶר, "tower of the flock."[21] Again, the future ruler in 5:3 will act as shepherd (רָעָה-verb) over Israel and shall do so בְּעֹז יהוה, "in the strength of YHWH." Moreover, the human leaders under this ruler are described as shepherds (רֹעִים) who will rule over (רָעָה) their enemy Assyria.[22] The motif is altered in 5:7; here "many peoples" are described by the image of flocks of sheep (עֶדְרֵי צֹאן). The flock/shepherd motif recurs in 7:14. Here YHWH addressed in prayer is asked to shepherd (רָעָה) his people with his staff and to let them graze in the fertile region of Bashan and Gilead. Moreover, YHWH's people are also here termed "the flock (צֹאן) of his inheritance."[23]

---

[18] The exceptions are in 1:8 and 2:10.

[19] The verb מלא sets up a similar contrast between the sections: in the first, the prophet declares himself to "be full of" (מלא) power, the spirit of YHWH, justice, and might (3:8); by contrast, 6:12 declares the rich men of the city to "be full of" (מלא) violence.

[20] Note the emendations; see p. 54 n. 45 above.

[21] Contrary to Willis (Dissertation, pp. 235 n. 4, 245) and Renaud (*Formation*, p. 279; *Structure*, pp. 28-29), I fail to see the motif in 4:6-7.

[22] Here Assyria plays the role of flock, but set in an adversary relation to her "shepherds."

[23] Note also the mention made of this motif by Willis (Dissertation, pp. 235, 243, 245-46) and Renaud (*Structure*, pp. 28-31; *Formation*, p. 279).

Several other motifs also occur in both chaps. 1-5 and 6-7, thus spanning the book. The remnant motif has been noted as a prominent feature in the first section of the book (pp. 70 & 85-86 above), it is introduced in 2:12 and recurs in 4:6-7 and 5:6-7. This motif recurs again in 7:18. Again, the concern for משפט, the governing theme of chap. 3, is also significant in chaps. 6-7. YHWH requires his people to do משפט (6:8); and YHWH himself does משפט (7:9). Finally, in both sections there is a concern that the people know (ידע) what YHWH is doing. Thus, according to 3:1 the leaders are expected to know משפט. However, not only does YHWH do משפט, he also does צדקה (6:5; 7:9). And so, the purpose of YHWH's recitation of the saving history in 6:5 is that the people know צדקה. Conversely, the nations know neither the thoughts of YHWH nor his plans in 4:2. While the term ידע does not occur in either 2:7 or 6:8, these verses seem to be related to this motif also. 2:7 presumes that the people should be able to recognize YHWH's doings. And, in 6:8, the representative of the people is expected to know (הגיד לך) YHWH's requirement that the people do משפט (which YHWH himself does according to 7:9).

IV. OTHER LINKING CORRESPONDENCES

In addition, one may note a miscellany of other correspondences between Micah 1-5 and 6-7 which further enhance the literary coherence of the book. For example, both sections make use of a universal setting, i.e. encompassing the whole earth. (See 1:2, 3; 4:13; 5:3; 6:2; & 7:2, 13.) Moreover, as Mays notes, the peoples/nations motif in 6:16 and elsewhere reveals an "interest in the world setting of YHWH's history of judgment and salvation."[24]

The following elements are also common to both sections: the importance of the "name of YHWH" (4:5; 5:3; 6:9); references to Israel's sacred history (5:1; 7:14, 15, 20); mention of YHWH's anger, rage, or wrath (5:14 twice; 7:9, 18); עין used together with a verb of seeing to express gloating over fallen enemies (4:11; 7:10). Compare also the reactions to shame in 3:7 and 7:16.

Note also the use of legal terminology which evokes a courtroom setting: עד in 1:2; שפט and יכח in 4:3; ריב and יכח in 6:1-2;[25] ריב in 7:7. In addition to such terminology, observe the summonses and the apparent roles involved of plaintiff, witnesses, and defendant.[26]

Consider also the parallel between 3:8 and 7:7. In each the speaker employs a disjunctive sequence and a first person singular pronoun (ואני in 7:7; ואולם אנכי in 3:8) to introduce a sharp contrast between himself/herself and a group of persons. In 3:8, the prophet declares himself to be filled with "power, the spirit of YHWH, justice, and might" in contradistinction to the false prophets

---

[24] Mays, *Micah*, p. 33.

[25] The root ריב occurs twice as a noun and once as a verb in 6:1-2. Note also the use in 6:2 of קום which, according to Watson ("Form Criticism," p. 64), reflects "the custom of the court for both plaintiff and defendant to stand before the court while addressing it."

[26] See pp. 24-26 & 89-91 above.

described in 3:5. Moreover, his mission is "to declare to Jacob his transgression and to Israel his sin" whereas the false prophets prophesy in favor of whomever will pay them. Similarly, in 7:7 the city declares her intention to look to and wait for YHWH in contrast to the behavior of her inhabitants described in vv 2-6.

Finally, Merwe draws attention to the relation between 1:12 and 7:7. In 1:12 the inhabitants of Maroth wait (יחל) for good; but in vain, as YHWH rather sends evil. Contrast to this the situation in 7:7-10. Here the city waits (יחל) for YHWH, expecting deliverance (an expectation which is confirmed in 7:11-13) and also openly confessing her sins and bearing her punishment. The contrast reveals that a valid and legitimate hope becomes possible only following judgment and repentence.[27]

V. THEOLOGICAL INTERRELATION

Moreover, chaps. 1-5 and 6-7 do function together theologically, i.e., the language of the text does provide keys which lead to meaningful construal of the book as a whole. Reading Micah 1-5 as a unit, the repeated עתה, "Now," establishes a temporal vantage point for the reader; the present is a time of judgment from which one looks forward to future salvation. So also in chaps. 6-7, the present is a time of distress (6:13; 7:1-6, 9). The reader is thus situated between judgment and salvation.

But how should one respond to this situation? Consider those texts in which the reader is led to join in with the communal response. Those responses are distributed between chaps. 1-5 and 6-7, but all occur within the salvation portions of those major sections. Yet, because within each section the judgment and salvation portions are interrelated, one must in each case consider the responses as consequent to the preceding oracles of judgment as well as related to the oracles of salvation which constitute their more immediate context.

Now, the indictment of chaps. 1-3 is clearly identifiable as referring to the pre-exilic situation, i.e., before the destruction of Jerusalem. Thus, for any conceivable reader of the completed book, the indictment is addressed to a "them." Following the oracle of salvation in 4:1-4, the first communal response is a confident confession of faithfulness on the part of YHWH's people. Then, after several more oracles of salvation, comes a second communal response – this time somewhat triumphalistic in tone. Their deliverance depends not only on the activity of the מושל of 5:1-3, but also on their own military initiative (see pp. 65-67 above). But is this the response desired of us the readers? A comparison with chaps. 6-7 will shed light on this question.

As demonstrated earlier, Micah 6-7 is composed of three cycles of dialogue. The first leads to the question of how one is properly to worship and to atone for one's sin and then to the climactic oracle which states what YHWH actually desires. The second cycle begins with an indictment of the specific

[27] Merwe, "Micah 1:12," pp. 45-53 (especially 51-52).

sins of the city's rulers and leading citizens. The city responds in the first person by identifying with the sins of her inhabitants. After this acknowledgment of her sin (7:1–6; repeated in 7:9), she then moves on to confident trust in YHWH. That is, she confesses her sin, bears her punishment, and waits for YHWH himself to work deliverance on her behalf trusting in his faithfulness. In vv 11–13 this response is affirmed which leads the reader to identify the city's speech as a proper response. Finally, cycle three leads to another communal response. Now, however, (as opposed to the situation in chaps. 4–5) the reader has been led to understand the indictment as applying to himself. Thus, while the response begins with a boast over their enemies, the master of their foes is clearly YHWH rather than any human leaders. After that, the community acknowledges the basis of their salvation: YHWH's forgiveness and faithfulness. This song of praise is at once an acknowledgment of sin and a confession of trust in YHWH.

The book thus ends with a chastened response. The indictment of chaps. 1–3 may be read as applying to a "them." But chaps. 6–7 clarify the situation; the whole book, words of both judgment and salvation, are directed to us — the audience (including the reader as part of that community). And this leads to a much more adequate response.

VI. THE FUNCTION OF THE SUPERSCRIPTION

Finally, though it functions in a manner somewhat different than the relations noted in the above sections, Micah 1:1 also plays a significant role in establishing the overall coherence of the book. As noted above (p. 77), Micah 1:1 is not connected directly to 1:2, but stands apart as a superscription.[28] As such, it names the coherence of what follows in an obvious and important way. To begin, the superscription does not belong to the genre of prophetic speech *per se*,[29] but to the genre of the book.[30] Thus, within the Book of Twelve, this superscription functions to set apart the book of Micah as a unit.

Moreover, the superscription provides the reader with a general characterization of the book together with the theological pre-understanding necessary for its interpretation. In particular, it identifies what follows as to its divine origin and source of authority, its speaker, its temporal setting, and its overall topic. It will be helpful to examine, in turn, each of these items.

First, Micah 1:1 is not a complete sentence, but rather a phrase — דבר

---

[28] According to Gene M. Tucker ("Patterns in the Prophetic Canon," in *Canon and Authority*, ed. George W. Coats and Burke O. Long [Philadelphia: Fortress Press, 1977] 57–58), a superscription is by definition a statement prefixed to a written work" which stands "outside the body of the work itself."

[29] Rather, Tucker (ibid., p. 65) notes, such superscriptions "refer in the third person, and retrospectively, to the activity of the prophet, and to the books which contain the prophetic words."

[30] See ibid., p. 59; Mays, *Micah*, p. 36.

יהוה — followed by two relative clauses.[31] Above all, the book is to be read as "the word of YHWH."[32] This concern is also reflected within both major sections of the body of the book. The דבר יהוה motif, as noted above,[33] is a prominent feature in Micah 1-5. So also, the speeches in 6:3-5 and 6:9-16 are identified as words of YHWH by their introductions in 6:1-2 and 6:9a. Both sections thus appeal to YHWH as their ultimate origin and source of authority.[34]

The first relative clause in the superscription states first that this divine revelation came through the prophet Micah. Certainly this is a necessary element as part of the title; all the prophetic books are associated with some prophet.[35] It is notable, however, how little information the superscription supplies regarding Micah — only that he is associated with the town of Moresheth. Moreover, his name never recurs in the body of the book, nor is additional information given about him other than the little one might glean from his prophetic discourses themselves. The second element of the clause is a phrase designating the general time period in which the prophet Micah received this "word of YHWH" and thus in which this book — or at least the material in it — originated: "the days of Jotham, Ahaz, and Hezekiah." This reflects a historical concern. Mays is most likely correct, as he states with regard to Amos, that the superscription indicates that the book is to be "read and understood as words for a particular time and place through one individual man. Rather than an embarrassment, their historicality is a key to their meaning."[36] These words were addressed by YHWH to his people through the prophet Micah within a given historical setting. However, I would hasten to qualify this; for while its historicality may be a key to the meaning of this message, this does not of necessity provide warrant to abstract the material from its literary context and historicize it — seeking to relate each oracle to a precise historical situation (or to excise material which does not appear to stem from the specified period). It is notable that neither chaps 1-5 nor 6-7 provide any such specific historical information, nor do they refer back to this information in the superscription.[37] Rather, this superscription functions as background information, not part of the

---

[31] Cf. Tucker, "Patterns," p. 60.

[32] See Mays, *Micah*, pp. 36-37; idem, *Hosea: A Commentary*, OTL (Philadelphia: Westminster Press, 1969) 20.

[33] Pp. 70, 86. Note the phrases דבר יהוה in 4:2; נאם יהוה in 4:6 and 5:9; צבאות דבר in 4:4; and כה אמר יהוה in 2:3 and 3:2. Note also דבריו in 2:7 (note the emendation; see p. 50 n. 20).

[34] Cf. Tucker, "Patterns," pp. 63-65, 68.

[35] Ibid., pp. 62, 65.

[36] James L. Mays, *Amos: A Commentary*, OTL (Philadelphia: Westminster Press, 1969) 20.

[37] Note, however, that the association of at least 3:12 with the prophet Micah and its provenance in the days of King Hezekiah are confirmed by Jer 26:18.

foreground of the text. While the significance of this information should not be discounted, neither should it be given undo emphasis.[38]

Finally, the second relative clause—after underscoring the nature of the book as divine revelation by its use of the verb חזה[39]—sets forth the claim that that which follows pertains to the cities of Samaria and Jerusalem. Thus, in chaps. 1–5 Samaria is mentioned explicitly in 1:5, 6; Jerusalem in 1:5, 9, 12; 3:10, 12; & 4:2, 8.[40] The judgments of these two cities are related in 1:5 & 9. In chaps. 6–7 neither Samaria nor Jerusalem is mentioned explicitly. However, 6:9 identifies "the city" as the addressee of 6:9–16. And, as noted above (pp. 98–99) "the city" is also the speaker in 7:1–10 and the addressee of 7:11–13. It seems most probable that Jerusalem is "the city" here in view. Moreover, as noted by Mays, Samaria is not entirely absent from view:

> The verse [6.16] uses established language and tradition to connect the guilt and punishment of Jerusalem with that of Samaria, and so introduces an echo of the Samaria-Jerusalem pattern present in the redaction of ch. 1.[41]

Thus, as anticipated by the superscription, both Micah 1–5 and 6–7 are concerned with the capital cities whether as centers of corruption, objects of divine judgment, or—at least in the case of Jerusalem—as future recipients of salvation.

In conclusion, Micah 1–5 and 6–7 are not simply two juxtaposed, but functionally independent units. Rather, they correspond with respect to structure; they display similar terminology; they interlock by virtue of common motifs and other linking correspondences; and they function together theologically. Thus, the two major sections of the book of Micah are bound together in such a way as to function as one larger whole. The superscription to the book (Mic 1:1) supports the same conclusion. Taken together with the results of previous chapters, this establishes my thesis, namely, that the book of Micah displays an overall literary coherence which renders it capable of meaningful construal as a unit.

---

[38] Similarly, while certain psalms are attributed to David and in some cases even linked to a particular situation in his life, it seems unlikely that they are to be expounded biographically; see Brevard S. Childs, "Psalm Titles and Midrashic Exegesis," *Journal of Semitic Studies* 16 (1971) 137–50. The superscriptions themselves reflect exegetical work according to Tucker ("Patterns," p. 67).

[39] See Tucker, "Patterns," pp 60–65.

[40] Note also the references to "Zion" in 1:13; 3:10, 12; 4:2, 7, 8, 10, 11, 13.

[41] Mays, *Micah*, p. 149. See also p. 33 where he observes in addition that "the selection of the block which features 'the city' means that chs. 6–7 like 1–5 are, though in a more subdued way, Jerusalem prophecy." Cf. Willis, Dissertation, pp. 164–69.

7
Conclusions

I. COHERENCE IN THE BOOK OF MICAH

The focus of this study has been a literary analysis of the book of Micah. By means of this analysis I sought 1) to demonstrate that the book of Micah in its final form displays such coherence as to be capable of being construed as a unit and 2) to display the concrete literary features by which this coherence is manifested. To recapitulate, chapter 2 opens with a review of scholarly proposals as to the structure of the book of Micah and then, after evaluating these on the basis of certain literary characteristics and applying an analysis of the summons "Hear" as a discriminant, arrives at a working hypothesis: the book consists of two major sections, chapters 1-5 and 6-7. A detailed literary analysis begins in chapter 3 which consists of a demonstration of the coherence of Micah 3. In the process of this demonstration, the various literary features which contribute to the coherence of Micah 3 are catalogued. Chapters 4 and 5 then extend the analysis and demonstrate the coherence of the book's two major sections. Finally, chapter 6 describes the interrelations which connect the two major sections of the book thus rendering the whole a coherent unit. The thesis is established; the book of Micah in its final form is characterized by an overarching coherence.

The Nature of this Coherence

Nevertheless, coherence is not an all or nothing matter. There are degrees of coherence and different ways of expressing coherence. To be sure, the coherence of the book of Micah is not as that of an original composition produced (all at one time) by a single author![1] There remains tension within the final form of the book. For example, I have noted the contrast between peaceful and militant pictures of the future in Micah 4-5. To emphasize coherence is not to harmonize all differences; such a "flat" reading would not be faithful to the inner tension within the text. As Robert Alter has observed with respect to biblical narrative:

> There is no point . . . in pretending that all the contradictions among different sources in the biblical texts can be happily harmonized by the perception of some

[1] Cf. Mays, *Micah,* p. 3.

125

artful design. It seems reasonable enough, however, to suggest that we may still not fully understand what would have been perceived as a real contradiction by an intelligent Hebrew writer . . ., so that apparently conflicting versions of the same event set side by side, far from troubling their original audience, may have sometimes been perfectly justified in a kind of logic we no longer apprehend.

In a similar fashion he elsewhere proposes:

> . . . the biblical writers and redactors . . . had certain notions of unity rather different from our own, and . . . the fullness of statement they aspired to achieve as writers in fact led them at times to violate what a later age and culture would be disposed to think of as canons of unity and logical coherence. The biblical text may not be the whole cloth imagined by pre-modern Judeo-Christian tradition, but the confused textual patchwork that scholarship has often found to displace such earlier views may prove upon further scrutiny to be purposeful pattern.[2]

For this reason I have sought to discern the inner relations within the book of Micah itself by which it displays its own variegated form of coherence. I do not merely contend that the book of Micah is coherent, but describe in terms of concrete literary features precisely how this coherence is expressed.[3]

---

[2] Alter, *Art of Biblical Narrative*, pp. 20, 133.

[3] It is not to be assumed that all biblical books are coherent, much less that they would all express such coherence in the same way. Various books may display coherence of a different nature which would affect their interpretation. Nevertheless, fruitful comparison may be drawn between the features noted in this study as contributing to the coherence of the book of Micah and those emphasized in other critical analyses of various biblical texts. For example, James Muilenburg, in his analysis of II and III Isaiah ("Isaiah 40–66"), emphasized the importance of stylistic characteristics and structural patterns and noted in particular some of the same features which I have observed in Micah such as: strong contrasts, repetition, triads (of words, phrases, or larger units), the use of particles, vocatives, imperatives, transitions, shifts in speaker or addressee, etc. Many of these same features are emphasized in his programmatic article "Form Criticism and Beyond" (*JBL* 88 [1969] 1–18); especially significant in light of the present study is the addition of the "inclusio." So, too, Holladay, in his rhetorical critical study *The Architecture of Jeremiah 1–20* points to a number of the same features.

Umberto Cassuto ("The Sequence and Arrangement of the Biblical Sections" and "The Arrangement of the Book of Ezekiel," in *Biblical and Oriental Studies*, 1:1–6 & 227–40 [Jerusalem: Magnes Press, 1973]) has suggested that "association," especially of words and expressions, is a basic principle underlying the greater part of biblical literature and has demonstrated his thesis as regards the book of Ezekiel. In a similar fashion, Good ("Composition of Hosea") has sought to display the "techniques of linkage" by which the individual units of the book of Hosea were combined. He concluded that the primary techniques in operation were association of words, images, themes, and sounds. Of course, the present analysis has excluded consideration of the compositional history of the book of Micah. Yet, the compositional techniques listed above would clearly result in features such as verbal repetition, thematic continuity, and recurrence of motifs on the literary level. Such have indeed been noted in this study.

Cf. also the studies noted above on p. 2 nn. 3 & 4; Yehoshua Gitay, "A Study of

Features Constitutive of Coherence

Coherence functions on a variety of levels and encompasses a variety of different phenomena, such as: grammatical and syntactical conventions, logical connectives, the structure of the composition (on various levels), thematic development, recurrence of motifs, and other stylistic and rhetorical features. Moreover, the means of expressing coherence varies from level to level. Coherence on the level of the sentence and coherence on the level of extended discourse do indeed show a family resemblance, but they are certainly not identical twins or examples of both similarities and differences between several levels of coherence. See table 3 (on p. 41 above).

Coherence results from a whole network of interconnections within the text. Some of these connections operate sequentially, i.e., by establishing relations between consecutive words, sentences, or larger units. Within chapters 4 and 5, I deal with such connections in the sections labelled "Linear Analysis." Among the important constituents which contribute to such linear continuity are syntax, connecting particles and adverbials, logical sequences, verbal repetition, sustained imagery, recurring motifs, and continuity of topic and theme. In this regard, I would emphasize the important role played by articulations between sections. However, while linear continuity is one important component of the coherence of the book of Micah, such continuity does not continue unbroken throughout the whole book. Coherence is maintained, nevertheless, by other literary characteristics which provide links which operate over some distance of text—rather than in a linear fashion. For example, among the most important features which serve to connect chaps 1-5 and 6-7 are extensive structural parallels between the two sections, the relation of each section to the superscription of the book in 1:1, terminological correspondences, correspondence with regard to specific sins under indictment, and common motifs.[4] In addition, I noted a miscellany of minor correspondences and references which, while perhaps of lesser importance, do indeed reinforce the connections between these sections.[5] So also have I noted such a network of connecting features within chaps 1-5 and 6-7. Though they have been discussed in previous chapters, I would like briefly to review three of these features.

The Inclusio

The literary technique of inclusion contributes in a very significant way to the coherence of the book of Micah, especially in chaps. 1-5. Within Micah 1-2, two such inclusios frame 1:8-16 and 2:6-11. Another inclusio extends from 1:5-6 to 3:12. And yet another encompasses the entire first section of the book

---

Amos's Art of Speech: A Rhetorical Analysis of Amos 3:1-15," *Catholic Biblical Quarterly* 12 (1980) 293-309, idem, "Deutero-Isaiah: Oral or Written?" *JBL* 99 (1980) 185-97.

[4] See pp. 116-20 & 121-24 above.

[5] See pp. 120-21 above.

(1:2–5:14).[6] This device does not enjoy the same prominence in the second section although, as noted above (p. 103), the binomination Israel/Jacob split between 6:2 and 7:20 may be construed as an inclusio framing the second section.

Organization

The overall structure or organization of the book of Micah is a major feature of its coherence. In this regard, the present study bears directly on other work within the field. That is, this literary analysis has proven useful in sorting out the various proposals offered regarding the organization of the book.

In chapter 2, I described and evaluated each of the four basic structures proposed for the book of Micah. Of these, two structures (1–5/6–7 and 1–2/3–5/6–7) appeared initially as having a good basis from a literary standpoint. I then employed an analysis of the function of the summons "Hear" as a discriminant to discern which of these is to be favored.

This analysis of the summons "Hear" led to the conclusion that while the summons does play a role as a structural indicator in the book of Micah, its significance in this respect must be carefully qualified. It is important to note that the summons is variously employed in its several occurrences. Not all function on the same level, the significance of the summons varies. Moreover, the summons "Hear" simply will not bear the weight of the structure of the book of Micah when considered alone. From this analysis I also concluded that the evidence of the summons does not support the three-part partitioning of the book for which it is most commonly cited as evidence.

Finally, I concluded that the two-part partitioning of the book of Micah, 1–5/6–7, is the most likely structure and, thus, adopted this basic outline as a working hypothesis. In determining the superiority of this structure I relied on several literary features as indicators. This structural hypothesis was confirmed by additional literary features adduced in the following chapters.

The Superscription

The superscription in Mic 1:1 contributes to the coherence of the book in at least three ways by delimiting the unit, characterizing its contents, and providing direct links to both major sections of the book. That is, the superscription sets the book of Micah apart as a unit within the Book of Twelve. Secondly, its several elements characterize the contents of the book as sharing a common origin, background, and general concern. Finally, two of these elements are reflected directly in the book proper. The opening phrase, דבר יהוה, functions as a prominent motif in Micah 1–5 and relates directly to chaps. 6–7 identifying the whole book as divine revelation. The final prepositional phrase, על שמרון וירושלם, points to a major focus of the book; that which follows

---

⁶ See pp. 47, 49–50, 58, & 84 above.

pertains to the capital cities of Samaria and Jerusalem. This concern also is expressed in both major sections of the book.[7]

Toward an Interpretive Mandate

This investigation has established 1) that the book of Micah as a whole in its final form displays such coherence as to be capable of construal as a unit and 2) that this coherence is manifested in a variety of concrete literary features.[8] It follows that an interpretation of the book of Micah should not only be concerned with the meaning of each individual pericope (or other such unit), but also be attuned to the relationships between such units — as well as the particular literary features by which these interrelations are established. That is, the message of the whole is greater than the sum of its parts. For example, to one who reads 3:9-12 in the context of Micah 1-3 the error of the leaders' theological reasoning in 3:11 is quite evident. First, 3:11 is linked by the טוב/רע motif to 1:12 and 2:1-3 which clearly demonstrate that YHWH's presence is no insurance against evil; for YHWH himself may work evil. Secondly, the use of the term ישר in 3:9 harks back to the rhetorical question in 2:7. The reader may note that while YHWH does good to the upright, the leaders because they lack uprightness have no basis for their assurance. Rather, they should be expecting evil such as 3:12 announces. Again, the identity of the יולדה in 5:2 remains enigmatic unless one turns to its wider literary context; one would then note that her identity is revealed in 4:10. Moreover, as shown above (p. 86), 4:10 also sheds light on 2:12-13 confirming the function of the latter as an announcement of judgment.

Focusing on larger units, one may note that within each major section of the book the judgment and salvation portions are interrelated. So too, the major sections themselves interact theologically.[9] As a result, the book presents a unified theological message of judgment and subsequent salvation. The reader stands between these two poles of God's working — but not without perspective. For the reader of the completed book (from post-exilic times to the present) the judgment announced is clearly past. Salvation awaits in the future. The book thus pronounces a message of hope and encouragement. The reader looks forward toward a glorious future under the kingship of YHWH and leadership

---

[7] See pp. 122-24 above.

[8] Thus, the following observation by Alter (*Art of Biblical Narrative*, p. 21) concerning an investigation of the function of narrative analogy and of syntax in biblical narrative applies also to an analysis of the literary features which contribute to the coherence of the book of Micah: "Attention to such features leads not to a more 'imaginative' reading of biblical narrative but to a more precise one; and since all these features are linked to discernible details in the Hebrew text, the literary approach is actually a good deal *less* conjectural than the historical scholarship that asks of a verse whether it contains possible Akkadian loanwords, . . ."

[9] See pp. 121-22 above.

of his משל, an age characterized by YHWH's forgiveness, compassion, faithfulness, and steadfast love. Nevertheless, the judgment of Samaria and Jerusalem is paradigmatic. It stands in the past, yet continues to function as a warning against the manner of behavior of which the book declares it to be the consequence. In this way the reader discerns the whole book, words of both judgment and salvation, as a meaningful and pertinent word of YHWH — historically conditioned, but of present significance.

In conclusion, the theological message of the book of Micah is to be discerned not only in its parts, but in the interrelation of those parts, and in the relation of the parts to the whole. These relations may be discovered by a careful attention to concrete literary features in the text. Any interpretation of the book which does not take into account its underlying unity must be evaluated as lacking in this respect.

II. IMPLICATIONS REGARDING THE HISTORY OF INTERPRETATION

This study also sheds light on the history of interpretation. I have discovered that many earlier commentators — free of source, form, and redaction critical questions — arrived at conclusions much in harmony with the present analysis. For example, as late as 1893 Orelli described the book of Micah as "a beautifully finished book" and "a well articulated whole."[10] Moreover, at two points in particular the reading suggested by this literary analysis differs from that advocated by most modern scholars, but displays a close relation to readings offered by earlier commentators. In chapter 5, I discussed at some length the dialogical character of Micah 6-7. Among recent commentators only Mays has construed the whole of chaps. 6-7 as an extended dialogue. However, as evidenced by the literature cited above,[11] this view was at one time widespread. Secondly, to interpret Mic 2:12-13 as an oracle of judgment also seems idiosyncratic in the context of modern interpretation; yet a variety of interpreters from Kimchi to Calvin interpreted it in a similar fasion — such that Pococke considered this one of three main readings of the text in the history of interpretation![12] These observations suggest that the advent of biblical criticism interrupted an interpretive tradition of reading the biblical texts as literature which made sense in its final form. Thus, such interpretation was not in error as the early critics thought; rather, their predecessors were reading the text at a later stage, i.e., in its final form.

In a similar fashion, Robert Alter has noted a correspondence between literary analysis and Midrashic exegesis. He writes:

[10] Orelli, *Twelve Minor Prophets,* pp. 186, 188.

[11] On pp. 107-11. As regards the dialogical character of Micah 6-7, see pp. 106-13 (also pp. 89-102) above.

[12] Pococke, *Micah,* pp. 22-23. See also pp. 53-54 above.

. . . in many cases a literary student of the Bible has more to learn from the traditional commentaries than from modern scholarship. The difference between the two is ultimately the difference between assuming that the text is an intricately interconnected unity, as the midrashic exegetes did, and assuming it is a patchwork of frequently disparate documents, as most modern scholars have supposed. With their assumption of interconnectedness, the makers of the Midrash were often as exquisitely attuned to small verbal signals of continuity and to significant lexical nuances as any "close reader" of our own age![3]

Of course, Alter is not suggesting a return to Midrashic exegesis; he goes on to draw distinctions between such exegesis and his own literary approach. I cite Alter, however, in further support of my own observation of a certain continuity between pre-critical exegesis and the results of the above literary analysis.

Finally, in his article "Patterns in the Prophetic Canon," Ronald Clements observes that the New Testament writers understood the message of the prophets as 1) unified and 2) concerned with the age of salvation. As Clements notes, both of these features of New Testament interpretation of the prophets are problematic for modern historical-critical scholarship. Nevertheless, Clements proposes that

. . . the basic features of the interpretation of OT prophecy which are evident by NT times do not represent a hermeneutic imposed upon the prophetic writings entirely from outside, but rather must be seen as an extension of patterns of interpretation which are woven into the literary structure of the prophetic corpus.

In particular he notes:

This message concerned the destruction and restoration of Israel, but special emphasis was attached to the latter. This was because this restoration was still looked for in the future, while the destruction was believed to have already taken place![4]

My analysis of the book of Micah in its final form is completely consonant with these observations of Clements. The book of Micah is unified. It is concerned with both judgment and salvation, but tacitly emphasizes the latter in that the destruction lies in the past whereas the age of salvation awaits. The reader is thus situated between judgment and salvation. This suggests that a certain continuity also exists between the type of literary analysis I have proposed and interpretation of the New Testament era.

III. IMPLICATIONS REGARDING "CANONICAL" INTERPRETATION

One prominent difference between the present analysis and the approach to interpretation suggested by Brevard Childs has to do with the matter of

---

[13] Alter, *Art of Biblical Narrative*, p. 11.
[14] Ronald Clements, "Patterns in the Prophetic Canon," in *Canon and Authority: Essays in Old Testament Religion and Theology*, ed. George W. Coats and Burke O. Long (Philadelphia: Fortress Press, 1977) 43, 45.

intentionality. The analysis I have carried out is purely literary in character. I have sought out keys within the text as to how a reader may best construe it. I have not claimed that such a reading will correspond to the intended meaning of any particular writer or editor. Neither does Childs seek the intention of any given writer or editor; however, he does seek to uncover a "canonical intentionality."[15]

The meaning of this term, "canonical intentionalty," is not immediately evident. Fortunately, however, Childs has elaborated somewhat on this concept. Childs contends that he has "no desire to separate an author's so-called 'real' intention from the meaning of the text." In his estimation, however, reference to intention is useful in distinguishing degrees of consciousness reflected in a text's composition. He notes that sometimes intentionality is clear; sometimes no conscious intention may be discerned; and sometimes the evidence points to accidental and fortuitous factors in the shaping process. Yet, regardless of the exact nature of the text's prehistory, "a new dynamic was unleashed for its interpretation when it was collected with other material and assigned a religious role as sacred literature." It is this role, the text's literary function within the community of faith, to which the term canonical intentionality refers![16]

Elsewhere Childs has characterized this distinction between approaches as follows: "the canonical approach differs from a strictly literary approach by interpreting the biblical text in relation to a community of faith and practice for whom it served a particular theological role as possessing divine authority."[17] Of course, though our approaches do clearly differ in this respect, my approach could well be extended to relate the text to a community. That is, after a literary analysis of the text itself to discern features which might serve as guidelines to its construal, one might then in light of this analysis reconsider the question of the intention of the final form of the book. For example, one might ask: At what time was the book read in this way as a unitary whole? What was the socio-historical locus of the reader? How was prophecy in general understood during this period of the post-exilic era? A reading of the text in light of such results would bear a close resemblance to Childs's concept of a canonical intentionality determined not by a particular editor of the book but by the community which received the text, understood therein a certain meaning, and valued and passed on the text with intent to preserve this meaning.

Childs also distinguishes his approach from a strictly literary approach in another way. He contends that "For theological reasons the biblical texts were often shaped in such a way that the original poetic forms were lost, or a unified narrative badly shattered." For this reason, "The canonical approach is

---

[15] Childs, *Introduction*, p. 79.

[16] Brevard Childs, "Response to Reviewers of *Introduction to the OT as Scripture.*" *JSOT* 16 (1980) 54 (in response to criticism from James Barr on pp. 13–14 of the same issue).

[17] Childs, *Introduction*, p. 74.

concerned to understand the theological shape of the text rather than to recover an original literary or aesthetic unity."[18] On this point I would agree with Childs, i.e., that original poetic forms and aesthetic unities were often lost. Yet this consideration does not inhibit the application of a literary approach such as I have employed which seeks to discern that coherence which may yet be present in the final form of the text![9] Rather, this approach is quite amenable to that of Childs. Indeed, I have found that the kinds of features to which I point as contributing to the coherence of the book of Micah are similar to or the same as those cited by Childs in the sections of his *Introduction* entitled "The Canonical Shape of . . ."[20]

It will be instructive also to compare in particular Childs's conclusions regarding "The Canonical Shape of Micah" with the resuts of this analysis of the book. The first item to which Childs points as being of signifiance to the book's canonical shape is its literary structure. With Childs I would agree that "The more usual division of the books [*sic*] into sections 1-3, 4-5 and 6-7 arises clearly from a historical critical evaluation of the history of the book's composition . . . and does not do justice to the present shape of the book." I would further agree that "The book of Micah gives every evidence of being arranged in a clear pattern of alternating sections of judgment and salvation."[21] However, the three part structure which Childs offers for the book is not to be preferred. As demonstrated in chapter 2, the summons "Hear" (שִׁמְעוּ) functions in a manner different from that supposed by this partitioning. Moreover, this partitioning places excessive weight on 2:12-13 as comprising a salvation section such as 4:1-5:14 and 7:7-20. As I have shown, not only is 2:12-13 capable of being construed as an oracle of judgment, but such a construal clarifies its function within the literary shape of the book. For example, 2:12-13 presents the convergence of the "gate of Jerusalem" and exile motifs and introduces the remnant motif. Furthermore, I have demonstrated also that the two-part partitioning 1-5/6-7 is in fact to be preferred.[22]

[18] Ibid.

[19] Cf. the chap. entitled "Composite Artistry" in Alter's *Art of Biblical Narrative* (pp. 131-54).

Nevertheless, one might also note differences between such literary shape and the "theological shape" which Childs purports to study. For that matter, the precise meaning of the term "theological shape" is not entirely clear.

[20] For example, such sections often include considerations of structure (e.g., organizational method; division into major sections; presence and function of introductions, conclusions, repeated phrases, order of material serving to emphasize or subordinate), topic/theme/motif (e.g., range and relation of topics addressed; major motifs and their functions; thematic development, tension, climax), and language or literary technique (e.g., use of specialized vocabulary; shifts in literary style; point of view; shifts of addressees; imagery; specific literary techniques). See also pp. 2-3 n. 5 above.

[21] Childs, *Introduction,* p. 431.

[22] See chapter 2 above. As regards the interpretation and literary function of Mic 2:12-13, see also pp. 51-54, 56-59 passim, and 85-86.

Childs next suggests that the literary pattern of the book is a result of an editorial process and that even a limited reconstruction of this development process "might aid in interpreting the present shape of the canonical text." However, he objects quite strenuously to redactional studies done up to the present in that

> ... regardless of which editorial hypothesis is used, ... the redactional model assumes the written tradition was "actualized" for a later historical period in Israel's history by a process of updating the material. The major incentive lying behind the editorial process was to adjust the biblical tradition, which was already in some sort of written form, to a different historical need.

Childs contends that this assumption is not only unproven from a theoretical standpoint, but also "highly misleading" with regard to the book of Micah in particular. Rather, he argues, the prime motive force behind the editorial process which led to the final form of the book of Micah was "the influence exerted upon its editors by the larger corpus of other prophetic material, particularly the oracles of Isaiah." After an examination of the relations between the books of Isaiah and Micah, Childs concludes that while each displays an integrity and independence in its overall composition, on the redactional level they reflect a "mutual influence from a common circle of editors" — a circle which operated in Jerusalem "from the beginning of the seventh century throughout the early post-exilic period."[23]

This reconstruction of this process and the influences which bore upon it is, of course, outside the scope of the present study. However, Childs then proceeds to suggest the effects of this process on the final shape of the book. At this point comparison is possible. First, Childs notes a "sharply defined theological pattern of recurring divine judgment and salvation." Now, the existence of a pattern of judgment-salvation I would affirm. However, this is not simply a pattern of recurring events; rather the dominant point of view in the book refers to the present as a time of judgment and eagerly anticipates the future as a time of salvation. Yet although the future horizon presents the bright hope of salvation, the indictment of sin along with an indication of its consequent judgment persists as a warning. Secondly, Childs avers that the book of Micah displays a liturgical stamp according to which the "community of faith is assigning its role as the worshipping body, standing in between God's judgment and salvation, and possessed by both memory and anticipation." From a literary standpoint, I have interpreted those parts which Childs refers to as liturgical as applying to the reading audience (as part of the worshipping community). The reader thus finds himself situated, as Childs suggests, between God's judgment and salvation — though not simply so, but possessed of a perspective which clarifies the relation between God's workings in judgment and salvation. Finally, Childs notes that "the present shaping of Micah's prophecy

---

[23] Childs, *Introduction,* pp. 432–33, 434, 435–36.

has interpreted the book by placing it within a larger context shared by the prophet Isaiah."[24] I would affirm that there exists a close relation between these books; however, as noted earlier, this relationship and its implications stand outside the purview of the present study. Nevertheless, I would underscore the importance of giving full consideration to the literary integrity of each book prior to an analysis of their interrelation.

To move beyond the realm of established results of research and into that of theological and hermeneutical reflection, I would suggest — as does Childs — that the starting point for interpretation be the final ("canonical") form of the biblical text. The final form of the text is the most appropriate starting point for interpretation because, as Childs observes, "it alone bears witness to the full history of revelation."[25] The coherence revealed by this study has roots far too deep in the literary warp of the material to be considered simply the product of a final redaction. Surely the final community of tradents which put the finishing touches on the book did not create all the detailed and absolutely intrinsic unifying stylistic features observed above. The emphasis here is not then on the last editorial level, but on the resultant product which does indeed bear witness to a process of revelation.

This study has shown that important interpretive dimensions may indeed be lost if the final form of the text and its distinctive literary shape are neglected. In the case of Micah I have shown this to be a coherent form capable of being interpreted as a unit — this despite its admittedly long history of development. Given this result, I suggest that one might reasonably expect to find such coherence displayed elsewhere within the Old Testament canon as well — though such is to be demonstrated rather than assumed.

Lest I be misunderstood, however, I should note that I do not advocate a flat, static reading of the text such as might result if literary analysis alone were to be taken as a proper method of biblical analysis. Indeed, as Bruce Birch aptly observes: "knowledge of the context and intention of earlier stages in the tradition process may be necessary to understand the way in which tradition materials are used to balance, supplement, or challenge each other in the final form of the text."[26] Nevertheless, it remains important to read the whole in its final form so as to see its literary shape and not reduce its inner dynamic to a sum of its editorial stages.

In conclusion, I have advocated and demonstrated with respect to the book of Micah the benefit of employing an approach which seeks to discern the unity which inheres within a text and to interpret the text in light of this. In chapter 5, I noted that a movement began with Gunkel toward viewing Mic 7:7-20 as a

[24] Ibid., pp. 436, 437, 438.

[25] Ibid., p. 76.

[26] Bruce C. Birch, "Tradition, Canon and Biblical Theology," *Horizons in Biblical Theology* 2 (1980) 120. Note also Birch's very clear statement of Childs's program on p. 123. Cf. Childs's response on pp. 204-5 of the same issue.

single unit rather than a collection of four unrelated units. In that seminal study, Gunkel made the following observation:

> Long ago Ewald saw the relationship of the four passages we have studied, but modern expositors seem to have overlooked his exposition. In their ignorance of this organic method of exposition, they have applied all kinds of mechanical methods. They say that our text does not at first sight read like one unit, and they concluded that the parts do not belong together. Objections were based on the presence of different metres, on the fact that there are several speakers and several persons who are addressed, and on the variety of the thoughts expressed, so they suggested deletions and alterations in order to get at the meaning of the chapter. In spite of all their endeavors, they failed to bring out the unity of the whole poem and fell back on the suggestion that two or three separate poems have been accidentally brought together. We hope we have shown that our method points a way towards finding in the entire passage one comprehensive unit.[27]

The intention of the present study is comparable; I have sought to point to relationships within the final form of the book of Micah which facilitate its construal as a single, coherent unit. Moreover, I have demonstrated that the book of Micah in its final form is indeed so shaped as to render the book a unified, coherent whole and thus capable of being so construed.

---

[27] Gunkel, "Close of Micah," pp. 148–49 (in German: "Der Micha-Schluss," pp. 177–78).

Appendix

A TRANSLATION OF MICAH 3 WITH BRIEF NOTES

1a   And I said:[a] Listen, O chiefs of Jacob
1b   and rulers of the house of Israel.
1c   Is it not your responsibility to know justice,
2a   O haters of good and lovers of evil?[b]

3a   They eat the flesh of my people
3b   and tear their skin from them
3c   and break their bones.
3d   They chop [them] up like meat[c] in the kettle,
3e   like flesh in [the midst of] the pot.
2b   Their skin will be torn from them
2c   and their flesh from their bones.

4a   Then they will cry to YHWH;
4b   but he will not answer them.
4c   He will hide his face from them at that time
4d   because they have made their deeds evil.

5a   Thus says YHWH concerning the prophets
5b   who lead astray my people,
5c   who—while they have something to eat[d]—
5d   cry out "Peace;"[e]
5e   but whoever does not give them something to eat[f]
5f   against him they declare[g] war.

6a   Therefore, it shall be night for you without vision;[h]
6b   it shall be darkness[i] for you without divination.
6c   The sun shall go down upon the prophets;
6d   [even] the day shall be dark for them.
7a   The seers shall be ashamed;
7b   the diviners shall be abashed.
7c   All of them will cover their mouths,[j]
7d   because there is no answer from God.

8 a   But as for me, I am filled with
8 b   power, with the spirit of YHWH, and justice, and might
8 c   to declare[k] to Jacob his transgression
8 d   and to Israel his sin.

9 a   Hear this, you chiefs of the house of Jacob
9 b   and rulers of the house of Israel,
9 c   who abhor justice
9 d   and pervert all uprightness
10 a   by building Zion with bloodshed[l]
10 b   and Jerusalem with crime.

11 a   Her chiefs judge for a bribe;
11 b   Her priests instruct for a price; and
11 c   Her prophets divine for money.
11 d   Nevertheless, they lean upon YHWH saying:
11 e   "Surely YHWH is in our midst is he not?[m]
11 f   Calamity cannot overtake us!"[n]

12 a   Therefore, because of you:
12 b   Zion shall be plowed as a field;
12 c   Jerusalem shall become a heap of ruins,
12 d   the temple mount [reduced to] wooded heights![o]

---

[a]ואמר. The LXX appears to read the same consonants vocalized, however, as third masculine singular perfect with simple ו. This reading seems unlikely; nowhere else in the book are Micah's words introduced by a third person introduction or third person narrative. Moreover, as Mays (*Micah,* p. 77) notes, ויאמר "would be the expected form here if the verb were in the third person." As regards the significance of ואמר, see p. 57 above. Cf. Mays, *Micah,* pp. 77-78.

[b]Here I follow the rearrangement suggested by Elliger in *BHS.* Note the discussion on pp. 30-32 above.

[c]For MT's כאשר read כשאר.

[d]Literally: "are biting with their teeth."

[e]For a smoother English translation of v 5bc, it would be better to rearrange the clauses and render thus: "who cry out 'Peace' when they have something to eat."

[f]Literally: "give concerning their mouths."

[g]Literally: "consecrate" (a reference to holy war tradition).

hJPS renders: "so that you cannot prophesy" and "so that you cannot divine."

iחשכה. Read noun form rather than the verbal form of the MT.

j"mouths:" so *NEB* (cf. Mic 7:16); Syr renders as from שפה, "lip." RSV translates as "lips," JPS and J. M. P. Smith (*Micah, Zephaniah and Nahum,* pp. 71-72) as "upper lip," and Mays (*Micah,* p. 81) as "beards." BDB and KB both suggest "moustaches."

kI have deliberately chosen a neutral translation. One might also render this explicitly as a purpose clause, i.e., "in order that I might . . ."

lI repoint the participle בנה as an infinitive absolute and construe v 10a as an adverbial clause of manner. Note the discussion on pp. 36-37 above.

mA rhetorical question expecting a very definite positive answer. See Gesenius, *Hebrew Grammar,* p. 474 (§150e).

nTranslated as "cannot" instead of "will not" in order to emphasize the logical force of the statement.

o"Temple mount" for "mountain of the house [of YHWH]." Instead of "wooded heights," JPS reads "a shrine in the woods."

Bibliography

I. ANCIENT TEXTS AND EXEGETICAL AIDS

Brockington, Leonard H. *The Hebrew Text of the Old Testament: The Readings Adopted by the Translators of the New English Bible.* Oxford: Oxford University Press, 1973. 169 pp.

Brown, Francis; Driver, Samuel R.; and Briggs, Charles. *A Hebrew and English Lexicon of the Old Testament.* 1st edition reprinted with corrections. Oxford: Clarendon Press, 1972. 1127 pp.

Driver, Samuel R. *A Treatise on the Use of the Tenses in Hebrew.* Oxford: Clarendon Press, 1874. 256 pp.

Elliger, Karl, ed. *Biblica Hebraica Stuttgartensia.* Fasc. 10: "Liber XII Prophetarum." Stuttgart: Deutsche Bibelstiftung, 1970. 96 pp.

Gesenius, William. *Hebrew Grammar.* Edited and enlarged by E. Kautzsch. Translated and revised in accordance with the 28th German edition by A. E. Cowley. Oxford: Clarendon Press, 1910. 598 pp.

Joüon, Paul. *Grammaire de L'Hébreu Biblique.* Deuxième édition anastatique corrigée. Rome: Institut Biblique Pontifical, 1947. 542 + 79 pp.

Labuschagne, C. J., et al. *Syntax and Meaning: Studies in Hebrew Syntax and Biblical Exegesis.* Oudtestamentische Studiën, Deel 18. Leiden: E. J. Brill, 1973. 213 pp.

Lambdin, Thomas O. *Introduction to Biblical Hebrew.* New York: Charles Scribner's Sons, 1971. 34 pp.

Meek, Theophile J. "The Co-ordinate Adverbial Clause in Hebrew." *American Journal of Semitic Languages* 47 (1930/31) 51–52.

———. "The Co-ordinate Adverbial Clause in Hebrew." *Journal of the American Oriental Society* 49 (1929) 156–59.

———. "Result and Purpose Clauses in Hebrew." *Jewish Quarterly Review* 46 (1955/56) 40–43.

———. "The Syntax of the Sentence in Biblical Hebrew." *Journal of Biblical Literature* 64 (1945) 1–13.

Muilenburg, James. "The Linguistic and Rhetorical Usages of the Particle כי in the Old Testament." *Hebrew Union College Annual* 32 (1961) 135–60.

Rahlfs, Alfred, ed. *Septuaginta.* 5th ed. Stuttgart: Württembergische Bibelanstalt, 1952. 2 vols.

Williams, Ronald J. *Hebrew Syntax: An Outline.* 2d ed. Toronto: University of Toronto Press, 1976. 122 pp.

II. COMMENTARIES, BOOKS, AND VOLUMES OF RELEVANT ARTICLES

Allen, Leslie C. *The Books of Joel, Obadiah, Jonah and Micah.* New International Commentary on the Old Testament. Grand Rapids, MI: William B. Eerdmans Publishing Co., 1976. 427 pp.

Alter, Robert. *The Art of Biblical Narrative.* New York: Basic Books, 1981. 195 pp.

Anderson, Francis I., and Freedman, David N. *Hosea.* Anchor Bible, vol. 24. Garden City, NY: Doubleday, 1980. 700 pp.

Beckson, Carl L., and Ganz, Arthur. *Literary Terms: A Dictionary.* New York: Farrar, Straus, & Giroux, 1975. 280 pp.

Brueggemann, Walter, and Wolff, Hans W. *The Vitality of Old Testament Traditions.* Atlanta: John Knox Press, 1975. 155 pp.

Bruno, Arvid. *Micha und der Herrscher aus der Vorzeit.* Leipzig: A. Deichertsche Verlagsbuchhandlung Dr. Werner Scholl, 1923. 213 pp.

Buss, Martin J., ed. *Encounter with the Text: Form and History in the Hebrew Bible.* Philadelphia: Fortress Press, 1979. 224 pp.

Calvin, John. *Commentaries on the Twelve Minor Prophets.* Translated by John Owen. Vol. 3: *Jonah, Micah, Nahum.* Edinburgh: The Calvin Translation Society, 1848 [written 1559]. 534 pp.

Caspari, Carl P. *Über Micha den Morasthiten und seine prophetische Schrift.* Christiana, 1852. 458 pp.

Childs, Brevard S. *Introduction to the Old Testament as Scripture.* Philaelphia: Fortress Press, 1979. 688 pp.

Coats, George W., and Long, Burke O., eds. *Canon and Authority: Essays in Old Testament Religion and Theology.* Philadelphia: Fortress Press, 1977. 190 pp.

Cohen, Abraham, ed. *The Twelve Prophets.* (Micah by S. Goldman) London: Soncino Press, 1948. 368 pp.

Coppens, Joseph. *Le Messianisme royal: ses origines, son développement, son accomplissement.* Paris: Editions du Cerf, 1968. 228 pp.

Crenshaw, James L. *Samson: a Secret Betrayed, a Vow Ignored.* Atlanta: John Knox Press, 1978. 173 pp.

Dahood, Mitchell. *Psalms I: 1-50.* Anchor Bible, vol. 16. Garden City, NY: Doubleday, 1966. 329 pp.

———. *Psalms II: 51-100.* Anchor Bible, vol. 17. Garden City, NY: Doubleday, 1968. 399 pp.

———. *Psalms III: 101-150.* Anchor Bible, vol. 17A. Garden City, NY: Doubleday, 1970. 491 pp.

Danell, Gustav A. *Studies in the Name of Israel in the Old Testament.* Uppsala: Appelbergs Boktryckeri-A.-B., 1946. 334 pp.

Deane, W. J., and Hillman, S. D. *Micah.* In *The Pulpit Commentary,* vol. 30. New York: Anson D. F. Randolph & Co., [1881-90]. 135 pp.

Donner, Herbert. *Israel unter den Völkern. Die Stellung der 8. Jahrhunderts v. Chr. zur Aussenpolitik der Könige von Israel und Juda.* Supplements to Vetus Testamentum, vol. 11. Leiden: E. J. Brill, 1964. 193 pp.

Douglas, George C. M. *The Six Intermediate Minor Prophets: Obadiah — Zephaniah.* Handbooks for Bible Classes and Private Students. Edinburgh: T. & T. Clark, n.d. 157 pp.

Driver, Samuel R. *An Introduction to the Literature of the Old Testament.* International Theological Library. 6th ed. New York: Charles Scribner's Sons, 1897. 577 pp.

———, ed. *The Books of Joel and Amos.* Cambridge Bible for Schools and Churches. Cambridge: Cambridge University Press, 1915. 251 pp.

Duhm, Bernhard. *Israels Propheten.* 2. Auflage. Tübingen: J. C. B. Mohr (Paul Siebeck) 1922. 263 pp.

Eissfeldt, Otto. *The Old Testament: An Introduction.* Translated by Peter R. Ackroyd. London: Harper & Row, 1965. 861 pp.

Ewald, Georg H. A. von. *Commentary on the Prophets of the Old Testament.* Translated by J. Frederick Smith. 5 vols. London: Williams & Norgate, 1876.

Fabianke, Paul, Hrsg. *Praktische Bibelerklärung.* Konstanz: Christlicher Buch u. Kunstverlag, n.d. T. 2, Bd.17b: *Die Propheten: Jonah, Micha, Nahum, Habakkuk, Zephaniah, Haggai, Zechariah, Malachi,* von S. Zeissig, A. Hering, P. Fabianke, B. Keller, u. W. Joft. (Micha erklärt von A. Hering) 96 pp.

Fohrer, Georg. *Introduction to the Old Testament.* Initiated by Ernst Sellin. Completely revised and rewritten by Georg Fohrer. Translated by David E. Green. Nashville: Abingdon, 1968. 540 pp.

Fokkelman, Jan P. *Narrative Art and Poetry in the Books of Samuel: A Full Interpretation Based on Stylistic and Structural Analyses.* Vol. 1: *King David (II Sam. 9-20 & I Kings 1-2).* Assen: Van Gorcum, 1981. 517 pp.

———. *Narrative Art in Genesis: Specimens of Stylistic and Structural Analysis.* Assen: Van Gorcum, 1975. 244 pp.

Gros Louis, Kenneth R. R.; Ackermann, James S.; and Warshaw, Thayer S., eds. *Literary Interpretations of Biblical Narratives.* The Bible in Literature Courses. Nashville: Abingdon Press, 1974. 352 pp.

Gunn, David M. *The Fate of King Saul: An Interpretation of a Biblical Story.* Journal for the Study of the Old Testament Supplement Series, no. 14. Sheffield, England: JSOT Press, 1980. 181 pp.

———. *The Story of King David: Genre and Interpretation.* Journal for the Study of the Old Testament Supplement Series, no. 6. Sheffield, England: JSOT Press, 1978. 164 pp.

Henry, Matthew. *Matthew Henry's Commentary.* Vol. 4: *Isaiah to Malachi.* McLean, VA: MacDonald Publishing Co., n.d. [written 1712].

Hirsch, Eric D., Jr. *Validity in Interpretation.* New Haven: Yale University Press, 1967. 287 pp.

———. *The Aims of Interpretation.* Chicago: University of Chicago Press, 1976. 177 pp.

Holladay, William L. *The Architecture of Jeremiah 1-20.* Lewisburg: Bucknell Unversity Press, 1976. 204 pp.

Holman, C. Hugh. *Handbook to Literature.* 3d ed. Indianapolis: Odyssey Press, 1972. 422 pp.

Hoonacker, Albin van. *Les douze petits prophètes.* Etudes Bibliques. Paris: Librairie Victor LeCoffre, J. Gabalda & Cie, 1908. 759 pp.

Horizons in Biblical Theology 2 (1980) 113-211. Section II of this volume consists of five reviews of Childs's *Introduction to the Old Testament as Scripture* plus a response by Childs himself.

Horton, Robert F. *The Minor Prophets: Hosea, Joel, Amos, Obadiah, Jonah, and Micah.* Century Bible. Edinburgh: T. C. & E. C. Jack, [1904]. 274 pp.

Jahn, John. *An Introduction to the Old Testament.* Additional references and notes by Samuel Turner and William Whittingham. New York: G. & C. Carvill, 1827. 574 pp.

Journal for the Study of the Old Testament 16 (May 1980). This issue is devoted to a discussion of Childs's *Introduction to the Old Testament as Scripture.* It comprises an introductory article and five reviews of this work together with a response by Childs.

Keil, Carl F. *The Twelve Minor Prophets.* Vol. 1. Clark's Foreign Theological Library, 4th series, vol. 17. Translated by James Martin. Edinburgh: T. & T. Clark, 1885. 515 pp.

Kelly, Balmer H., ed. *The Layman's Bible Commentary.* 25 vols. Richmond: John Knox Press, 1962. Vol. 15: *Micah, Nahum, Habakkuk, Zephaniah, Haggai, Zechariah, Malachi,* by James H. Gailey, Jr. 144 pp.

Kleinert, Paul. *The Book of Micah*. Translated with additions by George R. Bliss. A Commentary on the Holy Scriptures, vol. 14 [no. 7] of the Old Testament. New York: Charles Scribner's Sons, 1874. 59 pp.

Koehler, Ludwig, and Baumgartner, Walter, eds. *Lexicon in Veteris Testamenti Libros* with *Supplementum*. 2d ed. Leiden: E. J. Brill, 1958. 1138 + 227 pp.

Lippl, Joseph, and Theis, Johannes. *Die Zwölf Kleinen Propheten*. Die Heilige Schrift des Alten Testamentes, 8. Bd., 3. Abt./1. Hälfte. Bonn: Peter Hanstein Verlagsbuchhandlung, 1937. 227 pp.

Luther, Martin. *Luther's Works*. Edited by Hilton C. Oswald. Vol. 18: *Lectures on the Minor Prophets*. St. Louis: Concordia Publishing House, 1975 [written 1524–26].

Margolis, Max L. *Micah*. The Holy Scriptures with Commentary. Philadelphia: Jewish Publication Society of America, 1908. 104 pp.

Mays, James L. *Amos: A Commentary*. Old Testament Library. Philadelphia: Westminster Press, 1969. 168 pp.

———. *Hosea: A Commentary*. Old Testament Library. Philadelphia: Westminster Press, 1969. 190 pp.

———. *Micah: A Commentary*. Old Testament Library. Philadelphia: Westminster Press, 1976. 169 pp.

Morgan, G. Campbell. *Introduction: Job to Malachi*. The Analyzed Bible. New York: Fleming H. Revell, Co., 1908. 285 pp.

Nielsen, Eduard. *Oral Tradition: A Modern Problem in Old Testament Introduction*. Studies in Biblical Theology, no. 1/11. London: SCM Press, 1954. 108 pp.

O'Connor, Michael P. *Hebrew Verse Structure*. (Ph.D. dissertation, Univ. of Michigan, 1978) Winona Lake, IN: Eisenbrauns, 1980. 629 pp.

Orelli, Conrad von. *The Twelve Minor Prophets*. Translated by J. S. Banks. Edinburgh: T. & T. Clark, 1893. 405 pp.

Die Ou-Testamentiese Werkgemeenskap in Suid-Afrika. *Old Testament Studies: Papers Read at Eleventh Meeting Held at the University of Pretoria, January 1968*. Edited by A. H. van Zyl. Potchefstroom: Pro Rege, [1973]. 95 pp.

Petersen, Norman R. *Literary Criticism for New Testament Critics*. Guides to Biblical Scholarship. Philadelphia: Fortress Press, 1978. 92 pp.

Pococke, Edward. *A Commentary on the Prophecy of Micah*. Oxford: Printed at the THEATER, 1692. 2d impression. 111 pp.

Pusey, Edward B. *The Minor Prophets*. 2 vols. New York: Funk & Wagnalls, 1885.

Renaud, Bernard. *La Formation du Livre de Michée: Tradition et Actualisation.* Etudes Bibliques. Paris: J. Gabalda et Cie., 1977. 465 pp.

——. *Structure et Attaches littéraires de Michée IV-V.* Paris: J. Gabalda et Cie., 1965. 125 pp.

Robinson, Theodore H., and Horst, Friedrich. *Die zwölf kleinen Propheten.* 3. Aufl. Handbuch zum alten Testament, 1. Reihe, Nr. 14. Tübingen: Verlag von J. C. B. Mohr (Paul Siebeck), 1964. 275 pp. [Hosea bis Micha von Theodore H. Robinson]

Rudolph, Wilhelm. *Micha-Nahum-Habakkuk-Zephanja.* Kommentar zum Alten Testament, Bd. 13/3. Gütersloh: Gütersloher Verlagshaus Gerd Mohn, 1975. 317 pp.

Sellin, Ernst. *Das Zwölfprohetenbuch.* 1. Hälfte: *Hosea-Micha.* 2d & 3d Aufl. Kommentar zum Alten Testament, Bd. 12. Leipzig: A. Deichertsche Verlagsbuchhandlung D. Werner Scholl, 1929. 618 pp.

Smend, Rudolph. *Die Entstehung des Alten Testaments.* Theologische Wissenschaft, Bd. 1. Stuttgart: Verlag W. Kohlhammer, 1978. 237 pp.

Smith, George Adam. *The Book of the Twelve Prophets.* Vol. 1: *Amos, Hosea, and Micah.* Rev. ed. New York: Harper & Brothers, 1928. 237 pp.

Smith, John Merlin Powis. *A Commentary on the Books of Amos, Hosea, and Micah.* The Bible for Home and School. New York: Macmillan Co., 1914. 216 pp.

——. *A Critical and Exegetical Commentary on the Books of Micah, Zephanah and Nahum.* International Critical Commentary. Edinburgh: T. & T. Clark, 1911. 363 pp.

Trible, Phyllis. *God and the Rhetoric of Sexuality.* Overtures to Biblical Theology. Philadelphia: Fortress Press, 1978. 206 pp.

Ungern-Sternberg, Rolf F. von. *Der Rechtsstreit Gottes mit seiner Gemeinde: Der Prophet Micha.* Die Botschaft des Alten Testaments, Bd. 23/3. Stuttgart: Calwer Verlag, 1958. 179 pp.

Wade, George W. *The Books of the Prophets Micah Obadiah Joel and Jonah.* Westminster Commentaries. London: Methuen & Co., 1925. 156 pp.

Weiser, Artur. *Das Buch der Zwölf Kleinen Propheten.* Bd. 1: *Die Propheten Hosea, Joel, Amos, Obadja, Jona, Micha.* Das Alte Testament Deutsch. Göttingen: Vandenhoeck & Ruprecht, 1949. 261 pp.

——. *Introduction to the Old Testament.* London: Darton, Longman & Todd, 1961. 492 pp.

Wellhausen, Julius. *Skizzen und Vorarbeiten.* 5. Heft: *Die kleinen Propheten übersetzt, mit Noten.* 2. Aufl. Berlin: Georg Reimer, 1893. 214 pp.

Westermann, Claus. *Basic Forms of Prophetic Speech.* Translated by Hugh Clayton White. Philadelphia: Westminster Press, 1967. 222 pp.

Willi-Plein, Ina. *Vorformen der Schriftexegese innerhalb des Alten Testaments.* Beiheft zur Zeitschrift für die alttestamentliche Wissenschaft, no. 123. Berlin: Walter de Gruyter, 1971. 286 pp.

III. ESSAYS AND ARTICLES IN JOURNALS AND COLLECTIONS

Alonso-Schökel, A. "Hermeneutical Problems of a Literary Study of the Bible." In *Congress Volume: Edinburgh 1974* of the International Organization for the Study of the Old Testament, pp. 1–15. Supplements to Vetus Testamentum, vol. 28. Leiden: E. J. Brill, 1975. 277 pp.

Alonso-Schökel, Luis. "Die Stylistische Analyse bei den Propheten." In *Congress Volume: Oxford 1959,* pp. 154–64. Supplements to Vetus Testamentum, vol. 7. Leiden: E. J. Brill, 1960. 359 pp.

Barnes, W. Emery. "A Messianic Prophecy: Micah iv.8–v.6." *The Expositor,* 6th series, 10 (July-December 1904) 376–88.

Beyerlin, Walter. "Kultische Tradition in Michas Prophetie." *Vox Theologica* 31 (1961) 2–12.

Bright, John. S.v. "Micah." In *Dictionary of the Bible,* pp. 656–57. Edited by James Hastings. Rev. ed. by F. C. Grant and H. H. Rowley. New York: Charles Scribner's Sons, 1963.

Burkitt, F. C. "Micah 6 and 7 a Northern Prophecy." *Journal of Biblical Literature* 45 (1926) 159–61.

Carrier, A. S. "The *hapax legomena* of the Minor Prophets." *Hebraica* 5 (1889) 209–14.

Cassuto, Umberto. "The Arrangement of the Book of Ezekiel." In *Biblical and Oriental Studies,* 1:227–40. Jerusalem: Magnes Press, 1973. 2 vols.

———. "The Sequence and Arrangement of the Biblical Sections." In *Biblical and Oriental Studies,* 1:1–6. Jerusalem: Magnes Press, 1973. 2 vols.

Cathcart, Kevin J. "Notes on Miah 5,4–5." *Biblica* 49 (1968) 511–14.

Childs, Brevard S. "On Reading the Elijah Narratives." *Interpretation* 34 (1980) 128–37.

———. "Psalm Titles and Midrashic Exegesis." *Journal of Semitic Studies* 16 (1971) 137–50.

Clifford, Richard J. "The Use of HÔY in the Prophets." *Catholic Biblical Quarterly* 28 (1966) 458–64.

Condamin, Albert. "Interpolations ou Transpositions Accidentelles?" *Revue Biblique* 11 (1902) 379–86.

Coppens, Joseph. "Le Cadre littéraire de Michée V:1–5." In *Near Eastern Studies in Honor of William Foxwell Albright,* pp. 57–62. Edited by Hans Goedicke. Baltimore: Johns Hopkins Press, 1971. 474 pp.

Crook, Margaret B. "Did Amos and Micah Know Isaiah 9:2-7 and 11:1-9?" *Journal of Biblical Literature* 73 (1954) 144-51.

——. "The Promise in Micah 5." *Journal of Biblical Literature* 70 (1951) 313-20.

Dus, Jan. "Weiteres zum nordisraelitischen Psalm Micha 7,7-20." *Zeitschrift der Deutschen Morgenländischen Gesellschaft 115 (1965) 14-22.*

Ehrman, Albert. "A Note on רשׁי in Mic. 6:14." *Journal of Near Eastern Studies* 18 (1959) 156.

Eissfeldt, Otto. "Ein Psalm aus Nord-Israel, Micha 7,7-20." *Zeitschrift der Deutschen Morgenländischen Gesellschaft 112 (1962) 259-68.*

Ermoni, V. S.v. "Miche (Le Livre de)." In *Dictionnaire de la Bible.* 1908. Vol. 4, cols. 1064-67.

Gaster, Theodor H. S.v. "Micah." In *The Universal Jewish Encyclopedia.* 1942. 7:528-29.

Gehman, Henry S., ed. *The New Westminster Dictionary of the Bible.* 1970. S.v. "Micah, The Book of." Pp. 615-16.

Gemser, Berend. "The RIB or Controversy-Pattern in Hebrew Mentality." In *Wisdom in Israel and in the Ancient Near East: Presented to Professor Harold Henry Rowley by the Society for Old Testament Study in Association with the Editorial Board of Vetus Testamentum in Celebration of His Sixty-fifth Birthday, 24 March, 1955,* pp. 120-37. Edited by D. Winton Thomas. Supplements to Vetus Testamentum, vol. 3. Leiden: E. J. Brill, 1955. 301 pp.

George, Augustin. S.v. "Miche (Le Livre de)." In *Dictionnaire de la Bible, supplément.* Edited by Louis Pirot et André Robert. Paris: Letouzey et Ané, 1952. Vol. 5, cols. 1252-63.

Gevaryahu, H. M. I. "Biblical Colophons: as Source for the 'Biography' of Authors, Texts, and Books." In *Congress Volume: Edinburgh 1974* of the International Organization for the Study of the Old Testament, pp. 42-59. Supplements to Vetus Testamentum, vol. 28. Leiden: E. J. Brill, 1975. 277 pp.

Gitay, Yehoshua. "Deutero-Isaiah: Oral or Written?" *Journal of Biblical Literature* 99 (1980) 185-97.

——. "A Study of Amos's Art of Speech: A Rhetorical Analysis of Amos 3:1-15." *Catholic Biblical Quarterly* 42 (1980) 293-309.

Good, Edwin M. "The Composition of Hosea." *Svensk Exegetisk Årsbok* 31 (1966) 21-63.

Graham, W. C. "Some Suggestions towards the Interpretation of Micah 1:10–16." *American Journal of Semitic Languages and Literatures* 47 (1930–31) 7–58.

Gray, George B. S.v. "Micah, Book of." In *Dictionary of the Bible.* Edited by James Hastings. New York: Charles Scribner's Sons, 1909. Pp. 614–15.

Grollenberg, L. "Een Boete-Viering?" *Schrift* 17 (1971) 188–91.

Gunkel, Hermann. "Der Micha-Schluss: Zur Einfuhrung in die literaturgeschichtliche Arbeit am Alten Testament." *Zeitschrift für Semitistik und verwandte Gebiete* 2 (1924) 145–78. (English translation: "The Close of Micah: A Prophetical Liturgy." In *What Remains of the Old Testament and Other Essays,* pp. 115–49. Translated by A. K. Dallas. London: George Allen & Unwin, 1928. 187 pp.)

Hagstrom, David G. "Canonical Criticism." In *Handbook of Biblical Criticism,* by Richard Soulen, pp. 37–38. 2d ed. Atlanta: John Knox Press 1981. 239 pp.

Hammershaimb, E. "Einige Hauptgedanken in der Schrift des Prophet Micha." *Studia Theologica* 1 (1961) 11–34.

Haupt, Paul. "Critical Notes on Micah." *American Journal of Semitic Languages and Literatures* 2 (1909–10) 201–52; 27 (1910–11) 1–63.

Huffmon, Herbert B. "The Covenant Lawsuit in the Prophets." *Journal of Biblical Literature* 78 (1959) 285–95.

Innes, D. K. "Some Notes on Micah." *Evangelical Quarterly* 41 (1969) 10–13; 109–12; 169–71; 216–20.

Jeppesen, Knud. "How the Book of Micah Lost its Integrity: Outline of the History of the Criticism of the Book of Micah with Emphasis on the 19th Century." *Studia Theologica* 33 (1979) 101–31.

———. "New Aspects of Micah Research." *Journal for the Study of the Old Testament* 8 (1978) 3–32.

Jeremias, Jörg. "Die Deutung der Gerichtsworte Michas in der Exilzeit." *Zeitschrift für die alttestamentliche Wissenschaft* 83 (1971) 530–54.

Kapelrud, Arvid S. "Eschatology in the Book of Micah." *Vetus Testamentum* 11 (1961) 392–405.

King, Philip J. "Micah." In *The Jerome Biblical Commentary,* pp. 283–89. Edited by Raymond E. Brown, Joseph A. Fitzmeyer, and Roland E. Murphy. Englewood Cliffs, NJ: Prentice-Hall, 1968.

Ladame, François. "Les Chapitres IV et V du Livre de Michée." *Revue de Théologie et de Philosophie* 35 (1902) 446–61.

Lescow, Theodor. "Das Geburtsmotif in den messianischen Weissagungen bei Jesaja und Micha." *Zeitschrift für die alttestamentliche Wissenschaft* 79 (1967) 172–207.

———. "Redaktionsgeschichtliche Analyse von Micha 1-5." *Zeitschrift für die alttestamentliche Wissenschaft* 84 (1972) 46-85.

———. "Redaktionsgeschichtliche Analyse von Micha 6-7." *Zeitschrift für die alttestamentliche Wissenschaft* 84 (1972) 182-212.

Mays, James L. "The Theological Purpose of the Book of Micah." In *Beiträge zur alttestamentliche Theologie: Festschrift für Walther Zimmerli zum 70. Geburtstag*, pp. 276-87. Hrsg. von Herbert Donner, Robert Hahnhart, und Rudolph Smend. Göttingen: Vandenhoeck und Ruprecht, 1977. 580 pp.

Meek, Theophile J. "The Structure of Hebrew Poetry." *Journal of Religion* 9 (1929) 523-50.

Meyer, R. S.v. "Michabuch." In *Die Religion in Geschichte und Gegenwart*. 3. Aufl. 4. Bd., cols. 929-31.

Muilenburg, James. "Form Criticism and Beyond." *Journal of Biblical Literature* 88 (1969) 1-18.

———. "Isaiah 40-66: Introduction." In *The Interpreter's Bible*, 5:381-421. Edited by George A. Buttrick. New York: Abingdon Press, 1956.

Nowack, W. S.v. "Micah." In *Dictionary of the Bible*. Edited by James Hastings. 1906. 3:359-60.

Outler, Albert C. "The 'Logic' of Canon-making and the Tasks of Canon-criticism." In *Texts and Testaments: Critical Essays on the Bible and the Early Church Fathers*, pp. 263-76. Edited by W. Eugene March. San Antonio, TX: Trinity University Press, 1980. 321 pp.

Orelli, Conrad von. S.v. "Micah." In *The International Standard Bible Encyclopedia*. 1929. 3:2046-47.

Petersen, Norman R. "When Is the End Not the End?" *Interpretation* 34 (1980) 151-66.

Pope, Marvin. "The Word שחת in Job 9:31." *Journal of Biblical Literature* 83 (1964) 269-78.

Reicke, Bo. "Liturgical Traditions in Micah 7." *Harvard Theological Review* 60 (1967) 349-67.

Richter, Wolfgang. "Formgeschichte und Sprachwissenschaft." *Zeitschrift für die alttestamentliche Wissenschaft* 82 (1970) 216-25.

Schwantes, Siegfried J. "Critical Notes on Micah 1:10-16." *Vetus Testamentum* 14 (1964) 454-61.

Seligsohn, Max. S.v. "Micah, Book of." In *The Jewish Encyclopedia*. 1916. 8:534-35.

Sellery, Samuel. "The Book of Micah." *Canadian Methodist Quarterly* 5 (1893) 10-29.

Skipwith, Grey H. "On the Structure of the Book of Micah and on Isaiah ii.2-5." *Jewish Quarterly* 6 (1894) 583-86.

Smith, Louise P. "The Book of Micah." *Interpretation* 6 (1952) 210-27.

Smith, W. Robertson, and Cheyne, T. K. S.v. "Micah (Book)." In *Encyclopedia Biblica.* Edited by T. K. Cheyne and J. Sutherland Black. New York: Macmillan, 1902. Vol. 3, cols. 3068-74.

Stade, Bernhard. "Bemerkungen über das Buch Micha." *Zeitschrift für die alttestamentliche Wissenschaft* 1 (1881) 161-76.

————. "Streiflichter auf die Entstehung der jetzigen Gestalt der alttestamentlichen Prophetenschriften." *Zeitschrift für die alttestamentliche Wissenschaft* 23 (1903) 153-71 [§5, "Micha 7,7-20 ein Psalm," pp. 163-71].

Thomas, D. Winton. "Micah." In *Peake's Commentary on the Bible,* pp. 630-34. Edited by Matthew Black and H. H. Rowley. Edinburgh: Thomas Nelson & Sons, 1962. 1126 pp.

Volck, W., and McCurdy, J. P. S.v. "Micah." In *The New Schaff-Herzog Encyclopedia of Religious Knowledge.* Edited by Samuel M. Jackson. 1910. 7:362-63.

Watson, Paul. "Form Criticism and an Exegesis of Micah 6:1-8." *Restoration Quarterly* 7 (1963) 61-72.

Wharton, James A. "The Unanswerable Answer: An Interpretation of Job." In *Texts and Testaments: Essays on the Bible and Early Church Fathers,* pp. 37-70. Edited by W. Eugene March. San Antonio, TX: Trinity University Press, 1980. 321 pp.

Willis, John T. "Fundamental Issues in Contemporary Micah Studies." *Restoration Quarterly* 13 (1970) 77-90.

————. "Micah 2:6-8 and the 'People of God' in Micah." *Biblische Zeitschrift* 14 (1970) 72-87.

————. "Micah IV 14-V 5: A Unit." *Vetus Testamentum* 18 (1968) 529-47.

————. "A Note on ויאמר in Micah 3:1." *Zeitschrift für die alttestamentliche Wissenschaft* 80 (1968) 50-54.

————. "A Reapplied Prophetic Hope Oracle." In *Studies in Prophecy,* pp. 61-76. Supplements to Vetus Testamentum, vol. 26. Leiden: E. J. Brill, 1974. 169 pp.

————. "Some Suggestions on the Interpretation of Micah I 2." *Vetus Testamentum* 18 (1968) 372-79.

————. "The Structure of Micah 3-5 and the Function of Micah 5:9-14 in the Book." *Zeitschrift für die alttestamentliche Wissenschaft* 81 (1969) 191-214.

————. "The Structure of the Book of Micah." *Svensk Exegetisk Årsbok* 34 (1969) 5-42.

Wolfe, Roland E. "The Book of Micah: Introduction and Exegesis." In *The Interpreter's Bible*, 6:895-949. Edited by George A. Buttrick. New York: Abingdon Press 1956.

————. "The Editing of the Book of the Twelve." *Zeitschrift für die alttestamentliche Wissenschaft* 53 (1935) 90-129.

Wolff, Hans W. "Micah the Moreshite—The Prophet and His Background." In *Israelite Wisdom: Theological and Literary Essays in Honor of Samuel Terrien*, pp. 77-84. Edited by John Gammie, Walter A. Brueggemann, W. C. Humphreys, and J. M. Ward. Missoula, MT: Scholars Press, 1978. 314 pp.

————. "Wie Verstand Micha von Moreschet sein prophetisches Amt?" In *Congress Volume: Göttinen 1977* of the International Organization for the Study of the Old Testament, pp. 403-17. Supplements to Vetus Testamentum, vol. 29. Leiden: E. J. Brill, 1978. 417 pp.

Woude, A. S. van der. "Deutero-Micha: ein Prophet aus Nord-Israel?" *Nederlands Theologisch Tijdsschrift* 25 (1971) 365-78.

————. "Micha II 7a und der Bund Jahwes mit Israel." *Vetus Testamentum* 18 (1968) 388-91.

————. "Micah in Dispute with the Pseudo-prophets." *Vetus Testamentum* 19 (1969) 244-60.

Wright, William. S.v. "Micah." In *Cyclopedia of Biblical Literature.* Edited by John Kitto. 10th ed (1860). 2:333-35.

Wright, William A. S.v. "Micah." In *Smith's Dictionary of the Bible.* 1888. 3:1914-17.

IV. UNPUBLISHED MATERIALS

Bowman, Richard G. "The Crises of King David: Narrative Structure, Compositional Technique, and the Interpretation of II Samuel 8:15-20:26." Th.D. dissertation, Union Theological Seminary, Richmond, VA. 1981. 349 pp.

Hagstrom, David G. "Canon as Context: An Inquiry into the Interpretive Approach of Brevard S. Childs." Th.M. thesis, Union Theological Seminary, Richmond, VA. 1979. 124 pp.

Willis, John T. "The Structure, Setting, and Interrelationships of the Pericopes in the Book of Micah." Ph.D dissertation, Vanderbilt University. 1966. 385 pp.